DATE DUE

NOV 2 5 1997		

DEMCO 38-297

Technically Speaking

TECHNICALLY SPEAKING

Proven Ways to Make Your Next Presentation a Success

Jan D'Arcy

amacom
American Management Association

Library of Congress Cataloging-in-Publication Data

D'Arcy, Jan.
    Technically speaking : proven ways to make your presentation a
success / Jan D'Arcy.
       p.   cm.
    Includes bibliographical references (p.   ) and index.
    ISBN 0-8144-5016-4 (hardcover)
    1. Business presentations.   I. Title.
HF5718.22.D37   1991
658.4'52—dc20   91-53052
                                            CIP

Printing number

10 9 8 7 6 5 4 3 2 1

To
my
mother

Contents

Preface

This book is for scientific and technical professionals. It provides a system for the oral communication of complex information. It is a practical guide that will enable the reader to make presentations to fellow professionals and to lay audiences in an efficient, effective, and clear manner.

This book is the result of field research. Several years ago, I worked as a consultant in the Continuing Education Management Program at the University of Washington. I led special communication seminars for managers, approximately half of whom were from scientific and technical fields. Soon after I started presenting the seminars, I realized that the scientific and technical professionals have unique problems in relaying complex information:

- They must organize their material in strict sequential order.
- They must present it with unambiguous clarity.
- Their subject matter is rigidly defined.
- They must use specific terminology.
- They are sometimes uncomfortable establishing rapport with audiences and have difficulty retaining audience interest and enthusiasm.

I was particularly challenged by these (occasionally reluctant) students, but I was disappointed to find no up-to-date book that I could recommend to improve their communication skills and answer their particular needs. Although many texts provided general introductions to public speaking, none focused on the difficulties of oral communication of scientific and technical data.

In my private practice, I also found that I was increasingly concerned with the communication problems of scientists and technicians. I was receiving requests to work with engineers, aerospace personnel, physicists, environmental researchers, and computer specialists, and I resolved to develop methods particularly appropriate for them.

I conducted more than 200 interviews with personnel in high-tech companies. The basis of my interviews was a seven-point question-naire designed to elicit information about the circumstances under which oral presentations occur in such organizations. My initial contacts were with heads of corporate departments of research and development, education and training, public relations and communi-cations, and sales and marketing. At the completion of each inter-view, I asked my subject to name model communicators within his or her organization. I then interviewed these successful "star performers."

I was delighted to find that these top communicators were acute-ly aware of the special difficulties of communication in their fields and that they were eager to share their speaking experiences and expertise. I was excited about combining the information I was gleaning from model communicators in the scientific and technical fields with my extensive knowledge of the process and techniques of communi-cations.

During my twenty-five years as a communications specialist, I have conducted presentation skills seminars for thousands of people in col-leges and universities, corporations, government agencies, and finan-cial, legal, and medical institutions. In addition, I have individually coached business, professional, and government executives. I have written and recorded an audiocassette album, *Speak Without Fear—How to Give a Speech Like a Pro.*

Technically Speaking is arranged to lead the reader through the process of researching, organizing, and presenting complex informa-tion. I describe a ten-step approach that saves considerable prepara-tion time for speeches, briefings, and reports.

Each chapter (except the first) begins with an overview and concludes with an outline of key concepts. Checklists are included, such as an audience analysis checklist and a voice analysis checklist. Several chapters contain worksheets that enable the readers to define their strengths and areas needing improvement. There are simple warm-up exercises for the body and voice to ensure confident, vital delivery. There are suggestions for preparing audio-visual materials and a discussion of emerging techniques for visual presentations.

During the last few years, I have had considerable experience developing videoconferencing techniques. My booklet, *Dr. Jack's Ad-venture in Videoconferencing Land,* is a guide to communicating effectively on camera. I devote one chapter to this new medium because instantaneous exchange of information is essential within high-tech companies.

I emphasize techniques to deal with the anxieties that accompa-ny speaking. Such fears beset all speakers but are particularly unsettling to people who are accustomed to dealing with facts and figures rather than emotions and feelings.

Throughout this book, I show how humor, metaphors, and anecdotes can be used to clarify factual data. I include many examples gathered from interviews with model communicators.

This book can be used two ways: as a how-to instruction guide and as a reference tool. The novice technical speaker will learn the basic skills of oral presentation. The experienced speaker will use the book to hone communication skills and to update presentation techniques.

The physicist Richard Feynman believed that "making things as plain as day can also make them as sublime as the night sky." He demonstrated that the beauty of science is best conveyed not by wrapping it in mysticism or poetry, but by describing it simply, passionately, sometimes comically, and always clearly. With the help of *Technically Speaking*, I think you will be able to do the same.

Acknowledgments

I extend my thanks to Pam Bruton, Connie Bouressa-Shaw, Robert Schultz, and Larry Rader for their editing skills and feedback. Their good judgment and gentle but firm choices helped tighten the text. Special thanks: to my assistant Kathy Rollock for her many hours of typing and retyping and for the conversations and constructive criticism that helped clarify my ideas; to my children—Lisa, Paul, Shane, and Colleen—who have always supported my career and writing even though it took me away from their activities; to my youngest son, Tyler, for his encouragement, humor, and unfailing faith in my ability to convert my vision into reality; and to Jeanette Richards and my sister, Sarah Baltes, who listened patiently to all my trials and tribulations but kept me focused on finishing this book.

I wish to express my appreciation to Genigraphics, NASA's Jet Propulsion Laboratory, and Peninsula Partners for their contributions.

I want to thank the thousands of "students" who have been in my classes and seminars over the past twenty-five years from whom I learned so much. Finally, I am indebted to the people who answered my questionnaire and to all the model communicators who shared their ideas and inspired me to write this book.

Introduction

Canadian futurist Frank Ogden reports that information is doubling every eighteen months. Technological breakthroughs allow us to disseminate these data with greater speed than ever before through satellite communications, fiber optics, fax machines, and cellular telephones.

Yet, despite these advances, communicators are finding it increasingly difficult to capture and hold the attention of audiences. This trend particularly affects those who work in the scientific and technical fields. You must wade through reams of information, extract only the essential data, and communicate skillfully to bring about the desired response. The information that you have to convey is constantly being updated. The computer printout you have on the latest test results of your product's performance is superseded by a fax you receive in the morning, which is then made obsolete by a call you get on your voice mail or cellular phone on the way to lunch. At lunch, of course, you are supposed to present an intelligent overview of those same test results. When have you had a chance to absorb and synthesize the information that's bombarding you from all directions?

Companies battling to gain an edge on the competition need to translate the latest technological and scientific findings for the benefit of their customers. The ability of a company or research team to make a compelling presentation can be the deciding factor in determining whether a contract is awarded or a funding request is granted.

Scientists and technologists find themselves in unaccustomed roles that demand new communication competencies. They must bridge the different cultures within their company and communicate with technical, financial, sales, research, and generalist employees and managers to achieve organizational goals and objectives. They must not only be able to communicate with other professions in our borderless world but also inform the general public as well.

Technically Speaking was written for professionals in technology-oriented fields who want to improve their communication skills. The following pages offer time-proven, easy-to-follow steps and useful insights collected from my personal experience with thousands of clients for more than twenty-five years.

In the course of my work, I have found that scientists and technologists take pride in their resistance to being "packaged." They need not fear this author. I seek to make them more powerful by "unwrapping" their uniqueness. I want my readers to express their ideas comfortably, with confidence, and to get results on a consistent basis.

While we live in what is commonly referred to as the Information Age, the bottom line is, and always will be, that computers, telephones, fax machines, and satellites don't communicate, people do.

Part I
Being Comfortable, Confident, and in Control

1
Becoming a Model Communicator

"We are what and where we are because we have first imagined it."

—Donald Curtis

This time, you tell yourself you're going to give the perfect presentation. Given enough lead time, preparation, and self-confidence, you know you have the ability to present the kind of speech that will cause your audience to sit up and take notice.

You picture the surprised looks from the company's senior officer and the rapt attention of those seated in the back of the room as you make one insightful point after another. Hands shoot up to get your attention without your asking for questions. It's a lively give-and-take session. Applause follows and you feel a glow of genuine satisfaction as people crowd around you offering praise and congratulations.

Ah, if it could only be like that!

Reality sinks in. You realize that you'll probably end up giving another slapdash report thrown together at the last minute—due in large part to deadline pressure and lack of preparation time. Maybe you're stuck with soft information that needs verification. You're uncertain about your audience and what they want to hear. Maybe you're overwhelmed by other work responsibilities that demand your attention. Or you're busy attending to critical events in your personal life.

Frustrated, you think that if only you could take all those ideas running around in the corridors of your mind, isolate them, line them up in formation, and skillfully communicate them to your colleagues and the public, everyone would realize how brilliant and perceptive you are. And a myriad of problems would be solved.

Suddenly, your anticipation of getting the sale, convincing the review board that your project is on track, or having your research validated by your peers changes into the dreaded possibility of making a fool of yourself. The mental image you had of giving the perfect presentation is replaced with Murphy's Law: Everything that can go wrong does. And somehow you have equated the failure of the speech with failure as a person.

If you've ever felt like this, you're not alone. The fear of public speaking is a universal one. No matter how experienced, no matter how lofty the position, virtually every person faced with public speaking experiences some form of stage fright. And there are countless others who avoid speaking at all costs. Good communication is rarely an accident. Designing and delivering a successful presentation is a skill. The good news is that good communication, like any skill, can be learned.

I am cautious about agreeing with someone who says, "Well, I certainly learned from my mistakes that time!" I hear the catch in the voice, sense the tension in the muscles, and see the tightness in the jaw. Because, although it is possible to learn from one's mistakes, I also know that a technicolor imprint of those mistakes is ingrained into the memory forever. When that happens, it usually takes teeth-gritting willpower to block out negative memories and to face an audience again.

You can learn to swim and stay afloat without any coaching; it is also possible to muddle through reports and sales presentations all alone. Eventually you may succeed. In swimming, a coach can teach us how to stop thrashing about. We learn to breathe rhythmically and refine our strokes. We learn to merge with the water and not fight against it. And with every lap, we cut down the time it takes to swim from one point to another.

In speaking, we can also learn the refinements and the subtleties of getting our ideas across to our audience. We can learn to use our fears and anxieties to enhance our delivery. We can use techniques that will help save preparation time. Each positive experience will encourage us to look forward to opportunities for sharing information. Speaking in front of a group can bring satisfaction and pride. It can be a very enjoyable experience.

But the learning process begins with a conscious decision. Just as you commit yourself to excel in your profession, you must also commit yourself to excel as a public speaker and do what it takes to succeed. Let's get started!

2

Communicating Complex Technical Information

"Everything is simpler than you think and at the same time more complex than you imagine."

—Johann Wolfgang von Goethe

Overview

The information explosion does not necessarily mean there has been a knowledge explosion. We are data rich and understanding poor. Your audience needs to understand your ideas before they can accept them. A confused mind will say no. This chapter encourages you to look at the complex data you are presenting and find ways to tame, tailor, and illuminate that information so that you are transmitting useful knowledge that will be accepted by your audience.

A friend of mine was struggling to learn Akkadian, an ancient dead language. Making sense of the writing was an extremely frustrating task. Her teacher finally admitted that the only way to decipher an Akkadian tablet was to know in advance what it said. He explained that you need to know the subject, context, and jargon so you have a frame of reference and can choose the correct reading of a graphic symbol.

All of us must invest an enormous amount of energy in absorbing and processing information necessary to cope with daily life. When you are caught up in your ideas, it is easy to forget that other people don't have the same experience and familiarity with your technical discipline. Just as my friend needed prior information to learn Akkadian, you will need to provide basic references for your audiences.

Never overestimate your audience's knowledge base; at the same time, never underestimate their intelligence. A computer programmer told me that she had not been working in her field for eighteen months. When she went out for job interviews, she not only didn't know the workings of current software programs but didn't even understand the acronyms referring to them. She was depressed because she couldn't demonstrate how intelligent she was to the interviewers. They had already predetermined that she was not qualified because she didn't belong to the current "information club." She became competitive only after researching the market and taking time to update her skills. Assume your audience is smart, but not up-to-date in your discipline.

Model communicators make information simple and easy to understand. This is not to say that they water down their ideas. Albert Einstein said, "Everything should be made as simple as possible, but not simpler."

The most interesting discovery that I made in the course of my interviews is that model communicators illuminate and give insight; they don't dilute scientific and technical information. They don't talk down to their audiences; rather they feel that scientific concepts should be available to everyone. They empower their listeners. They "translate" complex concepts in a way that adds to a person's knowledge. Mike Sundell, the national sales manager for Basic Coatings (an Iowa company that produces wood and metal finishes), said, "I think in terms of bringing technology *up* to the level of my audience. A lot of audiences are intelligent and sophisticated; they simply haven't been exposed to this specific technology."

Publishing consultant Wendell Forbes remarked:

> No matter at what level of management we operate, and no matter what our job is, the challenge to all of us is to understand that whatever we are doing, the ultimate goal is wisdom. Even if we are on a production line, our data is what is delivered to us and our wisdom is what we should deliver to the next person. None of us operate exclusively at the wisdom level. We all start with our own equivalent of data and strive to end up with the ultimate satisfaction and reward that we here characterize as wisdom. One person's wisdom is another person's data.

Strive to pass on to your audiences useful knowledge and wisdom that will help them reach their goals.

Recognizing and Responding to Multilevels of Knowledge

How can you translate complex material so that your audience receives the information easily and can incorporate that knowledge into their experience base? Every individual in an audience has a different worldview, and there may be as many levels of knowledge as there are people. An audience analysis will help you understand how you should present your material.

Let's say you are going to address three different groups. The first audience may read *Reader's Digest* and *USA Today*. This audience will want and need to know very simplified versions of technical information. A second audience might read *Scientific American, Omni,* and *MacWorld* and attend computer user or environmental focus groups. This level would also include people who give business technical presentations. This audience will feel comfortable with some technical information. Another audience may attend technical conferences that present in-depth information, statistics, product details, demonstrations, references, samples, plots, schematics, and drawings. These audiences are interested in the hows and whys. Their reading material might include publications such as *American Institute of Aeronautics and Astronautics Journal, Journal of Applied Physics,* and *IEEE Transactions on Geoscience and Remote Sensing.* (IEEE is the Institute of Electrical and Electronic Engineers.)

A researcher should be able to convince a budget review panel that her project is valid and profitable for the company as easily as she would address her peers to describe the details of the process she followed. And she should also be able to adapt that same technical information to a general audience.

Many of the audiences you will face will have multilevels of knowledge. Begin your presentation by expanding and developing your information to cover some basics so that you won't alienate the people in your audience who have little knowledge of your subject. You can contract your topic by adding some in-depth points that will keep the interest of the more knowledgeable members of the audience. Expand by giving definitions of technical terms, and explain the acronyms. If it is necessary to describe a complex concept, give examples that include reference points familiar to everyone. However, you may contract again with a more specific and technical example. Reiterate your main points in simple terms as you go along. End your speech by expanding again and summarizing your message in general terms so that your entire audience can reach the same conclusion that you do.

How Much Detail?

David L. Harten reported in *Reader's Digest's* Campus Comedy that a liberal arts student scrawled the graffiti "Love makes the world go round." Underneath, a physics student added "With a little help from intrinsic angular momentum."[1] Scientists and engineers who think in precise terms often expect to communicate in the same manner, but you can alienate an audience by talking over their heads. Avoid exactness if the audience's knowledge level dictates a more general outlook. The perceptive expert will seek ways to diminish the gap between his knowledge and that of the audience. If the listener begins to feel ignorant, he will resent the presenter and his purpose.

Give the general idea or major findings before you give the details, the function, and the principles. Alert your audience that you are going to build a skyscraper, not a log cabin. Then you can describe it and show them how step by step. If you are describing characteristics, help your audience by zeroing in on the specifics. How big is too big? What do you mean by not enough time?

Decide how much detail your audience needs to know to do the job, make the decision, advise others, or achieve some clear purpose. While one audience may feel buried in particulars, a technical group of your peers may think that four days of in-depth talks and a four-inch notebook merely skim the surface.

Decoding Tech-Speak Into Concrete Images

There is nothing frivolous about depicting complex scholarly subjects in understandable concrete images. Choose images that are familiar to your audience. Illustrate the application of a theory or demonstrate your conclusion with words that engage the senses of touch, sight, smell, or taste. Robert M. Price, former chairman and chief executive officer of Control Data Corporation, clearly illustrates the complexity of parallel processing with this simple comparison:

> Without using parallelism, you could simply hire one person with one lawnmower to mow your lawn, but you have a

large lawn and it will take one person four hours. To shorten the time, you could contract with four people to do the job: one person for each side of your house. The control is simple: A mows the front, B mows the back, C mows the left side, D mows the right side. In this case, you have used parallel processing to reduce the time needed to mow your lawn from four hours to one.

Let's push this method and hire 240 people to mow the lawn. Can you expect that the job will be done in one minute? Not exactly. The problem is that you must spend a lot of time contacting each of these people and telling them what to do so that they aren't running over each other with their lawnmowers. With 240 workers, the simple job of mowing the lawn becomes a major task of control.

In state-of-the-art computing today, we know how to manage modest levels of parallelism. But we don't know how to manage *large* numbers of parallel processors effectively.[2]

Avoid "fat" words or abstract words. *Quality* and *change* are fat words. For example, if you say CADD (computer-aided drafting and design) is a high-quality software program, are you saying that it is faster (how fast?), is more interactive, or has more pixels per inch?

Defining Your Acronyms

One high-tech trainer told me, "We get so buried in our technical language that we forget that others don't have any idea what those acronyms are referring to." An audience may miss the whole object of your presentation because you assume they understand terms basic to your own profession. I gave a seminar to a group of nurses about the fear of public speaking and described how even CEOs of major corporations are often fearful. At the end of the session, a young nurse came up to me and asked, "What's a CEO?" My point that even chief executive officers experience fear was totally lost.

An overabundance of acronyms is especially prevalent in government circles. Washington state representative Steve Van Luen published a seventy-eight-page booklet that identified 3,187 of them. They range from FONSI, which stands for "finding of no significant impact," to LOVE, which represents "lots of vocational education," to SURF, which means "simple update reference file." Use all of the words in an unfamiliar acronym more than once so that your audience can remember exactly what it means. It might be advisable to include a cue sheet or glossary among your handouts.

If the words used to form the acronym are a meaningless abstraction, then the resulting acronym can be totally vague. For example, lasers are something we encounter daily in the bar code scanner in the supermarket and in medicine and dental equipment. Many people know the astronauts communicated with earth through laser beams. However, a recent poll asked over 2,000 adults if lasers worked by focusing sound waves. Thirty-six percent correctly answered it was false, but 29 percent thought it was true, and 35 percent didn't know. Even if they knew the acronym stands for *L*ight *A*mplification by *S*timulated *E*mission of *R*adiation, they might need a further definition of the terms to understand how lasers work.

People are intimidated by jargon but often won't ask for an explanation. A television commercial asked people on the street if they were familiar with Quinto, which is a new state lottery game. No one would admit they didn't know what the announcer was talking about. Passersby confidently said that it was a new dance step or a small Australian animal. One man confessed that he had an uncle who spent five years in Quinto.

Meaningful Definitions

"An inventor is an engineer who doesn't take his work seriously."

—Charles Kettering

Definitions only work when your audience is familiar with references in the definition. What is a Xanadu? If I said that a Xanadu has the tail of an elephant and the neck of a giraffe, you could start to imagine the creature. But if I said that it also had the body of a tripozip, your mind would have a difficult time searching for an association.

George A. Keyworth II, the director of research for the Hudson Institute, added to his audience's knowledge with a thorough definition:

> There's one word I want to use that sounds technical, but needn't be. The word is *digitization,* but think of it as a computer-age version of Morse code, the old Western Union language that had only dots and dashes. Like Morse code,

digitization consists of only two words. Those two words are
the means by which information is made so simple that it
can be treated by the computer as nothing more than a
series of ones and zeroes to be added and subtracted. But
what makes digitization significant is that virtually any
kind of information—and by that I mean words, numbers,
voice, music, photographs, or movies—can be converted
into those streams of ones and zeroes.[3]

Each word in your presentation can be made more explicit and
set forth by the words around it. For instance, author Bill Sweetman
explains the design of the Stealth bomber:

The idea is to avoid or minimize anything that might add
to the plane's radar reflectivity. That means no right an-
gles. For example, the rudders are canted outward in a V
shape rather than being vertical. In addition, there are no
curving surfaces which act as isotropic scatterers, that is,
curves that reflect glints from any viewing angle. What's
left is a prismatic gemlike shape composed of many flat
plates or facets.[4]

What Is It Like? Similes, Metaphors, and Analogies

Your audience will show discomfort, annoyance, and frustration if
they are unable to understand your presentation. No one likes to
think that he or she may lack the intelligence to grasp information.
Many scientific subjects are hard to describe; they can be difficult to
see, touch, measure, or imagine. A presenter should seek to find ways
to illuminate a concept in known terms with the least amount of
distortion. Aristotle said that people remember information better if
it is closely associated with something familiar, is sequential, or
contrasts with something they already know. Comparisons and contrasts are two of the best ways to translate your information clearly to
your audience.

Metaphors, similes, and analogies are comparisons that often can
lead to amazing insights. By using these devices, you can enliven the
dullest data and help people discover they know more than they
thought they did.

Simile: Makes a direct comparison between two dissimilar
                 objects and always uses connective words or

	phrases such as "like," "as," or "as if." For example, research "is like" a treasure hunt! Fresh, unique similes enliven your language.
Metaphor:	Assumes an identity between two things. A metaphor is a condensed simile. For example, research *is* a treasure hunt. Metaphors are useful descriptions that add color and express feelings: "The software marketplace is a jungle." You are substituting an image for an idea. The names of athletic teams are often metaphorical: Cowboys, Seahawks, Pirates.
Analogy:	An expansion of a simile or metaphor. It uses the similarity of attributes, uses, or circumstances between two objects or concepts to explain an unfamiliar object or a concept. Whereas similes and metaphors use vivid language to get an audience's attention, the analogy facilitates understanding by explaining the complex in simple, everyday terms.

When Maxine Singer, a biologist in the field of genetics, appeared on Bill Moyers' *World of Ideas,* she said:

> I'm interested in human genetics and in aspects of the structure of human DNA, what we call the human genome. The best way to look at it is that a gene is like a sentence in an encyclopedia. It's a piece of information, and it's buried in the genome, the whole encyclopedia, which is a vast store of information. The gene instructs the cell how to do some one thing, and all together the billions of cells in your body do all the things that make you who you are, that make a corn plant what it is, that makes a yeast cell what it is. It turns out there's a lot of DNA that doesn't really have any information, at least as far as we know now. It's as though you had an encyclopedia and on every third page there was a lot of jabberwocky. And two pages later, there it is again. It doesn't look like a meaningful sentence. I can't figure out what it is, and I'm certainly confounded by the fact that it occurs so many times.[5]

Mike Sundell of Basic Coatings says that he sometimes uses different analogies to make a point early in his sales presentation:

There are so many regional differences. An audience in the heart of New York City is a natural "doubting Thomas" with a show-me attitude. They listen differently to you than the people do in the central corn country of Iowa, where they don't lock their houses or cars at night. I check to see how my audience is listening to me and how they react. Then I know how to tailor the rest of my presentation and what type of analogies they will respond to.

I might just give the facts to a technical audience, but I could use the following metaphor with a nontechnical audience: To make products dry hard enough for floors, it has always been necessary to add catalysts or cross linkers. Think of polymer resins in solution as individual balls. If you tried to walk among the balls, you'd fall through. But if you tied string between them, you'd form a net that would hold your weight. That's what cross linkers do: They tie the polymers together.

John Moore, a software trainer at Hewlett-Packard, used the following analogy:

To explain virtual memory, consider that you are having a party at your house and are serving dinner. You have invited 100 guests, but have room for only 20 at your house. You rent a van to shuttle the guests back and forth from the Holiday Inn down the road whenever they wish to participate in the activities or eat at your party. For every 10 that leave, 10 more can be bused back to the party. By the same token, you can access a certain amount of memory but you have to commute the data back and forth. You can't have all the data there at the same time.

Moore used easily observed similarities to reduce the uncertainties of the people who were learning a software program. To avoid confusion, make sure that the similarities in your example outweigh points of dissimilarity.

You may agree that analogies help clarify and are an excellent way to increase understanding, but how do you make up an analogy?

- Think about the situation or idea you want to describe.
- Think about what you want your audience to feel, think, and do.

- Review your audience's background, particular interests, and knowledge (see Chapter 6).
- Find several things in your unfamiliar idea, process, sequence, action, or object that have similarities to a familiar idea, process, sequence, action, or object. What are the interrelationships? Analogies will eventually break down, so start with a strong relationship.
- Choose familiar objects, actions, places, people, myths, sports, or experiences that do not require any further interpretation. Your audience should be able to make an immediate connection and comparison.
- Make sure that the analogy you are making is short and simple and fairly general so that your audience can now view the idea in a new way.

One of my clients, Mike Carson, an engineer from EBASCO (Electric Bond and Share Company), was summoned to be an expert witness in a court case. He was testifying about the condition of a utility system, including the poles and other equipment, and the extent of depreciation in the utility district. It costs $2,481 to install a new utility pole. According to the tax laws, a pole has no "book value" after thirty-five years. Yet in the dry climate of northern California, poles may last twice as long as this. Therefore, the question was, What is the value of the average utility pole? The complex information would have overwhelmed a jury of ordinary citizens.

I asked Mike to think of something that the jury could relate to that would compare with the depreciation of telephone poles, as described above. We started to work out an analogy with a house depreciation and replacement cost. However, we were concerned that some of the members of the jury might not be homeowners and that they wouldn't recognize the relationship. We abandoned that analogy, and Mike suggested that almost everyone has bought and sold a car. Book value and depreciation rates would be familiar to them. When the attorney asked Mike to explain, he said, "It is similar to the depreciation of a car," and proceeded to make a clear comparison.

Because science and technology are constantly changing, new ideas and information can sometimes be explained only in terms of what we already know. Metaphors, similes, and analogies are useful tools to clarify communications.

Failure to Communicate

If the response you receive from your audience indicates that your material is hard to follow, ask yourself *why* it is obscure. Do you avoid analyzing and interpreting because you fear making inappropriate value judgments? Are you concerned that your views will conflict with those of a superior? Is using tech-speak your way of conforming and insulating yourself from others, especially outsiders? Are you overly conscious of criticism and therefore qualify every statement? Of course, one final possibility (and one that I hope isn't true) is that you haven't done your homework and have nothing insightful to say about your topic.

Your audience will appreciate your efforts to decode and interpret complex information. A judge who was presiding over a difficult trial said that the defense lawyer presented layers and layers of documentation that included federal antitrust litigation, laws from two state jurisdictions, environmental issues, and contract and employee rights litigations. She noticed that the jurors' eyes glazed over in confusion and boredom as they attempted to follow the bewildering onslaught of facts, statistics, and details over a six-week period.

The defense attorney gave a long and tedious closing argument, reciting multiple facts from the case and complex legal theories. After making a simple presentation in his closing argument, the plaintiff's attorney advanced toward the jury. "What we have here," he stated, "is a classic case of a fox getting caught in the henhouse. Now all you have to do is decide how much the fox has to pay," and he sat down. The jury members relaxed with a sigh of relief. They understood this language. The plaintiff was awarded the largest amount of damages in a state court in the history of Washington.

Some people can make the trivial complex. What is simple is always a matter of objective assessment. What is understood becomes simple. Changing the spark plugs in your car isn't simple if you're not sure how to do it. However, operating a broadcast camera might be simple if you knew how to use it.

An audience that doesn't understand the data you are presenting will remember little. Neither will they be persuaded to buy your product, fund your research, accept your bid, or be influenced by your ideas. Use distinctive language that does not obscure meaning. Understanding is a prerequisite to acceptance.

KEY IDEAS

- Empower your audiences by illuminating complex information.
- Strive for clarity and use concrete words and examples.
- Associate new information with the familiar so that your audience can see relationships.
- Use stories and analogies; they will be remembered longer than dry facts and statistics.
- Never underestimate the intelligence of your audience.

Notes

1. David L. Harten, in "Campus Comedy" column, *Reader's Digest* (September 1986). Reprinted with permission. Copyright © 1986 by the Reader's Digest Association, Inc.
2. Robert Price, "Supercomputers Propel Technology," *Vital Speeches of the Day* (March 15, 1988).
3. George A. Keyworth II, "Goodbye Central: Telecommunications and Computing in the 1990s," *Vital Speeches of the Day* (April 1, 1990).
4. Bill Sweetman, *Stealth Bomber* (Stillwater, Minn.: Motorbooks International, 1989).
5. Maxine Singer appearing on *Bill Moyers' World of Ideas* (#138). Used with permission of Public Affairs Television, Inc., New York, 1988.

3

Making Fears and Anxieties Work for You

"Of all the liars in the world, the worst are our own fears."

—Rudyard Kipling

Overview

You may be a brilliant engineer, scientist, or technologist, but if fears and anxieties adversely affect your ability to communicate, you will not be able to inform, influence, or persuade others. In this chapter, you will learn to specifically identify your fears and then develop a strategy to deal with them. If you minimize the perceived threat to your self-concept, you will find that your physical reactions will diminish.

Recently, I received a telephone call from the chief executive officer of a software company. He wanted to discuss his fear of public speaking. He said he was a "hard core" case and panicked at the very thought of speaking in front of a group.

When I met this gentleman, he confided that even though he had avoided public speaking, his company had grown and he was financially successful, because his product was in such demand. Now he was asked to speak about his product in the international market, and his buyers in Europe didn't want a substitute. In addition, he said he had some innovative ideas about civic causes that he wanted to address. He wanted to gain community support. Could I possibly help?

He is an articulate, dynamic, and exceptionally intelligent man. Yet I wasn't surprised by his admission. Over the years I have learned that no matter how lofty the position, the material success, or the social status, somewhere deep inside every one of us is the feeling that we just aren't good enough, that somehow we will make fools of ourselves in public.

I accepted the offer to work with the software executive but he told me he would have to postpone our first class. He was flying his plane to Montana for a week of survival training with an Alaska bush pilot. "But I would be scared to death to fly under the conditions they do," I said. "What's to be scared of?" he asked in puzzlement. A threat of real bodily harm was not as frightening as the perceived threat of an audience judging him and his ideas.

Virtually every speaker, every performer, experiences some form of stage fright. And there are millions like this CEO, who avoid speaking at all costs. Rex Harrison (who played Professor Higgins in *My Fair Lady*) said, "There isn't a performer with an ounce of talent that is completely relaxed in front of an audience." Take pleasure in the fact that only fools know no anxieties.

The path to success begins by acknowledging and accepting your fears. To deny you have fears is counterproductive and could lead to disastrous results. Everyone experiences fear to some degree. It's a normal, natural emotion that cannot, and should not, be suppressed. Recent evidence suggests that the intensity of the fear emotion can be attributed to genetics. Other studies report that the initial programming of a humiliating or embarrassing situation magnifies the fear. There is no one cause or one therapy. We can, however, learn how to make fear help, rather than hinder, our performance.

Analyzing Your Fears

I recently received a phone call from Dave, an engineer friend. "Jan, I have to make a presentation next week and I'm so anxious about doing well that I haven't been able to sleep for the past week. Can you help me?" His voice sounded as if he had been condemned to stand in front of a firing squad, and he wanted me to make it less painful.

"Can you tell me exactly what you are afraid of?" I asked. "I'll probably make a fool of myself," Dave answered. "What if I can't remember all the points? What if I can't answer all the questions? What if my speech goes overtime? I've wasted so much time worrying that I only have a few days left to prepare." Half-jokingly, he added, "Isn't there some scientific way to get rid of these fears?"

I told Dave that I would help him, but that there was no scientific way to eliminate his fears. Besides, to completely do so would make him an ineffective speaker. I added, "Fear is nature's way of helping you be alert, sharp, and up to doing your best—like the pregame tension of an athlete."

Most of us, like Dave, can drive ourselves to distraction and waste untold energy by dwelling on negative "what ifs." What caused Dave to procrastinate and fear speaking in public? Fear is caused by the perception of a threat. Some fears are real, but most are imagined. A scientist takes precautionary measures in the laboratory to avoid accidents; there are also measures that one can take to ensure success on a public platform.

"Small amounts of fear alert you," explains Phillip Gold, Chief of the Clinical Neuroendocrinology Branch of the National Institute of Mental Health. "We think better, we move faster, and we adapt better. But too much stress tips the scales the wrong way. Then we can't remember, we can't adapt to a situation. We make wrong choices. We feel demoralized and lose confidence in ourselves. It can be catastrophic."

One way to keep from being overwhelmed by our fears is to analyze what we're afraid of—such as forgetting our lines or not being able to answer everyone's questions. When we analyze these concerns, we realize that solutions can usually be found, whether by thorough preparation or by developing effective techniques.

I've noticed my scientific and technical clients are prone to stage fright because they tend to have an aversion to any kind of "performing." They are usually reactive in their communications, even in their social lives. Separating themselves from the group and taking center stage is unpleasant and foreign. They are more comfortable observing and reacting, which is why they excel in the question and answer period, rather than in making a prepared presentation.

We create our own insecurities and fears. Unfortunately, we make decisions based on the fantasies our imaginations conjure up for us, or we make decisions based on an attitude shaped by something that happened years ago—or what we think happened.

When I taught communications in the Management Program at the University of Washington, I sent a questionnaire to all my incoming students. I received a terse reply from one, an established manager of a well-known company. She wrote, "I will not be forced to get up in front of my peers and speak. I have completely avoided public speaking and am aware that it has cost me career advances."

I talked with her before class and she told me about an agonizing personal experience that she had. During her senior year in high school, she had spent a harrowing night defending her brother and sister from a raging alcoholic father. When she arrived at school the next morning, she suddenly remembered that she was supposed to give a speech. Not wanting to explain the real reason for her lack of preparation, she asked the teacher for a postponement. The teacher insisted she go to the front of the class. Paralyzed with fear, she stood silently for two minutes before being allowed to sit down. Exhausted and humiliated, she vowed never to make another speech, and she had since avoided public speaking in many ways that were actually ingenious.

I encouraged her to trust me and the class and try a brief presentation. "It's okay to be lousy," I told her. "No grades, no judgments; stop when you want to."

She reluctantly agreed. She hyperventilated at first, but then as she recognized the safe environment, she gained more and more confidence. She did a fine job and, she was pleased with herself for having taken that big first step. She had broken a link she had with the past.

One of my executive clients hired me to work with him on a speech. When I started to talk about fears and anxieties, he interrupted impatiently. "Let's skip that," he said. "I never get nervous." I asked him if he had ever had a bad speaking experience. Although he said no, he proceeded to tell how his boarding school headmaster had humiliated him in front of his peers. He swore then that nothing like that would ever happen to him again and he vowed to become an excellent communicator.

Two different reactions to a traumatic situation. One person viewed it as a defeat; the other one considered it a challenge and was driven to practice and excel.

Can you remember an embarrassing or humiliating experience speaking in front of a group? Reflect on your childhood. I am amazed when people immediately recall a long-ago situation and describe it in vivid detail. Their voices reflect the pain. When they've finished, I ask them to go back and create a happy ending. I tell them to relax and visualize the incident ending successfully several times. Your imagination doesn't know the difference between visualizing it and having it actually happen. Gradually, the negative feelings will diminish.

Physiological Reactions to Fear

To understand why fear can have such a tremendous effect on us, it may be helpful to understand how fear affects us physically. Imagine that you are asked to give a presentation and you agree to do so. Let's examine what happens to you physiologically before you speak.

The human stress response is derived from the "fight or flight syndrome" that served to keep our ancestors alive when they were confronted with a saber-toothed tiger. They could choose to face up to the tiger and fight it, or flee.

We have a similar reaction when we perceive a social danger to our ego. Making a fool of ourselves in public is today's tiger. We need to defend our image. As we get ready to speak, our body mobilizes its forces to meet this demanding situation. Hormones are released into the bloodstream to prepare for action. Within seconds, our heartbeat, blood pressure, respiration, and perspiration noticeably increase.

For our ancestors, an increased blood supply to the muscles enabled them to run from the tiger or battle with added strength. For us, the usefulness of increased muscle power is minimal. We have an intellectual encounter before us. We want to think well, remember clearly, and be creative, quick-witted, and, possibly, funny.

Normally, the brain uses one-fourth of the blood supply. In stressful situations, with the blood rushing to our muscles, the brain is shortchanged. We need to relax our muscles to redirect that oxygen-rich blood to the brain.

Excellent relaxation exercises are stretching, yawning, shaking arms and legs, and swallowing. You can include neck rolls, shoulder shrugs, and sighing. Suck on a mint to help you in the relaxing action of swallowing. Take a brisk walk up and down the hall. These movements help release tension.

Check your body to pinpoint sites of tension. Let's say, for example, you feel tension in your hands. If you can't shake them, visualize all those muscles becoming free and weightless. They will relax but also be ready to spring alertly into action. You want to work toward a state of restful energy. If you don't have a private place immediately prior to your speech, do relaxation exercises earlier in the day or while traveling to the site of your presentation.

Deep breathing will also help you to relax. Inhale to the count of six, hold to the count of six, exhale to the count of six, hold empty to the count of six. Do this several times, and concentrate on the numbers as if they were appearing in the middle of your forehead. Comfortably fill your lungs with air, and let all the tension flow from your body as you exhale. Your heartbeat will slow down and you'll feel calmer. You can do this exercise unobtrusively, even in front of a group.

Incidentally, when we eat or drink, blood rushes to the stomach to help the digestion process, and our brain loses out again. Therefore, it is best to eat or drink lightly, if at all, before speaking. Avoid alcohol.

You Are in Control

Years ago when I taught at a community college, I persuaded the administration to purchase a video camera so I could record my students giving presentations. The first week my students were apprehensive about being videotaped. They said the camera made them nervous. The second week they said the camera made them forget what they were going to say. The third week, a young woman stumbled through the beginning of her presentation, then stopped and said that the camera was making her uncomfortable. "Then please stop," I said. "We will all wait until the camera does something to make you comfortable." Twenty-three students stared at the camera. Finally one observed, "It isn't going to do anything." "I guess *I* made *myself* upset," the speaker said. The class learned the lesson that they had to accept responsibility for permitting their fears and anxieties to affect their behavior.

It is important to remember that a camera or an audience doesn't have control over you. You control yourself and your own tension. You decide if a camera or an audience will stress you out. I know from experience that if you wait for the audience to put you at ease, you will wait forever.

It's a matter of perception. You can either think of the audience as a ferocious tiger and magnify the threat or regard it as a group of eager listeners and minimize the threat.

Someday I'm Gonna Own This Town!

An excellent way to decrease the fear of speaking is to increase your desire to speak. General Chuck Yeager, the famous test pilot and the first man to break the sound barrier, says that he feeds on fear as if it were a high-energy candy bar. He is able to do so because he has learned to welcome challenges as opportunities to test his skill, a chance to prove that he is the best. Think of it as the "Someday I'm gonna own this town!" theory.

Here's how this theory applies to public speaking.

Karen Northrup of the U.S. Army Corps of Engineers had been forewarned that the general would be attending her presentation. She spent weeks designing slides and also preparing a duplicate backup of viewgraphs. After hours of practice, she felt completely confident that her presentation would go well.

But when the day arrived, the program dragged as speakers went beyond their allotted times. The schedule was already twenty minutes into her segment. Northrup's turn came, and she was walking to the front of the room when the general stood up and announced, "I have to leave in ten minutes to catch a plane. Can you conclude your presentation by 4:30?"

Northrup began to panic. "This is unfair," she thought, doubting that she could delete three-quarters of her presentation and still deliver a strong message. What if they were testing her, the only woman in the room? Wouldn't it be simpler to suggest postponing it until another time? But a small voice kicked in and quietly whispered, "You can pull it off and you will look terrific! Go for it!"

Everyone was staring at her, waiting for an answer. She decided to condense the introduction, flash quickly through the first ten slides, include two main points, give examples, and conclude with statistics.

"Certainly," she declared in a businesslike tone. Her eyes swept the room and made contact with the general. "Let's begin by looking at some new information," she said.

Northrup successfully responded to the last-minute challenge by adjusting her presentation to fit the situation. Her fear was put aside as she concentrated on actions that would bring about the response she wanted. She even felt that she won extra points because her audience recognized she handled a difficult situation creatively.

There are few times in public speaking when everything is automatically stacked in the presenter's favor. The difference between the amateur and pro is that the amateur gives up in the face of fear, while the pro considers a situation a challenge and plunges ahead. The person who stands up to speak and the person who is too fearful to get up have one thing in common: They both feel fear. But good speakers acknowledge the fear, harness it, and decide to use what abilities they have to accomplish their objectives. Their desire to succeed is stronger than their fear of failure. They also know that the only way to succeed is to take some risks.

Tips on Alleviating Fears

■ *Prepare 150 percent.* Preparation is essential and will make you feel more secure. Get started immediately even if you have a long lead time. Time and effort spent in design will translate into self-assuredness during the actual delivery.

■ *Acknowledge and accept your fears.* Accept nervousness for what it is: part of the preparation for speaking. Remember two things: First, our bodies initially react involuntarily and in proportion to the perceived degree of danger. Second, we can minimize further bodily reactions by our attitude and self-talk. We can make these reactions work for us.

■ *Label your physical reactions in a positive way.* You don't have to label the physical feelings of heart palpitations, quickening pulse, dry mouth, and sweaty palms as negative reactions. When you're in front of the audience, interpret your feelings as anticipation, exuberance, and joy. Say to yourself, "I'm very excited about being able to share my ideas."

■ *Avoid visions of doom and gloom.* If you have a vivid imagination, you probably have wild fantasies of what could go wrong in a presentation. Remember that if you perceive the situation as extremely threatening, your body will increase the nervous energy it needs to fight this big battle. Appraise your situation realistically. What is the worst thing that could possibly happen? Has it ever happened? Will anyone throw tomatoes at you? Will the audience get up and leave? Will you really fall in a dead faint in front of everyone? By being realistic about the "danger" of the situation, you will have more control, and you will reduce the stress response to that situation.

■ *Give yourself permission to make mistakes.* Give up perfectionism; it makes unrealistic demands. If you aren't making a few mistakes during every speech, you aren't taking risks and growing. Calculate how you can minimize your risks. Don't seek to be a keynote speaker at your company's annual convention if you really don't have the expertise or experience. But do challenge yourself. Do a few things that terrify you. Anything less is boring.

■ *Don't worry if memory lapses throw you.* What if you forget what you're going to say next? I've had it happen to me. There are several things you can say: "Let me summarize what we've covered so far," for example, or "Would anyone like to comment on my last point?" Or refer to a handout, or go to the next slide, even if it is out of context. These actions gain you some time to remember. The main thing is not to get rattled. If you maintain your composure, the audience may not even be aware that you lost your place.

■ *Trust in your abilities.* Believe in yourself, your ideas, and the value they have for other people. Act as if you are in control, even if you don't feel that way. Remember that you appear much more confident to your audience than you feel. Create mental pictures of your success as if it has already happened. Your confidence will build as you progress.

■ *Laugh.* Laughter releases tension. Has anyone said to you, "I laughed so hard that I fell off my chair"? The reason why it happens is because our muscles become totally relaxed when we laugh. Also stretch and do isometric exercises for relaxed alertness.

■ *Make a decision to do your best and then let go of your concerns.* Worry will use up a lot of precious energy and not be the least bit helpful. Relax and spend your time more productively visualizing and anticipating a successful outcome.

■ *Rate the difficulty of your presentation on a scale of 1 to 10.* Your presentation may have important consequences, but think back to other difficult situations you handled well. Acknowledge the critical or doubting voices in your head but replace them with positive thoughts of times when you were confident and in control.

■ *Become totally involved in the moment.* We feel fear when there is conflict: The body wants to do one thing, the mind says to do something else. The need to succeed and do everything perfectly becomes more emotionally charged when the stakes get higher. Your boss and key decision makers may be attending your talk and this presentation could propel your career forward (or slam doors in your face). Obviously, you have to be at your best even when part of your mind wants to exit quickly. Make the conscious decision to stay and be terrific. One remedy for fear is to tell yourself, "I would rather be here than anyplace else." It works!

■ *Make the audience your partner.* Remember that the audience wants you to succeed. They want you to be good; audiences don't come to hear a bad presentation. If you're comfortable, they will be comfortable. Direct your energy into becoming involved with your audience. Work toward generating thoughts and pictures in their minds. Make an emotional connection.

■ *Take every opportunity to speak.* Experience and practice will reduce your anxiety considerably.

Fear Can Be Helpful!

Fear can be very helpful. Remember the way you reacted to stress and anxiety by cramming for that statistics exam and acing the final? Take charge of the situation. Change your perspective. Use relaxation techniques. Totally concentrate on the moment. Prepare Plans B and C. Suddenly this whole anxiety-ridden situation is transformed into a challenge.

A doctor doesn't fall apart when she sees a car accident victim. A good tennis player doesn't crumble when he faces a strong opponent. A prepared speaker doesn't crumble before a large discerning audience. A small amount of fear can actually push us to perform beyond our accepted capabilities. The challenge is to recognize the fear, accept it, and make it work for you.

KEY IDEAS

- Understand and accept your fears. Minimize the perceived threat to your ego.
- Redirect the energy from stage fright into stage presence.
- Laugh. It releases tension.
- Do deep breathing and relaxation exercises.
- Make the audience your partner.

Part II
Creating a Powerful Message in Ten Steps

I asked one of my clients how he divided his time in preparing for his presentations. "I spend about 30 percent of my time in research, 40 percent in actually writing it and creating graphics, and about 5 percent in rehearsal." "But that only adds up to 75 percent," I said. "What about the other 25 percent?" "Oh," he replied, "I spend 25 percent of my time worrying about it before I ever get started."

One of the biggest problems facing any presenter is procrastination. I have developed a ten-step system that will help you get started immediately. The order can vary, but each of these steps must be accomplished.

Like any efficient system, this one will require modification with feedback or as new information is obtained. For example, you may need additional graphics for clarification if you find your audience lacks the expected expertise in your field. Your short-term objective may change because of last-minute information from a colleague. When you give a more interactive presentation, as in a consulting situation, you may wish to delete information on the spot.

If you master this system, you will be able to get the response you want on a consistent basis.

Ten Steps to Effective Presentations

Step 1 Target Your Objective, Tailor Your Message
Step 2 Define Your Image
Step 3 Analyze Your Audience
Step 4 Design the Finish First, the Start Second
Step 5 Choose Main Points

Step 6   Select Supporting Points
Step 7   Say It With a Visual
Step 8   Organize Your Content
Step 9   Add Variety
Step 10   Rehearse, Rehearse

4

Targeting Your Objective and Tailoring Your Message

"Those who cannot tell what they desire or expect still sigh and struggle with indefinite thoughts and vast wishes."

—Ralph Waldo Emerson

Overview

If you're going on a trip, you need to know your exact destination in order to plan which route to travel and what to take with you. Target your specific objective in order to decide which approach is best, what information to include, and what information to omit. In this chapter we discuss four criteria for targeting your objective.

Once you have decided on the response you want from a particular audience, tailor a message that will bring about that response. Your message should include the main idea plus the profit value to the audience for accepting and acting upon your information. Preplanning and time spent deciding on your desired outcome will give your ideas direction and focus. It will simplify your preparation and save time, money, and frustration.

During the Middle Ages, knights were trained with innovative "teaching machines." The knight on horseback charged a wooden figure mounted on a pivot. If the knight struck the shield exactly in the center, the wooden figure would fall over. But if it was struck off center, the figure would swing around and hit the knight with a club. That is instant feedback!

It's not necessary to employ such drastic measures for those presenters who stray from their purpose; but many audiences resent a speaker who wastes their time. Target your objective and customize your message to get the response you want. Fail to do so, and you leave the audience response to chance. If you know what you're aiming for, you will be able to evaluate whether you succeeded.

Establishing Your General Objective

Ask yourself, "Why am I speaking on *this subject* to *this audience* at *this particular time?* Is it because I have something worthwhile to say due to my background, credentials, or personal experiences that gives me unique insight?"

Your general purpose may be to inform, to persuade, to consult and recommend, to inspire, to entertain, or a combination of these.

You may want to:

- Inform customers, the general public, or investors about your industry, research, products, and services.
- Report progress on a project to management.
- Explain new concepts, goals, or regulations to employees.
- State your ideas for a professional association meeting.

Instruct others on:

- The use of new equipment or software
- Methods and policies
- Job requirements

Persuade others to:

- Accept and support your ideas.
- Give you resources: time, personnel, equipment, financing.
- Accept changes in operational procedures.
- Start or continue projects.
- Buy a product or service.
- Select your company for research or design.
- Accept the validity of your research.

In Chapter 3, I suggested you consider your audience your partner, not the adversary. You're actually asking them to duplicate your thinking and feeling. Take them by the hand and guide them along step by step through the maze of information to your destination.

Criteria to Target Your Specific Objective

Once you have decided on your general purpose, decide what *specific* response you want to elicit from your audience. What do you want them to do when you finish? Do you want them to take immediate action? Future action? What do you want that audience to feel? What attitude changes do you want?

■ Everything should be geared from the listener's point of view. Say to yourself, "After hearing my presentation, the audience will be able to...," or "The purpose of my speech is to have my listener...." Keep a specific purpose in mind and chances are much better that you will hit the target.

■ Use active, explicit words such as "identify," "contrast," or "cooperate" to describe the response you want. For example, "When I finish speaking and answering questions, the clients should be able to *identify* or *describe* three reasons why it is of value for them to *purchase* my product, service, or idea and they will *welcome* my suggestions." This objective, worded from the audience's viewpoint, is distinctly different than saying, "I want to sell them a new phone system." These verbs give you specific responses to aim for. Avoid such vague objectives as "I want my audience to understand or know about my product or situation." Choose two or three active verbs from the following columns that describe the response you want.

To Inform	*To Persuade*	*To Entertain*
Analyze	Accept	Amuse
Compare	Buy	Enjoy
Contrast	Contribute	Laugh
Define	Convince	Like
Demonstrate	Cooperate	Please
Describe	Disagree	Smile
Explain	Follow	Welcome
Identify	Help	
List	Join	
Plan	Offer	
Repeat	Participate	
Summarize	Volunteer	

- Your results should be measurable. If you gave the audience a test, could they actually do what you ask? For example, can they describe to someone else three reasons why she should sign a contract or continue funding your project? Or do they sign the contract or give approval to your project? Are your results measurable?

- Have realistic expectations. A common mistake is to take on too broad a subject, one that can't be covered adequately in the allotted time. You will be more effective if you limit your message and cover your points well. One of my clients called and said that it had taken him three years to get an appointment with a prospective customer, who was satisfied with an out-of-town competitor. My client would have ten minutes to tell his prospect why he should stop doing business with the other company and hire him.

What could he possibly accomplish in ten minutes? I suggested changing his long-term objective of getting a contract to a short-term goal of gaining the prospect's rapport and trust. My client decided the prospect needed to recognize two reasons why it would be valuable to consider him and his company. His message emphasized what clearly differentiated him from the competition: (1) His prospect's expanding company could benefit from his experience and innovative ideas, and (2) his customized, local service would enable him to work closely with staff. He had to limit his objective to selling himself and his uniqueness before he sold his services.

Focus and simplify your message. The person able to wade through vast amounts of complicated information will be successful. You don't have to tell everything you know. Size your message and the amount of detail to the amount of time and knowledge of your audience.

What Is Your Payoff?

Your emotional state is an important outcome. What do you want to feel when the presentation is over? Did you reach your objective if your department agrees to work overtime for a special project, but only because you made people feel guilty? Was there a way to accomplish your objective and maintain a good relationship for future endeavors?

Your emotional objective in a presentation might be to feel that you have been helpful and have efficiently presented your information. You might like to be perceived as caring and concerned. In order to feel good about the experience, you may need to have the audience indicate their time was well-spent. You will feel successful if there are numerous requests for additional information, an enthusiastic question and answer period, or requests for you to speak again. Target your emotional objective and pay attention to the factors that will help achieve that objective.

Tailoring Your Message

Your message should capture the essence of your presentation. Be brief. Be specific. One of the best messages I have ever seen was a sign along the dusty road through a wild animal park. It said: TRESPASSERS WILL BE EATEN.

Note the distinction between your objective and your message. Your objective describes the response you want. Your message is what you say to elicit that response. Your message contains the main idea plus the profit value to the audience.

The personals in our local newspaper are filled with vague advertisements: "Looking for someone who wants to add excitement to her life,..." "...who wants some laughs,..." "...to share times and personal growth," "to enjoy all the Northwest has to offer," "lifetime relationship...." But one recent ad said, "Need date for series of seven champagne and lobster picnics on one of the most exclusive, private islands in the world. Lady should be attractive, bright and possibly a little daring." This gentleman stated his objective and profit value succinctly!

Why should anyone invest precious time listening to you? Does the content of your message help them be more productive, make more money, or save time? Tailor your message and profit value to your specific audience to help you reach your objective. Ask yourself the following questions:

- What are the goals of my audience?
- What information do they need to reach those goals?
- What obstacles stand in their way of obtaining those goals?
- How can my ideas, products, or services reduce or eliminate those obstacles?
- What innovative ideas, products, or services will my audience need in the future that they aren't aware of now?

A commando leader addressed his platoon before battle:

Men, tomorrow's raid will be the toughest and bloodiest we've ever tackled. The enemy knows we're coming and they're reinforced by tanks and paratroopers. It'll be 200 of them to each of us. I don't know if our planes will have enough fuel to get back—if there are any survivors. Now, we leave promptly tomorrow morning at 0700. Anyone that's late doesn't get to go!

The profit value must be enormous today to break through the preoccupation barriers of your listeners. It's a "scratch and sniff" world and even lottery officials realize they must offer instant winners. The public is impatient to find out what they've won just as your audiences will immediately want to know if your information is valuable to them.

Project updates are fairly common occurrences but they can be stressful when a great deal is at stake. Greg Baron, a project manager at Lockheed, told me his objective for periodic updates was to convince management that all problems on the project were being identified and addressed, and that work was on schedule and within budget. His message was that the review board could be comfortable that the project was being handled well:

> Of course, I always like to report good news. But if an unexpected problem surfaces, my objective changes. Then I need to convince them that the problem was identified at the earliest possible moment and request assistance from the board. I make several recommendations about acceptable solutions and give the board options because I have already solicited feedback from key decision makers. The meeting becomes an informed decision-making session instead of a problem-solving session. One of my guidelines for the update is reflected in a sign in my office that says:

YOUR LACK OF PLANNING
DOES NOT AUTOMATICALLY
BECOME MY CRISIS.

Paths to Your Objective

There may be many routes to your destination. Your long-term objective may be to get a contract signed with a large company. But you may not be able to get an appointment with a key decision maker. When you do speak to a representative, your short-term objective may be to have that person identify the value of setting up an appointment with a key decision maker. You want the representative to clearly relay critical information that will influence a senior officer to meet with you to discuss your product or service.

Be wary of thinking you can disregard your audience's objective and substitute your own. A software executive was asked to demonstrate his product in such a manner that the audience would be encouraged to investigate all the different brands on the market. The demonstration was an excellent way to spotlight the best features of his product for prospective buyers and portray his company as an educational resource. Instead, he continually referred to his product as superior to anything on the market and the audience was turned off by his commercialism. He not only lost a wonderful public relations opportunity but also blemished his company's reputation by pursuing his personal objective even though he knew that it conflicted with the audience's objective. The audience would likely have been sold had he chosen to inform rather than try to influence them to buy his product.

Objectives May Change Within a Presentation

Audiences are not static. They may completely change their attitude as the speech progresses. That is why you must be attuned to what is happening within your audience to accurately target their responses. Have the flexibility to change if you aren't on the right road or press your advantage if you are. Some people will press on even if they are going in the wrong direction and even if they don't have any followers.

The situation is like the American who was with a group tour in England and went to Stonehenge. The tour leader told an elaborate story about the people who built the austere monument. He thought he had an attentive audience. He dramatically waved his arm and finished by saying, "And now, they are all gone."

"When did they leave?" asked the tourist.

"1215," the tour leader replied.

The American glanced at his watch and said, "Just my luck. Missed 'em by half an hour."

Actively interpret the feedback from your audience so you can underscore a point, heighten an advantage, or stimulate them when they begin to stray. If someone is looking at his watch—or worse, shaking it to see if it is still working—it is time to take a detour without losing sight of your objective. One trainer gives instruction for several hours and then stops for a midcourse correction. She asks the participants to write down on colored cards one question that hasn't been answered and one item they want covered during the rest of the session. She reads the cards and posts them on a bulletin board. The participants are asked to remove their card when the requested material has been covered in the class.

If you have a volatile subject, a short-term objective may be to avoid open conflict. In another situation, your feedback may indicate the need to change your objective to keeping negotiations open and scheduling another meeting. Sometimes attaining your objective may have to be delayed while you reassure the audience that they are getting reliable information from a credible source.

Hidden Agendas of the Presenter

When I asked one client to describe his objective for an upcoming presentation, he said he wanted to be the best speaker at his convention. I replied that everyone wants to be liked and come across well and repeated, "What is your professional objective?" He reiterated, "To be the best speaker and be asked back again." This is not the best choice for an objective. Seeking personal approval will dilute your body language and tone of voice. Your objective should not be "to be liked" but rather to be respected for your competence.

Most people have hidden objectives. Your objective at a scientific conference may be to give a good presentation that will enhance your personal image and represent your organization well. These are hidden objectives. Your professional objective should be paramount.

A technical consultant said that he used to give answers as a troubleshooter but has added another role as a salesperson. He wants his customers to perceive the company's support is valuable and his counsel is worth the monthly service fee. He needs to make his customers comfortable with the system they have bought; but his secondary agenda is to recommend additional products as he identifies a need.

Right Objective, Wrong Message

A local company decided to honor its staff during National Secretaries Week. A committee came up with the idea of presenting the secretaries with chef-style aprons imprinted with the words, "You're a key ingredient to our success."

The response? Most staffers chucked their aprons in the nearest wastebasket, incensed at the symbol of female servitude. One accepted the gift and said it would look great on her husband. The objective was well-intended, but the message was open to negative interpretations. Seek feedback from your colleagues before your presentation to ferret out any possible misinterpretations of your message.

Same Objective, Different Message

One of my clients, Sherill Jones of Generic Software, was on a trade show tour to four different cities. She had a thirty-five-minute presentation and her *objective* was to have dealers purchase CADD (computer-aided design and drafting) software to sell to their customers. Her *message* was that this software would be a profitable addition to the dealers' inventory because so many of their customers—from home-makers to architects—would be potential buyers. She wanted to emphasize that the dealers didn't have to learn CADD. The home office would give them plenty of support.

Jones also sold directly to customers. Her *objective* to sell software remained the same, but she changed her *message* because of the needs of a different audience. She emphasized that CADD, which replaces the pencil and eraser, would save them time, money, and frustration. Your objective may be to sell your service or product to different clients, but you need to adjust your message for each audience.

Clear Objective, Strong Message

Raymond Hull, coauthor of *The Peter Principle* and a frequent adviser, would make me write my objective with a magic marker on a large sheet of paper above my typewriter or computer. He would glance at my objective as he read my writing. If the material rambled from my objective, he tossed it in the wastebasket. I winced when a favorite example or choice quote met its fate, but he said that every line had to serve my purpose.

Mikhail Gorbachev spoke at Stanford University in June 1990. His objective was clear. He wanted his audience to identify strong reasons why U.S. companies should invest money in the Soviet economy. His bold message stated that it would be profitable but investors must act now or be left out. Tentative, lukewarm messages arouse the same kind of tentative, lukewarm emotions in the audience. Bold statements voiced with conviction will engage an audience from the start and keep them alert and attentive.

Do your data or evidence deepen the audience's understanding? Do your supporting points contribute and progress toward your objective? If they don't, eliminate them.

As you go along, and as new facts come to light, modify and make refinements to your purpose but essentially stick to your plan. An architect told me that once a client had decided on the design of a building, the client had to bite the bullet and give the go-ahead for construction. There could be minor modifications, but if the design kept changing, the building would end up outrageously expensive and would never be finished.

Be precise and clear in your mind about your destination. When the Spanish conquistador Hernando Cortez began his conquest of Mexico, his men balked at storming the unfamiliar shore and climbing the perilous mountains. Cortez ordered his ships to be burned on the Gulf of Mexico shore in full view of his army. He destroyed them so that his troops would concentrate exclusively on their objective of victory.

Once you have targeted your objective and tailored your message, you will know what type of data and evidence you should look for. You will have guidelines to analyze the material you find. The time spent on sharpening your objective and customizing your message will simplify the rest of your preparation.

KEY IDEAS

- Determine the outcome you want for your audience and for yourself.
- Be specific and have a measurable outcome.
- Narrow your subject to realistically fit into the allotted time.
- Emphasize the profit value to your audience in your message.
- Realize that your objective may stay the same but your message may change.

5

Defining Your Image

"You attract whatever you radiate."

—Jan D'Arcy

Overview

People buy you first; then they buy your services, products, or ideas. This chapter will help you make specific choices that build a well-defined, distinctive image for a particular speaking situation. We will discuss characteristics of the ideal communicator in scientific and technical fields. You will learn the best image is to be yourself. And you will learn how you can communicate your strengths. We will discuss how your self-image affects the way you communicate. An appropriate image will increase your chances of obtaining the response you want.

"Can you make me charismatic?" asked an engineer. "I have to speak to this committee next week and they really intimidate me." Then he laughed. "Actually I'd settle for coming across more confident and decisive. Can you do that?"

"I'm sorry," I said, "I can't make you more confident, or more decisive, or more creative or give you any of those qualities."

He sounded very disappointed. "I thought that's what speech consultants were paid to do."

"If I show you how to appear confident and you don't already possess confidence, I would be teaching you to act, to pretend. I can show you how to communicate in a stronger, clearer way those qualities that you already do possess. You probably have lots of excellent qualities that other people aren't even aware of.

"Can you think of a time when you felt self-assured, on top of the world, and you were proud of something you accomplished?" I asked.

"Well," he reflected, "I remember a baseball game in high school. I was confident of my ability as a pitcher because I had a no-hitter going as we started the ninth inning. There was a scout present from the Cardinals baseball team."

"Were you nervous?" I asked.

"You better believe it! The other team had their two best hitters coming up and everyone in the bleachers was screaming."

"Did the scout intimidate you?" I asked.

"Not really. I wanted to show him he hadn't wasted his time coming to see me. Of course, there was pressure, but I felt I could pull it off. I pitched a perfect game and we won. The scout asked me to sign a contract instead of going to college. I decided not to sign, but it was a great feeling to be asked."

"We've got something to work with," I said. "I'll help you visualize that situation again and transfer the exhilaration, challenge, and confidence to your upcoming speech situation. We'll show that committee they aren't wasting their time."

Maybe you haven't pitched a perfect ball game, but perhaps you can remember a situation in your life when you felt in control, when you had high self-esteem and confidence. It might have been when you completed a difficult project before the deadline, beat your time running a mile, or were complimented by your boss for solving a tricky problem. Visualize that moment again. Immerse yourself in the positive feelings. Transfer those emotions of high self-esteem to your present situation, and your body language and voice will communicate a strong image that helps you get the response you want.

Image Is Communication

When we talk about image, we are talking about communication. The first moment a person meets you, he takes in thousands of impulses. He selects, interprets, and filters information based on his expectations, his past experiences, the circumstances surrounding the situation, and his self-esteem at that moment. He makes an instantaneous judgment of whether he will trust you or deal with you before he hears a word you say.

Your image begins with your physical presence. You are judged first by the tone of your voice and then by the words you say. Words carry information. But your feelings, attitudes, physical state, and self-image are revealed by your voice and body language.

Studies indicate that more than half the information we receive is from body language, another third is from tone of voice, and less than a tenth comes from the actual words themselves. Your body language, facial expressions, and tone of voice make up your image. Those three elements must be in harmony with each other for you to communicate effectively.

For example, a woman runs into the room, jumps up and down, and declares in a loud, excited voice, "I won the lottery!" There is no confusion here. Her body language, voice, and words clearly communicate the same thing.

Or, you are listening to a paper being delivered at an association meeting. The presenter's words indicate the research is of critical value, but his voice lacks conviction and drones on in a monotone. His body language lacks energy, and he rarely has eye contact or acknowledges the audience. You have the feeling he would rather be somewhere else. If the presenter is bored by it all, is this important research? When a presenter sends conflicting signals, an audience will select body language as the most accurate message.

Your image isn't necessarily what you are or what you want to be but how you are perceived. And perception is reality. You may be sending unintended messages. If you are the least bit foggy, unfocused, or inconsistent, you leave room for other people to interpret you any way they want.

Clearly define how you want to come across to others, and your body language and tone of voice will be more in harmony with your words. There will be less chance that you and your message will be misunderstood.

Sell Yourself!

Historically, it has been acceptable in the scientific and engineering community for presentations to be factual, dry, and without personality. But the rules have changed; so has the game. Science and technology are front-page news. There is an expectation now that scientific and technical information not only will be of value to an audience but will be presented in a compelling fashion.

In today's climate, scientists and technologists must sell themselves. Clients want to talk to the actual people who do the work for them, not upper management. The general public demands to know and understand the data that control their lives.

An avalanche of information can anesthetize audiences and make it difficult for anyone to capture and retain attention. Since many of the topics that you discuss are not captivating to everyone, it behooves you to use every means available to engage your audience. Clients may not be looking for polished oratory but there shouldn't be anything to detract from an image of professionalism.

The Ideal Image

In my research during the last three years, I asked hundreds of people to name characteristics of the ideal professional image in scientific and technical fields. These diverse characteristics were mentioned frequently:

- Technically accurate, knowledgeable
- Thoroughly prepared
- Organized, structured
- Enthusiastic about subject
- Witty, humorous
- Confident
- Comfortable with subject and situation
- Good appearance—appropriate, unobtrusive clothing

But three characteristics were mentioned by almost everyone:

- Experienced
- Trustworthy
- Credible

Experienced

It is extremely important in the scientific and technical field that you come across as being experienced. You must appear to have been "in the trenches."

Your company also needs to be seen as having leadership and an excellent track record. Every time you speak, you are in a position to enhance or detract from your company's image. The audience is not listening to you as an individual. Your audience is listening to Mr. IBM or Ms. Hewlett-Packard.

If you are speaking with a potential customer, it is critical that you refer to your previous performance on other jobs and how key issues were handled and problems solved. However, experience isn't enough. Arnold Silver, known for his work in superconductivity for TRW, said, "There is a current need in technical fields to be perceived as more than competent. A customer must believe you have the ability and intelligence to solve *his* problem."

It is comparable to being introduced to a potential date at a cocktail party. Will it benefit you to recite what wonderful things you did for a previous companion? Or is the person you meet more interested in how you will behave with him or her? In the theatrical world, the reviews of your last play aren't as important as whether or not you can sell tickets for the current one.

Perhaps you were proficient using a software program last year but the upgrade leaves you in the dust. The rapid updating of technology mandates that you are perceived as someone who can *adapt your experience to the present situation, keep up with frequent changes, and deliver exceptional-quality products and services.*

Do other people perceive you as experienced? In addition to your words, people look for self-assurance, strong presence, and direct eye contact. Your tone of voice is important. There should be no hesitations. Your voice must convey authority. You need to appear comfortable with yourself and with your material.

Trustworthy

A presenter must be perceived as having integrity. Jim Collins, faculty member of the Stanford Business School, defines integrity as "telling the truth, fulfilling your commitments, living up to your word, and not cheating others—even if you can get away with it." Collins makes the distinction between being ethical and having integrity. "Having ethics means having values or a moral code. However, having integrity is withstanding the pressure of compromising that moral code."

Today, when the actions of so many business executives, clergy, and public officials have been revealed as corrupt, it is important for your audience to be able to rely on you and your information. If agreements are made between you and your audience, they need to believe you will keep your part of the bargain.

Salespeople in technology need to project an image of professionalism, competence, and product knowledge. The people buying your product or service may not fully understand it, but they must be absolutely convinced that you are proposing the right solution for them. They must feel comfortable and trust you.

A trustworthy person has open body language and appears vulnerable. He has direct eye contact. He projects a feeling that he will follow through with whatever he says he will do. There's no evasiveness or hesitation in his speech. He is relaxed and sincere.

Credible

Expertise in your field and trustworthiness give you an image of credibility. A CEO of a software company told me, "Investors do not put their money into products or services but they do invest in people. That is why professional image is so important. People buy you first." If I perceive you to be an expert and I perceive you are fair and reliable, then I will be more apt to believe you.

Credibility is especially important for women in technical and scientific professions. Women need to focus and carry off a strong image to avoid being stereotyped and misinterpreted. One woman in sonar technology sales wears a lab coat when she demonstrates equipment and talks about her twelve years as a technician to emphasize her credentials and to gain trust.

It is harder for women to define their image because they do not have many role models in science and technology. The rules change and women are unsure whether they should be feminine, masculine, or androgynous. Many women feel pressure to be something they are not.

I asked a man why he felt that a certain woman had risen to the top of her field. He replied, "Her expertise and her presence. She looks comfortable with herself. In our industry, such an attitude is an indication to me of professionalism." What he is suggesting is that women can be themselves without relinquishing their authority and leadership qualities.

A weak image, awkward and nervous delivery, and lack of presence can be the deciding factors in whether or not you are perceived as credible and whether others are willing to accept what you say.

Choosing the Appropriate Characteristics to Reflect

Make a clear choice of the image you want to project for your next presentation. Ask others for feedback. Look within yourself and assess what strengths you possess. Can you project them more clearly?

Select five adjectives from the following list that will help you get the response you want. Perhaps you want to project the three characteristics mentioned for the ideal image: experienced, trustworthy, and credible.

- Knowledgeable
- Enthusiastic
- Sincere
- Confident
- Interesting
- Warm
- Committed
- Supportive
- Fair
- Realistic

- Open
- Unflappable
- Futuristic
- Organized
- Caring
- Attentive
- Innovative
- Consistent
- Reliable

- Cheerful
- Resourceful
- Independent
- Decisive
- Intelligent
- Adaptable
- In control
- Witty
- Prepared

A young engineer in one of my classes at Westinghouse remarked, "How can I come across as knowledgeable when I don't know everything about my product? Besides, I look much younger than my age of twenty-six. Youth might be an asset in the computer industry, but it's a strike against me when I'm selling high-ticket items on complex projects."

I had him come to the front of the room. I told the class that if you are young or look young, people will question your experience and intelligence. You will need to compensate by having impeccable content and superior presentation skills. Naturally, you should have as much product knowledge as possible. However, *being knowledgeable simply means knowing where to get information.*

I had a class member ask this young engineer a difficult question. I instructed him to appear bewildered and answer, "I don't know." He shrugged his shoulders and looked down as he answered. He looked uncomfortable.

"When unexpected questions come up," I told him, "remember that your listener gets most of his information from the body language and tone of voice. Keep your posture aligned, make eye contact, and answer, 'I don't know' in a strong voice. Tell them you will get the information to them as quickly as possible. In this way, you can still convey that you are a knowledgeable person even though you don't have a specific answer to the question." He tried it again and the class agreed he came across as intelligent and concerned.

I asked another engineer to name one of her strongest characteristics. She felt that she was organized, but feedback indicated that her audiences didn't think so. When we videotaped her, I noted she rambled when she spoke and it was difficult to follow her thoughts. She also became involved with her viewgraphs and excluded the audience. We worked on simpler viewgraphs and I encouraged her to establish frequent eye contact with her audience. I advised her to introduce one section with "Let's divide this into two areas of discussion" or refer to her ideas as "number one, number two." In addition, I suggested she give a short preview of her presentation and also write it on a flip chart. This way, both she and her audience had an outline to follow. This situation demonstrates how one's perception of oneself may not coincide with the audience's view and the important need for feedback.

Be aware that your strengths are also your potential weaknesses. For example, many engineers and scientists feel a need to be precise. Although this is a desirable trait, it can be carried to unfortunate extremes if a presenter gives detailed, minute statistics that overwhelm and confuse the audience. A presenter can be so organized and structured that he discourages questions. A presenter can be so knowledgeable that she inhibits creative feedback and involvement of the audience. Moderation is the key.

Being Real

When Ralph Waldo Emerson first heard the abolitionist Wendell Phillips speak, he wrote in his journal, "The first discovery I made of Phillips was that while I admired his eloquence, I had not the faintest wish to meet the man. He had only a platform existence and no personality." In other words, Emerson did not perceive Phillips as genuine.

The best image is a real one. When I talk about projecting an image, I am not suggesting that you fake one. Your image should not be a deception or a veneer to conceal who you are, but rather it should accentuate your best qualities and strengths. Think of image as a tool for communicating your competence and credibility because it will underscore everything you say.

The closer you get to your real self, the more powerful you become. We shouldn't need to rehearse to be ourselves. But many times, we think we aren't salable the way we are and we assume a facade.

It was thought-provoking to hear the story about a reporter who gushed to one of Hollywood's most famous stars, "What's it like to be Cary Grant? Everyone wants to be Cary Grant." And Mr. Grant replied, "Hell, I wish I were Cary Grant. I became the person I wanted to be and he became me or we met someplace in the middle." Various stories reported that Mr. Grant was an insecure person in search of an identity with which he could be comfortable.

Roger Ailes, communications consultant to many top U.S. executives, stresses that:

> Once you reach a comfortable, successful level of communi-
> cations, you *never* have to change it, no matter what the
> situation or circumstances or the size of the audience. The
> key element is that you not change or adapt your essential
> "self." *You are the message* and once you can "play yourself"
> successfully, you'll never have to worry again.[1]

Have courage in your convictions and trust in your common
sense. Be careful about following every best-selling author who claims
to know the perfect formula for instant success. If an author tells you
to put a pumpkin on your head and waltz around your office, there are
bound to be people who will try it. Walt Disney's advice makes more
sense. He said, "The more you are like yourself, the less you are like
anyone else and the more unique you are."

I ask participants in my technical presentations classes to give
persuasive speeches about their favorite causes. We videotape these
presentations. All of a sudden, their body language is transformed as
they try to persuade the audience to adopt their beliefs. They have
energy, their voices have more variety, and eye contact is strong. The
video reveals that they can be compelling. All they need to do is
transfer that enthusiasm and energy they have to their on-the-job
presentations.

I was called in to work with a financial officer in a technical
company who had to deliver a speech to an accountant association.
His expertise was immediately evident but his delivery was bland. He
objected to exercises that I hoped would loosen him up and allow more
of his personality to show through. "I'm not interested in learning all
those creative techniques. I just want to get up and have something
worthwhile to say."

I asked him to name someone that he would be anxious to hear
speak. He mentioned an executive. When we started to analyze why
the speaker was compelling, he had to admit that the executive was
enthusiastic about his subject, was comfortable in front of a group,
asked questions, and used humor and other creative techniques to
convey his substantive material.

A Sense of Theater

When I suggested to one of my technical clients that a presentation is
a performance, he protested by saying, "I'm not an actor, nor do I want
to be! I don't want to change my personality. I want to come across
naturally, as myself."

I told him I had no intention of changing him. Rather than packaging him, I preferred to unwrap his best qualities. But he needed to take an inventory of his assets and liabilities. Which ones were holding him back from getting his ideas across and which ones could be communicated in a clearer way?

Although the best image is a genuine one, develop a sense of theater. Without a sense of the dramatic, you may have *efficient* speaking but not *effective* speaking. It's the difference between getting the audience to *understand* what you say and getting them to *do* what you want. Dynamic, purposeful, energetic speakers can propel their beliefs and ideas with efficiency and ease and break through the preoccupation barrier. Stimulate your audience to get involved.

Self-Talk

The most important elements affecting your communication are your self-image and your self-talk. No matter what techniques you use, if there are negative thoughts running around in your head, they will destroy any attempts to project a strong positive image. If you don't like yourself, your negative body language will overshadow any positive words.

A presenter who is uneasy with himself appears weak. It is important to know and be comfortable with yourself. My mother told me about Jack Kennedy's presidential campaign train coming through our small town in upstate New York. When he spoke from the back of a railway car, she was captivated by his energy. The mesmerizing quality that he had comes through in videos years later. He had total delight in himself and in the job of the presidency. When someone walks away from your presentation, do they believe you like yourself and your work?

"Humble Doesn't Play Well" (Jackie Gleason)

An IBM engineer specializing in artificial intelligence asked me to help him with an acceptance speech. He had been chosen engineer of the year by an international engineering fraternity.

I stopped him after he'd read the first few words of his speech.

"What is the image you wish to project to the audience and the board who selected you?"

"I think I should be humble," he said.

"If you spent hours on a committee to select a distinguished, young engineer in the United States, would you be happy with a humble person who apologized and said, 'I don't deserve this'? What did you feel when you were notified of the award?" I asked.

"Me? Wow! That's terrific! I'm honored!"

"That's what you should project," I counseled. Sir Laurence Olivier, acclaimed in his lifetime as the world's greatest actor, astutely acknowledged that "the most difficult equation to solve is the union of the two things that are absolutely necessary to an actor. One is confidence, absolute confidence, and the other an equal amount of humility toward the work. That's a very hard equation."

I explained to my client that humility is necessary for a speaker but it also needs to be balanced with confidence. Would you like it if a person opened a gift from you and then said you should find a more worthwhile recipient? Wouldn't you prefer to see a person who enjoys the recognition of such a prestigious group and who exhibits strong leadership qualities and confidence in his work?

The engineer decided on a different image and his whole approach changed. When he accepted the award, he told the audience about the many years of disappointment and failures, and the nights spent in research and experiments. Then he said, "On any one of those discouraging nights I never would have imagined I'd be standing here accepting this award. This makes it all worthwhile. Thank you for recognizing me and my work."

Feeling Comfortable

Have you ever lost a contract to a competitor and felt you never were told the real reason? You spent weeks doing research, employed state-of-the-art equipment, and had an outstanding reputation in the field. The written proposal was excellent and professionally bound. You knew you were on track because you were a finalist. What happened? What was the deciding factor?

An engineer told me that his department head received a phone call from a prospective client. "We were impressed with your ideas and appreciated all the time and effort you put into research. However, we've decided to work with another company," the client informed the department head.

"Could you give me some feedback on why we weren't chosen?"

"We felt more comfortable with their team" was the only answer.

"We were shocked we didn't get the contract," the engineer told me. "We have more years of experience. I know our bid was lower. More comfortable—what does that mean?!"

Effective speakers, no matter how technically expert, must project human qualities that show others they are *easy to deal with*. This translates into being comfortable with someone. Of course, there may simply be a personality conflict. It is said that 25 percent of your audience will love you, 25 percent will hate you, and 50 percent will have a "show me" attitude. You can't do anything about the 25 percent that have no rationale for their dislike (you may remind them of a cousin they loathed), so concentrate on the 50 percent that you can persuade.

What to Avoid

The image you project of yourself, and of your work, department, or company, should reinforce positive traits and avoid perceptions that could have an adverse affect.

What image do you want to avoid?

A project leader should not appear out of control, disorganized, or incompetent. A salesperson should be perceived not as insensitive but instead as caring and concerned about customer problems. Even though your knowledge may be superior to that of everyone in the audience, an arrogant or abrasive attitude may turn off your listeners.

More people are fired because they can't get along with others than because they lack technical expertise. Managers don't make it up the career ladder if they have personality conflicts. I have seen brilliant people in line for top jobs get passed by because they had a "short fuse" and couldn't control their anger.

One employee was called the "Grim Reaper" because every time he came in the office, he was gloomy. It was difficult to deflect his negative energy. Are you positive, upbeat, humorous in your communications? You will be welcomed with open arms if others perceive you as someone that will not be unduly upset by daily hassles.

We live in a stressful, unpredictable world and we aren't always feeling in top form, rested, and focused. Defining your image will be especially helpful in those impromptu moments when you are asked to say a few words in front of an important committee or unexpectedly meet a potential client. Your body language and tone of voice will reflect the predetermined behavior that will help you achieve your purpose.

KEY IDEAS

- Recall a time when you felt high self-esteem and transfer those emotions into the present situation.
- Be real and genuine.
- Project an image of being experienced and trustworthy to be perceived as credible.
- Be easy to get along with.
- Be aware that your strengths are also your potential weaknesses.

Note

1. Roger Ailes, *You Are the Message* (Homewood, Ill.: Dow Jones-Irwin, 1988).

6

Analyzing Your Audience

"If you know the enemy and know yourself, you need not fear the result of a hundred battles. If you know yourself but not the enemy, for every victory gained you will also suffer a defeat. If you know neither the enemy nor yourself, you will succumb in every battle."

—Sun Tzu
The Art of War

Overview

You want your audience to listen attentively; therefore it is important to find out what is of value to them. This chapter explains a system that will enable you to determine the level of knowledge of your audience. It will help you zero in on the information most valuable to the audience. You will be able to anticipate how the audience will react to your material and to you. You will be able to select appropriate material for your presentation and organize it in the most effective way.

It has been accepted in the technical, scientific world that facts speak for themselves. But sometimes those facts don't say anything to nonscientific or nontechnical audiences. Scientific and technological terms are often viewed as foreign language. The public is unfamiliar with the vocabulary. Maybe it seems too difficult to translate the complex technical concepts into something useful in everyday life. And facts can mean different things to different people. In that sense, each of us speaks a separate, individual language. Presenters must speak the "language" of the audience if they wish to avoid misunderstandings, misinterpretations, or boredom.

Effective communication that seems effortless is not accidental. In interviews with model communicators in scientific and technological fields, I found that they take responsibility for the audience's understanding of their topic. They realize it is not what they say but rather what each listener *hears* that is important. They take time to find out how they can be on target.

Model speakers know that their audiences are inundated with overwhelming amounts of information and that it is critical to present only that which is pertinent and of value to their listeners. You can create strong, clear, concise messages. You can command rapt attention if you take the time to analyze your audience, respond to their needs, and speak in a language that they can easily understand.

Getting Started

If you are like most people, you delay working on a presentation until the last moment. I devised the audience analysis checklist in Figure 1 from twenty-five years of working with clients. The first few questions are factual and easy. You can start working on a plan for your speech the minute you are requested to speak. And if you can answer all the questions, the speech is off to a sound start. The checklist gives you the security that you've covered all the bases and will help you develop the best approach to your content.

Do you have a presentation coming up in the next few days or weeks? Read the audience analysis checklist to see how many questions you can answer right now about your prospective audience. The first few questions are obvious but essential. The rest of this chapter will expand on the checklist and explain in detail how the answers should affect the way you write your speech. When you finish reading the chapter, review the checklist and start the detective work to find answers to as many of the twenty-six questions as possible.

Detective Work

Before you begin gathering information or writing your speech, make contact with someone responsible for the meeting. Find out who is going to be present and obtain background information about the audience. Your liaison usually is the person who originally requested you to speak, but it could be someone in the same department or a program chairperson. Request phone numbers of audience participants and inquire about their high-priority concerns. Ask the group for its annual reports and newsletters. Make a trip to the library for industry magazines and recent publicity.

Figure 1. Audience analysis checklist.

Situation

1. Requested topic _____
2. Name of person, group, client, department, etc. _____
3. Liaison's name_____
    Phone numbers: Work (_____) _____   Home (_____) _____
4. Address or location of speech _____ Room number _____
5. Occasion _____ Date _____ Time _____
    a. Business meeting? _____ Formal _____ Informal _____
6. Meal _____ Refreshments _____
7. Attendance: Voluntary _____ Required _____
8. Other speakers _____
    a. Topics _____
9. Length of presentation _____ Q&A _____
10. Title of speech _____
11. Person introducing you _____

Audience

12. Size of audience _____ Men _____ Women _____
13. Age levels _____
14. Occupations _____
15. Educational levels _____
16. Knowledge of the subject _____
17. Unknowns to define or explain _____
18. Profit value or goals of audience _____
19. Fixed beliefs and attitudes because of professional, social, departmental,
    religious, or cultural affiliations _____
20. Specific concerns of audience _____
21. Expectations of the group _____
22. Recent event, situation, or local color that you should take into
    consideration? _____
23. What example, story, personal anecdote, historical reference, or humor will
    "bond" you to the audience? _____
24. Decision maker or key person(s)? _____

Speaker

25. General attitude toward you: Known _____ Unknown_____
    Friendly _____ Hostile _____ Indifferent _____ Show me _____
26. Perceived credibility on subject: High _____ Medium _____ Low _____

I often send out a short questionnaire to be completed and returned to me by several people who will be in the audience. That questionnaire can have variations on the questions on the checklist. For example, *concerns:* "What specific question do you want to have answered in the meeting?" *Level of knowledge:* "How long have you owned a personal computer?" *Attitudes:* "Would you install equipment for solar energy in your home?"

If you are speaking at a meeting, ask to be sent a copy of the agenda. Request an advance program of a formal conference. Sometimes final programs are not known or printed in time. After a last-minute program change, I had the unenviable experience of having my presentation, "Charisma in Communications," follow a frightening discussion of "Medical Horrors of a Nuclear Attack." Don't apologize for asking a series of detailed questions—a group should feel flattered that you intend to complement the rest of the program.

Familiarity Breeds Confidence

George Novak is the NASA's chief ACTS (Advanced Communications Technology Satellite) projects analysis officer. This is how he approaches his monthly in-house progress reports:

> The objective of the meeting is to report the status of the project to the center director and his staff. If any activity on the "critical path" slips or is behind it can cause problems in the whole system. The meeting is held in the administration building and I am familiar with the room. There are usually ten to fifteen people present, depending on "who's in town." It's mandatory for the director of the project and his deputy but voluntary for the rest of the staff.
>
> Since it's a small group I don't use a microphone and I know that I will be using viewgraphs for visual aids. I can speak fairly fast but if it was a larger group, I would have to slow down my delivery.
>
> There are two other presenters. The program manager

gets up and gives a technical analysis and the safety and
quality assurance manager gives a report. Prior to the
meeting, we discuss at length what we each will be saying
to avoid any surprises.

Normally it is from 1:30 to 4:00 P.M., right after lunch.
I always eat a light lunch, and I get physically relaxed by
walking the three-quarters of a mile to the administration
building.

Prior attention to details will put you at ease and give you more
control. If your presentation is at another site, make sure that you get
the liaison's name and phone number both at work and at home. You
may need to check with him for any last-minute changes in the
audience or location, or if you have a personal emergency.

Your Audience's Map of the World

A painter, geologist, and rancher were all looking down into the
Grand Canyon. The painter said, "I can't wait to come at dawn and
paint the sunlight breaking over the horizon and the incredible mix of
colors." The geologist remarked, "Look at the different strata. I want
to go down and collect some ore samples." The rancher gazed down
the vast chasm and exclaimed, "That's a heck of a place to lose a calf!"

Everyone has his own "map of the world" or unique worldview. To
understand people and to connect with them during a presentation,
we must recognize that they do not respond and behave according to
our perceived "reality" of a situation but to their perception of
"reality." Two scientists working together in the same field who have
had different educational and work backgrounds and have read different books may be worlds apart in communicating because their
perceptions, vocabulary, and images are different. Difficulties are
compounded when communicating across organizational lines, such as
research and development to sales and marketing.

Recently I attended the open house of an architect. He is a patron
of the arts, and beautiful paintings and sculptures were on display
throughout his new offices. In the reception area was a print of the
famous painting *The Doctor* by the Scottish artist Sir Luke Fildes.
The masterpiece shows a country doctor at the bedside of a very sick
child. The crisis is near. The doctor looks puzzled and gravely concerned. The mother has her face buried in her arms, sobbing in
desperation. I paused to look at the exquisite colors and precise detail.

A medical doctor was standing next to me studying it. "What do you think, Doctor?" I asked. He peered at the painting closely, stepped back, and announced, "Acute appendicitis!"

Any audience you address will make associations and call up images based on their unique background, experiences, and knowledge. Could I read your speech and be able to write a profile of your audience? Model communicators make an extra effort to thoroughly plan and prepare. They know that if the audience fails to understand, the reason is not that the audience is stupid but that they failed to present the information in ways that the audience could readily comprehend. One presenter said, "I'm here for understanding, not to convince them how smart I am."

Start From Where They Are

When I first bought a personal computer, I was so intimidated by it that I didn't use it for the first two months. Finally, my son, who was ten at the time, said, "Mom, you are going to learn to use the computer. You have an IBM Selectric typewriter. Well, I am going to show you how the computer is like your typewriter and then I am going to show you some things that are very different." He knew his audience well and began with similarities before plunging into the unknown.

Mixed Audiences

Years ago, there were few women in science or technology, but today's world is very different. Be aware that men and women not only will describe the same situation in a different way using different language, but also that the men and women in your audience will hear and interpret your information in a distinctive way. If you adhere to only the way that men process information, you may be setting yourself up for some miscommunication. It will be worth your while to read some literature on gender differences.

For example, some male presenters predominantly use sports analogies. Even though many women are avid sports fans, presenters should select metaphors that have meaning for everyone in the audience.

Women are also more likely than men to actively signal their attention by nods and *mmhmm*s. A common misperception occurs because men tend to interpret such actions as signifying agreement with what they are saying; however, the woman's intent may be to show that she is listening and comprehends, not necessarily that she agrees.

Gender differences can also be found in nonverbal communication. Conventions of posture, facial expression, tone of voice, and use of pauses differ between the sexes.

Avoid using sexist language. Rephrase statements to include men and women or use neutral descriptive terms. For example, say "work force" instead of "manpower," "supervisor" instead of "foreman" and "artificial" instead of "man-made." For help in using nondiscriminatory language, consult the various references available.[1]

The Generation Gap

What is the age range of the audience? Age categories will indicate the eras and general experiences your audience members have lived through and the associated facts they carry around in their heads. You can be fooled by stereotyping individuals or groups because of age but the age range of your audience may reveal some commonalities.

Many social scientists describe the over-fifty generation as traditionalists. There is one acceptable way to do things. Things are black and white. However, the baby boomers in the thirty-to-forty-five-year range usually need options. They demanded the salad bar and twenty kinds of toothpaste in five different flavors. The twenty-to-thirty-year-olds are said to be challengers and don't exhibit as much loyalty to tradition or to their employers. They will probably question everything you say.

You will find a multitude of exceptions to these classifications, however. I know one CEO over fifty who refuses to have a computer on his desk and another older CEO who insists on personally using the latest updated software. Most audiences have a wide age range and it is best to remember that individuals in these audiences will respond to different logical and emotional appeals. Use analogies, references, and facts to call up images familiar to the entire audience, but try to include some examples that will touch time frames of different age groups.

What Do They Really Want or Need to Know?

If you are selling technical equipment you will speak before individuals with very different needs. Flexibility is important, since the focus of the audience can be technical or business-oriented. An audience can consist of engineers, architects, computer wizards, business executives, security analysts, consultants, prospective buyers, or current customers.

For example, the chief executive officer and upper management of a company are concerned about profits. These executives don't usually concern themselves with software details or computer technology but want to know whether or not your system is a good business investment. They need to understand your product in terms of costs and benefits: Will this system allow them to meet their corporate objectives?

One manager said, "When I give instructions, my staff doesn't always follow through correctly. Now I realize that my biggest fault is assuming they know the fundamentals. I can remember my office assistant spending several hours creating a detailed graphic. I asked her to print it out and assumed she knew the printer needed to be on before she gave the print command. The computer froze and the graphic was lost. Sometimes people won't ask questions or admit they don't understand. But they will always tell you if you are giving them information that is too basic."

At technical conferences, the research papers presented are intended to increase the audience's knowledge, but the information may not be of immediate use. Audience members will watch the clock or may doze off if the speaker does not mention data of specific value.

Tech-Speak

Today the scientific and technical world is being enriched by an infusion of different cultural perspectives. Your audiences will increasingly be made up of multilingual people for whom English is a second language. At Digital Equipment Corporation's Boston plant, for example, 350 employees speak nineteen different languages. Identify with your listeners and consider the difficulty of understanding complex, technical information in another language. Choose your words carefully and use universal associations that will evoke accurate images in the minds of your listeners.

Regardless of the background of your audience, it is essential to explain unfamiliar terminology. Joe Warner, a district manager for Compaq Computer Corporation, was addressing a nontechnical audience of writers on the use of various word processing programs. He began by issuing a challenge to the audience and putting himself on the line. "If I introduce a concept, a word, or an acronym without giving you a concrete example or explaining it in your terms, raise your hand and I will give you a quartz clock." Everyone was eager to catch Warner, but he only needed to give out three clocks during his ninety-minute talk. Not only did he ensure the audience's attention with his pledge, he let the audience know that he cared enough to speak in their language.

One technique Warner used was to break down groups of unfamiliar words such as *file allocation table:*

> All of you are familiar with files in a file cabinet. The word *allocate* means to distribute, and you can allocate your information into different files. As writers, you know that a table of contents helps you find information in a book. Now you know what a file allocation table does. If you walked into a library, you would need a card catalog or some system to find out where certain books are located. Your computer has to know where information is located. A table of contents or file allocation table asks the disk to find it for you.

Specific Concerns

Someone once said that "the illusion of concern has given great leaders their magnetic spell." What are some specific views held by members of the audience because of professional, departmental, social, religious, or political affiliations? Find out some group commonalities and concerns, but be mindful that each person in the audience also brings individual attitudes that need to be addressed.

A U.S. Navy spokesperson addressed many different audiences concerning the controversial subject of building a navy home port for a super aircraft carrier in Washington state:

- Realtors—who wanted to know about the influx of population in regard to housing availability and sales
- School officials—who were also concerned about the increase in population but in regard to their services and operational budgets
- Emergency services—who were mainly interested in police and fire services, sewers, and electrical power for an increased population

- Political groups—who wanted to know the exact plans and the funding to be provided by Congress
- Engineers—who were curious about technical details of the proposal such as the confined aquatic disposal technique

The navy spokesperson sent out a questionnaire to determine the knowledge and composition of each group, requesting the answers in writing. His careful audience analysis revealed that each group required different information and a differing approach, even though the basic topic was the same. All of the groups except the engineers required translating the technical terms into language understandable and useful to each audience.

Remember you do not allay the fears of your audience by giving them information they already know. You can eliminate fears by clearing up misconceptions and half-truths and inaccuracies, but you first need to determine their present state of mind.

Perhaps you own a small start-up company and wish to give a presentation to a prospective investor. The investors know the statistics of the enormous risks involved and the failure rate. How can you convince them your products or services will survive the competition? How can you align your objective with the hopes and goals of the investors?

Underlying Values and Attitudes

If your audience believes that your profession is only out to make money and is not concerned about the client or the societal impact of a business transaction, then you need to acknowledge these feelings and start from where they are before they will even listen to you. You can't ignore deep-seated resistance if you wish to persuade or influence them; gradually build credibility with facts, information, and recognition of their concerns.

Rick Daniels of Waste Management of North America, Inc.'s Oregon subsidiary was facing a very hostile audience. He was the project manager on a proposed landfill in a small town in Oregon. It is now the third largest landfill in the United States.

A community meeting was called. Rick's only prior knowledge about the town was that it was undecided on the landfill. He wasn't prepared for the twenty people that showed up. Rick said he felt that he was in front of a lynch mob ready to hang him. They yelled at him,

"No landfill, no trash! Are you moving up here? You're just an outsider sending your smelly trash up here!"

Rick said:

> I didn't give a presentation. It was time to do an on-the-spot analysis. So I asked them about their fears and concerns, and I listened. I took notes and asked more questions. At the end of the meeting, I told them that I wanted to make sure I understood what they were concerned about. I read back my notes; they wanted to know about litter, traffic, smell, and so on. I got agreement that I had accurately understood and recorded their questions. Then I read them the conditions under which they would agree to having a landfill. I told them, "We are committed to doing this in accordance with your wishes. Stick around; I'll be back in two weeks when I have the answers."

Two hundred people out of a town of 454 showed up at Rick's next meeting, and he patiently started through his list item by item. It was a free-for-all exchange of ideas, but Rick described it as a very positive meeting. He would be back again to continue to answer questions about their environmental concerns and also to tell them about the economic value that the project would have for the small town. By the fifth community meeting, when Rick had addressed every concern and fear and given adequate guarantees that the local environment would not be affected, not one person spoke in opposition.

The presenter who is aware of the audience's attitude can avoid provoking or increasing hostility and can use the audience's shared values effectively.

Audience Expectations and Beyond

When the audience heard or read that you were speaking on a subject, what were their expectations about your presentation? How did the meeting announcements, publicity, and newsletters describe you and your talk?

I learned a famous scientist was coming to a local university, and I called to find out his subject matter. I couldn't understand the title and the person on the phone couldn't explain what it meant. I decided to take the time and make the effort to go, but I finally left after listening to thirty minutes of a lecture that had nothing to do with the author's books or field of specialization. I can respect the fact that he may have wished to speak on something other than his world-famous research, but the title and advertisements should have been clearer.

You will have much more control over the expectations of your audience if you prepare a short paragraph that describes your talk and submit it to your liaison. They may not use everything for publicity but at least there is a better chance of the basic details being accurate.

Once you have determined how best to fulfill the expectations of your audience, you should decide how to incorporate the unexpected into your speech. How can you be innovative? You can establish your objectives and then ask the audience for additional areas of concern or interest. You need to be in command of your topic but the audience must be immediately aware that you will address their specific concerns. Promise to address these concerns later. At one presentation, I stood at the door and as I greeted the attendees, I asked them to submit a question on a piece of paper. This gave me more time to think about the answers.

Fulfill the expectations of your audience and then have something unexpected. You might use wit and humor in your serious speech. You might have colorful handouts, unusual animated graphics, or a completely different approach to your topic that surprises the audience.

Model communicators know that a dramatic presentation aids in retention of data. Phillipe Kahn, president of Borland International, is able to give practical technical information because he is a programmer himself. But he also knows how to grab his audience's attention. Kahn introduced and reviewed new software for a computer users group amidst fanfare, birthday cakes, and balloons and distributed a thousand T-shirts. The members vividly remember his presentation.

Finding Common Ground

What example, story, personal anecdote, or historical reference will bond you to the audience? When Rick Daniels faced hostile townspeople about the proposed landfill, he told them that although he didn't live in the town, he was a fellow Oregonian. He was a native of the state and he was as concerned about environmental issues as they were.

Sometimes it is difficult to find common ground with your audience. One day I got a phone call. A voice drawled, "You are getting shoved down our throat. We don't want you coming down here to teach us to articulate. Stay home!" Well I didn't.

I opened my sales seminar by saying, "Last night I heard you talk about hunting. I used to be very comfortable with a rifle. I also went fishing all the time and had rabbits, owls, dogs, and five raccoons as pets." The audience members began to sit up and listen because they were all hunters. "When I was a teenager," I continued, "I had my own trap line for muskrat and mink. I'm here to teach you to make better sales presentations and more profits for this company. We can swap some hunting and fishing stories at the coffee break." And we did. I could relate to them and talk their language, so they decided to give me a chance. They worked hard on their presentations and they turned out to be a great group!

However, a word of warning: A common bond must be real. If it is forced, you will come across as a phony and do yourself more damage than good.

Getting to Know You

Your credibility will depend on whether the audience perceives you as competent and credible. What or whom do you represent? What is the general attitude toward you? Are you known or unknown? Are you the best person to give the presentation? Are you viewed as an authority in regard to your topic? Is the subject so technical that you will need an expert with you to answer specific questions? Does the audience perceive you as closely allied to their values? Is the audience friendly, hostile, indifferent, or does it have a "show me" attitude? Unless you are a well-known figure, most of your audience will expect to be shown that you deserve their attention.

Key Decision Makers

Is there a decision maker in the group? If you are selling a large computer system to a company, will it be to your advantage to focus on the engineer in the group? Will the engineer make the final decision or will the CEO sign the check? Is there more than one decision maker?

What is this person's style? Does the decision maker want all the alternatives spelled out, lots of analysis, computer printouts, graphs and visuals, quick-action steps, committee work, or studies? We all employ various styles of behavior but there is usually one governing style.

- An analytical person will expect facts, trust facts, and remember facts. Be prepared with additional convincing details if delaying a final decision is suggested.
- A socializer who is more intuitive and creative will be more comfortable with hypothetical concepts. Socializers have large egos; beware of taking away any sense of their power.
- A compliant, amiable type may be easier to convince, but you must get a commitment from him to follow through. Include information about how your proposal will affect the people involved.
- A dominant, driver type of personality will be results-oriented and want you to immediately get to the substance of your presentation. Do your homework and don't have any frills!

Use the Figure 2 checklist to analyze key decision makers. Your answers should influence your approach to your presentation.

Adapting to the Audience

What if your lead time is so short that you cannot do an audience analysis? Even if you have one hour, you can still run through the audience analysis checklist to formulate an approach for dealing with an unfamiliar audience. If you get in the habit of using the checklist and considering the variables in each audience and situation, you will find even those impromptu speeches easier to write and present.

What if there is no way you can conduct an audience analysis? This is normal for many speaking situations. John Moore conducts five-day classes on specialized software at Hewlett-Packard with employees he has never met. He constantly seeks feedback and monitors his audience. He tells the class, "My first objective is that you have a good time and have fun this week. My second objective is that you learn something. You don't have to memorize everything I say. It's okay if you don't know or understand the concepts in the beginning— that's why you're here."

He asks numerous questions to determine their level of knowl-

Figure 2. Analysis of the key decision maker.

1.   Who is the key decision maker? _____

2.   Is there more than one key person? _____

3.   How much do these people know about the proposal, report, or briefing?
     _____

4.   What is their background and viewpoint (financial, marketing, R&D, etc.)?
     _____

5.   Did you request their presence? _____ Or did they ask you to
     present the information? _____

6.   Do you know if they react differently one-on-one than in a group? _____
     _____

7.   What has been the fate of similar proposals? _____

8.   Will the proposal reduce the power or influence of the decision maker?
     _____

9.   Will it have any impact on "pet projects"? _____ Will it fit in with stated
     goals of the key decision maker? _____

10. Has the decision maker been on the record as opposing such a proposal?
     _____

11. What is the decision maker's style? _____
     Do they want all the alternatives spelled out? _____ Lots of statistics,
     computer printouts? _____   Visuals and graphs? _____
     Quick action steps? _____ More committees and studies? _____

12. Are they analytical, drivers, socializers, or amiable types? _____

13. What is your best fall-back position, if any? _____

14. What is the next step? _____

15. What criteria must be met? Budget? Time? Personnel? Equipment? _____
     _____

Address major concerns of the key decision maker(s) up front so that they
know you are aware of them. Be aware that there is a built-in bias against giving
up the status quo, as this may indicate that things were done "wrong" before.
Therefore, major changes will meet with more reluctance than minor changes.

edge. He makes eye contact after presenting an important concept and often he repeats a concept. He only goes forward when new information has been assimilated.

Moore says he "senses" when the class is confused. If they become very quiet or write noisily, he gives more examples to explain a complex command. He is very responsive to body language and the "energy" of the individuals. He is never buried in his material but is totally involved with checking responses and selecting the best way to coach his students.

Putting It Into Action

Here's a suggestion. As soon as you schedule a presentation, select a bright-colored folder with a pocket. Write across the top with a large felt pen the audience, date, subject, and title. Fill in as many questions as you can on the audience analysis checklist (Figure 1). You might want to copy the checklist from the book and enter it into your computer. Start collecting anecdotes and statistics and put them inside the folder. Do your detective work and complete the checklist. You will have a revealing audience profile—their "map of the world."

This profile will give clues that will influence your choice of objective, the organization of your presentation, and the style of delivery. It will aid you in relating your exact message to the needs and beliefs of your audience and will help you get the response you want on a consistent basis.

KEY IDEAS

- Determine the profit value of your objective to the audience.
- Find out the level of knowledge of your audience and start from where they are.
- Realize that everyone has a different map of the world.
- Fulfill expectations, but then do the unexpected.
- Anticipate audience reaction to you and your message, but be flexible.

Note

1. Francine Wattman, Frank and Paula A. Treichler, *Language, Gender, and Professional Writing* (New York: Modern Language Association of America, 1989). Rosalie Maggio, *The Nonsexist Word Finder* (Boston: Beacon Press, 1988). Deborah Tannen, *You Just Don't Understand Me* (New York: William Morrow and Company, 1990).

7

Designing Your Finish
First and Your Start Second

"A speech is like a love affair. Any fool can start one but it takes considerable skill to end it."

—Lord Mancroft

Overview

In this chapter, we discuss how to make compelling first and last impressions. The finish of your presentation should be planned first. Design your conclusion so that your final words will move your audience to acceptance or action. What they hear last they remember the most. This chapter also suggests ways to help you get off to a strong start and involve your audience with your opening words.

Finish First

Plan your finish first. It may seem strange for you to begin with your ending, but your objective and finish determine and prescribe the body of your presentation. Every runner knows that races can be won or lost in the final lap. By the same token, your final words can be the deciding factor that determines your ability to reach your objective. A savvy runner plans the race and saves energy for the critical "kick" at the end. You too should plan and pace yourself in order to make a strong finish.

Your finish is not your last main idea. It is a separate part of your speech that ties everything together. A well-thought-out game plan can anticipate and minimize the following hazards. Avoid:

- *Introducing new ideas in your finish*. This may confuse your listeners. A lawyer never brings up new evidence in a closing argument.

- *Rambling or fading away*. Don't leave critical, persuasive points up in the air.

- *Presenting unclear ideas of what the audience is supposed to think or do*. Uncertain audiences won't do anything.

- *Misjudging your time*. You don't want to rush, condense, or eliminate your finish.

- *Going overtime*. This is a thoroughly unprofessional tactic and one that won't be appreciated by the audience or other speakers.

Your finish should:

- Restate your message.
- Heighten the emotional connection.
- Reinforce why this information is of value.
- Summarize the use of the information.

Follow these four strategies as you prepare your concluding remarks.

1. *Wrapping things up with a quotation that restates and reinforces your main theme*. You can make some final comment about the quote in your own words. James Fletcher, former NASA administrator, finished his presentation "Space, Thirty Years Into the Future" by commenting on a quote from Antoine de Saint Exupéry, the French flier, novelist, and philosopher. "'When it comes to the future, our task is not to foresee it, but rather to enable it to happen.' If we can do that, if we as professionals can enable the future to happen, then we will not be trapped; we will triumph."[1]

A quotation can refer back to opening statements and answer questions you raised in the beginning. One client began his presentation to the Sierra Club by emphasizing the necessity of providing for proper land usage. He ended his presentation with an eloquent passage from a 1971 television documentary about the native Americans' reverence for the land: "Teach your children what we have taught our children—that the earth is our mother. Whatever befalls the earth befalls the sons of the earth. Man did not weave the web of life; he is merely a strand of it. Whatever he does to the web, he does to himself." By using this quote my client restated his theme of everyone's responsibility to preserve our planet, and the rhythm of the words had a finality to them that sent a clear signal to the audience.

2. *Heightening the emotional connection.* It is important to heighten the emotional connection between you and the audience as well as to reinforce the logic of your message. Your final words will strongly influence the feelings of the audience toward you and your message and their desire to take any action. Are you challenging them, increasing their desire, putting them at ease, or stimulating them to increase their productivity? You may want to challenge your listeners to take action so the future will be a promising one. Stimulating the imagination of your audience can help you reach your objective. Showing how their work is going to be easier in the future will grab everyone's attention. Earle H. Harbison, Jr., president and CEO of Monsanto Company, finished his presentation to the World Forum by stressing the need for cooperation in biotechnology:

> From Zimbabwe to St. Louis, this planet is our home and our futures are connected. If we work hard to build consensus, I believe we can offer the world a technology that will make it proud of us. Industry and government, each performing its rightful role, can cooperate to produce, in timely fashion, an unending string of beneficial products and technological developments for the good of mankind.[2]

3. *Restating why this information is of value to the audience.* If you are speaking at an association meeting, you may want to confirm your audience's feeling about the worth of their profession and the values the association upholds. In sales, you try to build a relationship with your client and therefore must reinforce the idea that you will be there to personally service and support your products. A chemical engineer was selling chemical processing equipment in the detergent industry to a foreign client. He finished his final sales presentation by reinforcing the products' benefits to the client. The client, he said, could expect better performance and lower maintenance costs by using this equipment. This would enable the client to manufacture a better quality of detergent for its customers, which would lead to higher profits. And he assured the client that superior technical support would be available.

4. *Summarizing the use of the information.* Ask your audience for an order, an action, or a change of belief. It may be a challenge for the

group to act. Many times the audience knows what you want them to do but doesn't know the first step. Make the "What do I do next?" step or plan of action explicit.

One client's request for action wasn't clear at the end of her presentation. In the following question and answer period, the audience members got so caught up in the intriguing interchange that they all left debating the points of the Q&A without taking any action. You can encourage your audience to act by advising them: "I strongly recommend we adopt this plan by voting 'yes.'" "We can promise delivery in two months if you sign the contract today." "I believe that you will agree we should allocate funds for further research in this area."

Attention to these four goals will help you shape your ending. Succinctly and effectively bring all the loose ends to a crisp close. Even if you are in the midst of research and do not have conclusions to present, you can still summarize what has been accomplished so far and announce the plans and goals for the future.

Strive to make your concluding remarks as brief as possible. President Ronald Reagan once commented to the Governors Association:

> Well, I've gone on long enough. You know, there's a story about Henry Clay, the senator from Kentucky who was known for his biting wit. One time in the Senate, a senator in the middle of a seemingly interminable speech turned to Clay and said, "You, sir, speak for the present generation, but I speak for posterity." And Clay interrupted him and said, "Yes, and you seem resolved to speak until the arrival of your audience."

Start Second

"Life is uncertain. Eat dessert first."

—Unknown

Time has become our most precious commodity. The days of long-winded presentations that take forever to get to the point are no longer tolerated. During the opening remarks, audiences now ask, "Where's the punch line?"

Emerge from the starting gate with a purposeful, dynamic beginning. Let your audience know immediately what they will gain from your speech. Suspense has its place in mystery books, movies, and theater but is not appropriate for scientific and technical presentations.

A technical documentator told me that his first question is, "Does the presenter know what he's talking about? Is this another time waster? I want to know what's new. I came to hear his insights, his conclusions. Don't waste my time."

Your start should avoid:

- Establishing a fake bond
- Using humor only because you think you should
- Creating expectations that you can't fulfill
- Asking if it's too hot, cold, or noisy, unless you can remedy the situation
- Being too humble in front of a special audience
- Apologizing for anything, except if an audience has been kept waiting
- Complaining about your short lead time or lack of time to discuss your subject

The goals of the start are to:

- Get the attention of your audience.
- Establish your credibility.
- Announce your intentions in terms of subject, purpose, scope, limitations, and plan of development or approach.
- State the profit value of your subject to the audience.

Use the following strategies as you prepare your opening remarks.

■ *Break through the audience's preoccupation barrier and capture their attention.* Involve the audience as soon as possible. Ask a question, have them write in their handouts, get them to laugh at a story, or make a dramatic statement—anything to interact with the audience within the first ninety seconds. Professor Don Jardine began his speech to an American Society of Training and Development convention with the provocative pledge, "I have not come here to bring you drink, I have come to make you thirsty!"

Louis W. Cabot, chairman of the board of Brookings Institute, captured the interest of his audience with opening words that unequivocally set forth his objective:

> My purpose is to erase any complacency you have about science in your lives and to replace it with a sense of urgency and alarm. I believe man will do more to shake up the human race in your generation and the next 10 generations than in all the 100,000 generations of man that have gone before us. And we are not prepared for it.
>
> Even in periods of great aversion to it, science does march on. And like it or not, the affairs of man can only be managed by people who have the skills and concepts of a quantitatively trained mind and the competence for scientific, critical thinking. People who don't know how to work things out, who are not quantitatively and scientifically literate, are at the absolute mercy of people who are.[3]

If you can tie your beginning into the remarks of a previous speaker, do so. If you can ad-lib about the department, the group, or the occasion before starting your memorized opening statements, do so. This demonstrates you are in tune with this specific audience and the circumstances. You will show that you care about the audience and are in control.

Even at an in-house meeting, the presenter's first few words should get everyone's attention focused on the subject at hand. Your audience members may be absorbed in a prior work situation or be thinking about a personal matter.

A humorous story can focus the audience and set a friendly mood. A self put-down can bring a smile. Combine humor with a reference to the occasion or a brief observation concerning the setting, or pay a sincere compliment to your audience and their expertise. One client began a speech to a group of hospital managers by saying,

> I asked David how many would be in the audience today. He told me about two-hundred-odd people. Well, you were right about the number, David, but I must say I've had a chance to talk with several of the managers and they're not strange at all! In fact, I have been very impressed with their knowledge and their deep concern for their employees and the hospital patients.

If your story is relevant, makes an appropriate point, and you feel comfortable using humor, use it. It will make you seem positive, approachable, and in control.

■ *Sell yourself and establish credibility.* Credibility needs to be established with your opening words, body language, and tone of voice. This is particularly true if a presenter is an outsider to the profession of the audience members. Your audience needs to perceive that you are trustworthy and an expert in your field, and therefore they can safely place their confidence in you and your material. Carefully select words and ideas that will reflect your experience and indicate your concern and commitment to your topic.

Demonstrating common ground with your audience will build rapport and credibility. What do you share with your audience? President Jack Kennedy established common ground with a group of civil servants in Albany, New York, by his greeting "Mayor Horning, Congressman O'Brien, and fellow government employees...." Are there geographical associations or common origins that would have significant meaning in regard to your credentials or topic? Did you attend a local college or can you relate a positive experience in the city? If you are an outsider, mentioning your friendship or former working relationship with someone within the organization can help to establish a common bond. Find some way to indicate that you are familiar with the audience's world.

One speaker said she had been told that the key decision maker who would be at her presentation was aloof and impersonal. The speaker was warned to get down to business without delay. However, she found out the woman was an avid golfer and worked the subject of golf into her opening remarks. She felt she established rapport immediately and her information was accepted more readily because of this common interest.

Schoichiro Irimajiri, president of Honda of America Manufacturing, began a speech at Stanford University by referring to his interest in engineering:

> I will admit I am comfortable speaking to those of you who are engineers, because engineering—and not business administration—has always been the field I have wanted to pursue. When I was first interviewed for a job at Honda, one executive asked me what my future goals were. I responded, "I want to design racing engines. There is an idea I have about valve train design and I want to test it

out. If Honda will not let me do it, I don't want to work here." The executive looked stunned at my last comment. But he was not impressed by my goal. He said, "Young people these days do not seem to have very big dreams. I was expecting you to say that your goal was to become president of the company." Well, now I am president of Honda of America, but at heart, I am still an engineer.[4]

■ *Preview your material.* Tell your audience what is coming and give them a blueprint to follow. If you tell them that you are building a condominium and outline what steps you will go through, they can take your facts and ideas and build them in the same way you put them together. If they don't have any direction or plan they can end up with a pile of bricks or a rickety bridge.

An in-house presentation doesn't need a detailed preview, but you do need to set a level of expectation. You might give one or two statements to bring the listeners up-to-date on what has happened since the last meeting. You may simply choose to begin with "Today, I wish to focus on two new procedures," or "At our last meeting we outlined the problem of.... Since then I have spoken with several staff members and I would like to present my recommendation," or "My purpose is not to discuss why the staff has been reduced, but to talk about how the work will be redistributed."

■ *Sell your subject by emphasizing the value of your presentation to this particular audience at this particular time.* Tell your listeners why they should pay attention. How will your information make their job easier and more satisfying, save them money, give them power and control, or improve the quality of their personal and professional life?

William T. Esrey, chairman of United Telecom/U.S. Sprint, engaged the interest of the National Association of State Telecommunications Directors by immediately informing them how his information would benefit them. "I want to talk about a vision of what the telecommunications industry could become in the year 2000 and how you— individually, and collectively as NASTD—can guide how far and how fast we grow in the nineties."[5]

An enthusiastic photocopier salesman asked a friend of mine a few pertinent questions about his profession. Then the salesman introduced his product by saying, "Let me show you how this copier will save you time, money, and service calls. You can't afford down-time in your business." My friend listened intently.

One project manager said that he tells a reviewing board in the beginning of his presentation how a specific project is going. That way, the audience doesn't have to wait two to four hours to find out the project's status. He said this gives the board some control. They can say, "Skip the viewgraphs detailing the good stuff and get to the areas where there are potential problems." He believes this is the best use of time for both presenter and audience.

Scientists and technologists usually state their results up front and then proceed to prove their points and show how they reached their conclusions. This is an efficient technique. Audience members are more willing to give careful attention to complex material if they don't have to start out for a destination blindfolded.

Finish Strong, Start Strong

Audience attention is highest at the start and the finish of a presentation. Take advantage of this. Your opening should signal that you are enthusiastic about your message and comfortable speaking in front of a group. Therefore, the audience can be at ease, yet stimulated and eager to hear something of value. Wrap up with a strong finish that clearly asks for the response you want and motivates the audience to take that action.

Now that you know where you are going and how you will begin, you will find it easier to start planning the route you will take.

KEY IDEAS

- Write your finish first as a guide to the direction and focus of the body of the speech.
- Announce your objective in the beginning of your speech and preview the pattern you will follow.
- Tell your audience in the beginning what the profit value is for listening to your message.
- Make an emotional connection with your listeners in the beginning and again in your ending.
- Have a strong finish. Your audience will remember most what they hear last.

Notes

1. James Fletcher, "Space, 30 Years Into the Future," *Vital Speeches of the Day* (November 15, 1987).
2. Earle Harbison, Jr., "Technological Innovation and Political Leadership," *Vital Speeches of the Day* (September 15, 1990).
3. Louis W. Cabot, "Sci-Humanists Unite," *Vital Speeches of the Day* (May 15, 1989).
4. Schoichiro Irimajiri, "The Winning Difference, the Honda Way," *Vital Speeches of the Day* (August 15, 1987).
5. William T. Esrey, "Infonics," *Vital Speeches of the Day* (November 15, 1990).

8

Narrowing Your
Main Points

"Nothing astonishes men so much as common sense and
plain dealing."

—Ralph Waldo Emerson

Overview

*Your presentation should give the audience detailed information, but
you also want to give them the benefit of your insight, your analysis,
and your recommendations. In this chapter, we discuss the analytical
and intuitive ways in which you can gather information for the body of
your presentation. Step back and get another perspective on your
subject. You will save time by being selective and categorizing your
information as you collect it. Each piece of material must contribute to
and help you progress toward your objective and that of your audience.*

You have targeted your objective, defined your image, and analyzed your audience. You've planned your finish and your beginning.
You know how you will grab your audience's attention right from the
start. Now you are ready to gather the material that develops your
message and advances your objective. You can create your main
points by breaking your message into subdivisions.

Your objective determines what your main points will be: what to
emphasize, what to leave out, and what to develop in detail. Formatting
your main points is similar to packing a suitcase for your vacation. If
you don't know where you are going, you might include fishing
equipment, a tennis racket, swimsuit, books, casual clothing, formal

attire, and so on. But if you know that you are headed for San Francisco to attend a round of formal parties, you will skip the blue jeans and fishing pole and take evening dress.

By focusing on the main points of your speech, you are examining your current knowledge base and putting it in order. By structuring the information so that others will be able to see clear relationships, you create something new and useful. Almost everyone finds that when you try to explain a concept to someone else, you end up understanding the concept better yourself.

Rediscover Your Material

Make an attempt to rediscover your material. Adopt the point of view of someone in the audience: Step back and look at your subject from a different perspective. When I make a video or a film, the camera often starts with a closeup. It might be a tight shot of two people talking. You can't tell much about the environment they're in because you only see faces. Then the camera pulls back for a medium shot revealing the man and the woman sitting next to a campfire. There is a wagon train and you begin to get more of an idea about the scene. The camera pulls back for a long shot; you see a prairie and a wide river, and the cavalry is charging over the far hill. You now have an entirely different perspective and perhaps an entirely different reaction.

Sometimes we never step out of that closeup shot in our communications. Our egocentricity can severely limit our ability to influence our audience. When a scientist or engineer is too close to her information, she may be able to present a brilliant discourse on a high level but may be unable to supply the basics. The audience will lack a frame of reference to understand the main points.

One of the most common mistakes is taking on too broad a subject. Focus your topic so that you can present more in-depth information or step back and give an overall view. Michelangelo didn't say to his model, "I'm sorry that I eliminated your head, but I didn't have enough room for it on the canvas." An artist calculates the dimensions of the canvas and either paints a small area in detail or paints a large area from a distance. Speaking is also an art form, and a presenter must consider limitations of time, space, and situation.

Imagine a target (see Figure 3). In the center is a bull's-eye. That bull's-eye represents your main points, the 20 percent of your speech that will make 80 percent of the impact. For you to achieve your

Figure 3. Your main points target.

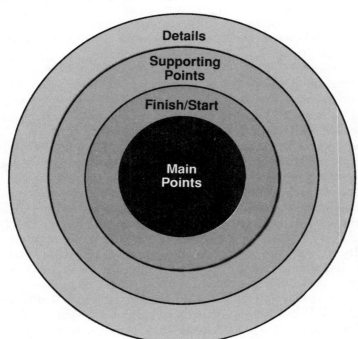

purpose, your audience must thoroughly understand these central points.

Surrounding the bull's-eye on the target is a blue circle that is the 20 percent of your presentation devoted to the start and the finish. Around that is a yellow circle of 40 percent that contains your supporting points. The final green circle of 20 percent represents the additional details, frosting on the cake, that are helpful but not essential. If you have to cut your presentation short, you could easily eliminate this final ring and not destroy the core of your presentation.

Basic Research: Analytical/Intuitive

"Basic research is what I'm doing when I don't know what I am doing."

—Wernher von Braun

Beginning research can leave you feeling overwhelmed, but think about this: The best way to climb a mountain is step by step. Taking the first few steps will start those creative juices flowing.

There are two approaches you can use to gather material for your presentation. One is intuitive; the other is analytical. The intuitive approach uses brainstorming techniques, free association, branching, or mind-mapping ideas instead of using a linear outline. We know from research that the brain relates most efficiently to information when it is organized in patterns than to the same information in sequential form.

One way to free-associate ideas is to write your topic, such as interplanetary space travel, in a circle at the center of a piece of paper. State your objective under the circle, which might be to convince your audience: Travel to Mars is possible! Start to draw lines branching out from this circle. Recall anything you know about your topic and start writing down words, thoughts, and draw pictures and symbols for at least ten to twelve minutes in any pattern that naturally evolves. You might cluster pictures and words relating to the propulsion and communications systems and group other ideas in a box or circle under long-term effects of space travel. Your finished picture may reveal that financial considerations and scientific experiments should be main points and you should only briefly mention the long-term effects of space travel. This exercise will undoubtedly stimulate ideas you haven't considered and will suggest innovative approaches to your information.

Here's another exercise to engage your intuition. Turn off the screen on your word processor so you won't be able to judge your ideas. Type as rapidly as possible for ten to twelve minutes on your subject matter. Even if you have nothing to say the first few minutes, don't quit! When you turn on the screen, you will probably be amazed at some of the perceptive ideas that have materialized. You might even try some of the new "thinking software" to help you generate ideas. These programs ask you specific "what if" questions, reverse your objective, encourage metaphors, and gently but persistently goad you into new avenues of thought.

A good time to think about your topic is before you go to sleep or when you wake up. Some people free-associate better when they are jogging, walking, driving a car, or taking a shower. Keep a notebook handy to jot down notes. Talk into a tape recorder. Don't try to judge or analyze your thoughts; this can limit your creativity. You are looking for a variety of ideas.

The analytical approach is a systematic search for relevant facts and data. The journalist's questions of who? what? where? when? why? and how? are good starting points. For instance, ask yourself these questions about a process or an object:

- What is it?
- Who uses it?
- Where is it used?
- When is it used?
- Why is it used?
- How does it work and how can it work most efficiently?

If your topic is about an object, additional questions might be:

- What is it made of?
- How do the parts relate to the whole?
- What is the synergistic effect of components in the system?

Start your research with the basic facts. The library's encyclopedias, indexes, and computer databases will provide you with current and accurate information. Computer searching allows you to research a multifaceted scientific or technical topic involving multiple key words much faster than using printed indexes. Scientists, engineers, and researchers can use a database such as Dialog, Orbit, or STN (Scientific and Technical Information Network) to locate the exact references they need from millions of scientific journals, technical reports, patents, as well as chemical, thermodynamics, materials science, and biomedical research documents.

For example, one of my clients was asked to give a thirty-minute informative presentation about an expert systems software. Her objective was to have her audience be able to identify the pros and cons of using the software. Her approach was to describe the software, how it works, why she used it, when she used it, the results, pros, cons, and the success stories of other users.

She started a computer file and noted her own experience using the software. Then she conducted personal interviews with other users. In the library, she looked up computer magazine reviews on expert systems software, searched other key words on databases, and found an article written by one of the people she had interviewed.

My client then logged onto Dialog for about thirty minutes and went into several databases that supplied her with abstracts of articles, books, and papers. She had the option of downloading articles and storing them for later perusal and printing or having them printed out immediately. The database source would also mail a copy of the material to her. But she wanted to keep the expense down and went back to the library and looked up the references provided by the databases.

In this instance, she found that her people network was more valuable than some of the databases. The reviewers and writers of the articles on the databases seemed to write positively about the software, but the users gave her examples of how the software did or did not solve their problems. She felt that their comments were more realistic and useful.

You may want to gather current data or get information from other experts in your field or solicit the reactions of the person on the street to your particular subject. If you expect to interview people, always prepare questions beforehand and know where and how you are going to use the information. Otherwise you may have a stimulating chat, but the interview will be wasted. You can make notes, but taped interviews are more accurate. Most people will not object to having their conversation recorded.

As you gather your material, evaluate and classify it. Then make a list of active verbs you could use for determining your specific objective (see Chapter 4). "When I finish talking," you might say, "I want my audience to be able to *identify* my main points, *restate* or *explain* them, and *compare* or *contrast* them to other information." By using these verbs, you can identify and qualify the material as you collect it. For example, if you expect to have your audience compare your process with another process, look for information that will help make that comparison.

Many speakers set up individual files on their word processor and then store quotes, ideas, and other pertinent information. If your topic is interplanetary voyages, use one file to store information on Mars, another for propulsion and communications systems, another for the long-term effects of space travel, and so on. You can import and merge information between files as you begin to organize the information into clusters or themes or put it in sequential order. Each file would list all the sources and contain information about that aspect of the subject.

One engineer told me that he couldn't work exclusively on a word processor. "The advantage of serendipity is lost if you just use a computer," he said. "You can only retrieve whatever you remember you stored away. If I don't remember what I put in, I'm not going to find it. In order to know what I have said, I print out all the information so that I'm not limited only to a screenful of information."

Set Limits on Your Research Time and Process

At some point, you have to bite the bullet and begin a final outline or actually write out your presentation. Once you start and find gaps, you can always go back to the library for more research or conduct further interviews.

Do you have more information than you can use? Will this one particular bit of information help reach your goal or should it be eliminated? Get rid of dead weight. If the point, no matter how fascinating, does not logically relate to your objective and move the presentation along, eliminate it. Continue this weeding-out process right up to your final rehearsal.

Perhaps some of the material that you feel needs to be included but isn't quite essential can be documented and given as a reference. A handout can supply your audience with resources, statistics, abstracts, or a bibliography.

Develop Your Main Ideas

Help Your Audience Remember

Can you recall all of the main points from a presentation you heard last month? Or an important conversation last week? What was the essence of a phone call yesterday?

Twenty-four hours after your presentation, your audience will have forgotten 75 percent of your material. For that reason, you should repeat and reinforce the main ideas (the 20 percent in the bull's-eye) in different ways to help your audience retain the information you've prepared.

When you have all your information assembled, list the three fundamental points the audience needs to know at the end of your presentation. Your audience will remember the points better if you speak in triads or groups of three such as three points, three examples, or three sets of numbers.

John G. McDonald, president of British Petroleum Oil Company, in his speech to the City Club in Cleveland realized the value of narrowing his topic. "To keep the topic today to manageable proportions, I intend to focus my comments only on one important element of the debate, the impact of automobile emissions on air quality. There are three main areas of current concern arising from conventionally fueled automobiles and they are air toxics, carbon monoxide, and smog." After he enumerated the three problems, he continued, "It is my hope that our industry can help in three ways," and went on to enumerate those solutions.[1]

Robert M. Price, former CEO of Control Data Corporation, began a presentation, "Today I would like to discuss four aspects of supercomputers: (1) the nature of the supercomputer industry, (2) its importance, (3) parallelism and growth in computing power, and (4) actions the U.S. government can take to help ensure continued American superiority in supercomputing."[2]

Each of your main points should carry the same weight and relate to the whole picture. If the fourth point in Price's presentation had been finding a job in the supercomputing industry, it would not have had the same importance as the other three points.

Just as you might begin assembling a picture puzzle by grouping the colors, start to group the ideas you find under different headings. How do they interlock? What are the dominant relationships? You may quickly see the interrelationships of your ideas because of your familiarity with your field, but someone else with another map of the world needs to be told how your ideas contribute to the whole picture.

Associate unfamiliar ideas with the familiar. Relate your information directly to the needs of your audience. Use vivid imagery, contrast and comparison, hands-on experience, handouts, repetition, and especially visual aids to help your listeners put the main points into their long-term memory.

Be Concise

Have you ever asked a teenager if he liked a certain movie? He can go on forever telling the details, explaining everything twice, analyzing what the characters were doing, what they didn't do and why, why the leading character was or wasn't appealing, and who sat behind him in the theater. He can go through more plot twists than the screenwriter or director did when shooting the movie. But all you wanted to know was if you should go see it.

Speakers dilute their power and authority by rambling. Strive to be concise; edit your words. Express your ideas simply, clearly, and above all briefly. Keep in mind that with the overwhelming amounts of information people are receiving, they will thank you for synthesizing information and selecting the most pertinent and essential data. Memorable presentations are lean and clean.

Even the experienced speaker has to change his or her style to adapt to our faster-paced world. We're used to *USA Today* with lots of pictures and simple language. Audiences have become accustomed to the accelerated images on MTV. Audiences are used to slick broadcasters and unconsciously compare speakers to these professional presenters and their four-minute interviews. Even politicians are changing the way they speak. The average sound bite has shrunk from forty-five seconds in 1980 to fifteen seconds in 1984 to nine seconds in the 1988 presidential campaign. Candidate Jesse Jackson said that he did not mean to be trite with his short, clipped phrases. They were purposefully intended to be lead-ins for TV news or newspaper headlines.

Clarity

Your audience's level of knowledge will determine the kind of material needed to clarify or prove a specific point. Socrates said that a good speaker offers "to the complex soul, elaborate and harmonious discourses, and simple talks to the simple souls." If you address a computer user group that meets every month, their information needs may be very specific and sophisticated. A group of novice computer users would be baffled by the same information.

When it comes to briefings, Larry Ross, the director of NASA's (National Aeronautics and Space Administration) Lewis Research Center, advises "clarity before truth or accuracy." Ross is referring to research engineers who prepare a briefing in "painful detail." Engineers try to be as exacting as possible, but if the audience can't clearly understand the material, its accuracy is of little value.

Many times, this tendency to provide too much information and detail is especially evident when staff members make recommendations to their superiors. One department head said, "This is not high school algebra. I don't want you to explain in detail how you worked out your solution. I only want your final answer."

Clarity also means choosing points that are appropriate. A vice-president of sales and marketing for a high-tech medical equipment company had been turned down for his proposed $750,000 budget. He was denied the increase because he had come in under budget the previous year and management felt that he could do it with less in the future. Sound familiar? He came to me and said it wasn't possible for him to accomplish his goals in the coming year with less money.

We started over on his presentation. I told him to omit the details that had detracted from his main points. Instead of dwelling on why it was unfair to cut his budget, I suggested he describe: (1) which worthwhile projects would have to be eliminated due to lack of funds, (2) what could be accomplished if he kept his same budget, and (3) how his departmental goals were closely aligned with the company's goals. It worked: He got another hearing and the $750,000.

What Is Relevant?

If you were seated in the audience, what would you need or want to know? Sales representatives are finding that clients want products and services that are topical, environmentally conscious, healthy, worthwhile, and fascinating, and that give them an immediate, profitable, and gratifying return on their investment. Take another look at your audience analysis checklist in Chapter 6 and then ask yourself:

- Are these main points of value to your audience?
- Are they relevant?
- Is this new information?
- Will it make the audience's job easier, more productive?
- Is the information significant?
- Does it address specific needs and concerns?
- Will listeners be repeating this information to others?
- What can the audience do with this information?

Many of the model communicators that I interviewed said that they are called on to give so many speeches that they develop a "core speech" of between three and five main points. Then they analyze their audience, write a different ending and beginning, and adapt their main points to each audience. They feel more secure about accepting speaking engagements because much of their preparation is already done.

Do your main points support your message? If not, either rewrite your message or revise the main points. Sometimes you discover significant material that should be included and therefore need to change your message.

Anyone can recite a laundry list of facts and data. Your audience wants your interpretation of those facts. What insight can you contribute to your topic? Your main points should constantly reflect your awareness of the audience. Your content demonstrates that you know who the audience is, why they have come together, and what will be valuable to them.

KEY IDEAS

- Assess what you know.
- Be selective as you gather facts.
- Contribute creative insights with intuitive analysis.
- Limit your main points to between three and five concepts.
- Seek clarity rather than exact accuracy.

Notes

1. John McDonald, "Gasoline and Clean Air," *Vital Speeches of the Day* (August 15, 1990).
2. Robert Price, "Supercomputers Propel Technology," *Vital Speeches of the Day* (May 1, 1988).

9

Selecting
Supporting Points

"There are only two parts to a speech; you make a statement
and you prove it."

—Aristotle

Overview

*Supporting points should clarify, illustrate, substantiate, and make
your assertions memorable. This chapter discusses how to select vivid
and interesting supporting points that will help your audience make
associations with and visualize your ideas. If you can identify the
values and beliefs of your audience and present appropriate logical and
emotional appeals that match their values, you can encourage them to
accept your main points.*

Lyman Frank Baum, the author of *The Wizard of Oz,* chose to
send a lion, a tin woodsman, and a scarecrow off in search of courage, a
heart, and brains. Two thousand years ago, Aristotle described similar traits that were necessary for an effective speaker to be persuasive. A speaker, he said, must have ethos, pathos, and logos. The
ethos, or moral character (courage), of a person is the key factor in
having an audience accept information and be persuaded. Aristotle
said that we believe "good men" more fully and more readily than
others. In addition, Aristotle believed that unless you could move
your audience members through pathos, or emotional appeals (heart),
it would be difficult to persuade them to change their beliefs or take
action. Social psychology indicates that most people decide to act

based on their emotions. They validate their actions through logic, or logos (brains). A speaker who uses logos is appealing to the audience's intellect through organization and logic.

Audiences can be very selfish and egocentric. They are, after all, composed of individuals and it is said that each of us thinks about our own interests about 95 percent of the time. A speaker can keep the listeners attentive and alert by being constantly aware of their desires and needs. Your audience analysis checklist will provide you with clues of what type of supporting evidence will help you reach your objective.

Whether your audience is technical or nontechnical, your presentation will be weak if ethos, pathos, or logos is missing. If you were addressing a nontechnical audience about environmental concerns, you would probably rely more on establishing your credibility and providing emotional proof than you would on using a multitude of statistics. However, highly sophisticated nontechnical audiences will demand corroborating data. If you were addressing a technical audience, you would rely more on facts, scientific analysis, and statistics to prove your points, but you still should include emotional appeals.

Now that you have sharpened the focus of your presentation by a clear choice of main points, you are ready to select your supporting points. You can give evidence to support your points in the form of examples or statistics. You can offer opinions about your main points in the form of testimony from appropriate sources. You can clarify your main points by using quotations, explanations, and anecdotes or by restating the ideas in different ways. You can provide contrasts, comparisons, mental pictures, action, and color. You can exaggerate, anticipate points, identify evidence, and summarize.

Statistics

Technical presentations contain many statistics. Statistics reduce masses of information into generalized categories and are useful in substantiating disputable claims; but can you dramatize those numbers for better comprehension and retention? Speakers should translate difficult-to-comprehend numbers into more understandable terms, round off complicated numbers, and use statistics fairly. Who collected the data and are they objective? How current are the statistics? Too many statistics will only confuse your audience. Showing figures graphically on a viewgraph, slide, or computer or linking numbers to key concepts will help retention.

Irving B. Harris, chairman of the Ounce of Prevention Fund, used startling statistics in his presentation:

> Last June, our high schools graduated 700,000 students who could not read their diplomas. 700,000 more students dropped out before high school graduation, for a total of 1,400,000 students who are functionally illiterate. Since eighteen years ago, only 3,700,000 children were born in the U.S. This means that 37 percent of these eighteen-year-olds, more than one-third of our nation's youth, are functionally illiterate. And with technology advancing all over the world, employers now expect the average new employee who starts with them and stays with their company to experience five job changes over the next forty years.[1]

Note how Harris gave specific numbers, changed them into a percentage, and then a fraction. Then he explained what they meant.

William D. Ruckelshaus, former head of the Environmental Protection Agency, told me:

> The same statistics can be interpreted in vastly different ways by scientists and the public. For example, one out of every four people runs the risk of getting cancer. One out of five people, or 20 percent of the population, will die of cancer. When a scientist talks of a chemical causing ten cancers per million population, the average person panics. They don't understand that since 250,000 out of a million will get cancer anyway, increasing that figure by ten is not a great cause for alarm.

Your audience may lack expertise in interpreting statistics. It is your responsibility to translate your statistical data into a form that your audience can accurately comprehend.

Anecdotes

Anecdotes are short narrations, serious or humorous, that make a point. They support and clarify an issue but shouldn't be expected to prove your main points by themselves. Historical vignettes or tales from other cultures can be intriguing anecdotes.

Harold L. Adams, FAIA (Fellow of American Institute of Architects) chairman of the board, RTKL Associates, Inc., pointed out that technology can serve as a trap or as a triumph, and the challenge is to determine what technology can and cannot do. He vividly illustrated this idea with an anecdote:

> When the art of writing on papyrus was first developed, an example of this new technology was rushed to the king. It was explained that now he no longer had to rely on memory and the kingdom could retain a history of what had gone on before. The king looked at the example with sorrow and said, "No. From now on, everyone will forget." The king couldn't anticipate that two thousand years later, the world— and you and I—would be suffocating under mounds of paper. And he was right, people would forget.[2]

Audiences enjoy and retell anecdotes and war stories. Start collecting and compiling them long before you need to use them. Unique anecdotes can be found daily in newspapers, magazines, and conversations.

Examples

Your audience will not be persuaded if you make too many abstract generalizations and don't support these statements with statistics, facts, or examples. In the audience analysis checklist, I ask my technical clients to predict if the audience will be friendly, hostile, or have a "show me" attitude. The majority indicate that their audiences will have a "show me" attitude. Examples are an excellent way to satisfy this attitude. If you make a general statement, give an example. Examples illustrate a concept, condition, or circumstance. Use descriptive adjectives that will narrow down a generalization and help your audience form a clear mental picture.

There are two kinds of examples. A factual example describes a situation in detail. This type of example is highly persuasive. William Van Dusen Wishard of WorldTrends Research used a factual example in his speech to AT&T Corporate Strategy and Development:

> Some experts think that computers now give us more information than we can possibly use. For example, a decade ago, 90 to 95 percent of new package goods introduced into the market failed. Today, despite the increase in

computers and sophisticated technology to assist in product design and market research, 90 to 95 percent of all new products introduced into the market still fail. We may have reached the point of what one expert calls "negative information," that is, so much information that useful knowledge is actually reduced rather than increased.[3]

Wishard made a statement, clarified it with a striking example, and made a concluding statement. By using this example he gave credence to his initial statement that we have more information than we can use.

Hypothetical examples also provide a valuable means of clarifying an idea. They involve the imagination of the audience but are not as powerful as factual examples. This type of example involves the "what if" scenario. Washington State Governor Booth Gardner set up a hypothetical scenario in a speech he gave to the Education Commission for the States. Governor Gardner said:

Imagine that today, outside this hotel, two thousand children are holding a rally and chanting, "We want to learn! We want to learn!" How would we respond to them? If we went to the window and looked down at that sea of young faces, what would we observe? We would notice that some of them are hungry, that some of them are neglected, and that some of them don't speak English. We would see a rainbow of children, and we would understand immediately that their educational needs and cultural expectations were as diverse and wide-ranging as the roots of America itself.[4]

This emotional example painted a striking picture of the needs of children.

Use typical examples and not deviations from the rule. How many examples should you mention? One example may not be enough, and although you may give one example in detail, it may be best to use one or two others for your listeners' reference so they can see patterns. If your topic is controversial and your audience is thinking of all the negative examples that refute your example, then one example will not carry enough weight. Avoid sprinkling your presentation with too many details and examples and not providing enough general statements that tie them together.

When giving examples, think globally especially if members of your audience represent international companies. Illustrate comments with references to cities like Hong Kong or Paris rather than Dallas or Los Angeles. If referring to yourself or an industry, use North America instead of United States.

Explanations

Explanations are usually simple expositions or descriptions that serve to make a term, concept, process, or proposal clear and intelligible. They are often reinforced by examples, statistics, or other forms of supporting evidence. Explanations also tell your audiences how something came to be, how something happened, or how something is done.

University of Illinois professor David F. Linowes used this cause and effect type of reasoning in a speech to the White House Conference on Libraries and Information Services. He explained how the capability of some nations to collect, store, manipulate, and disseminate information "has caused a greater disparity among developing nations and sophisticated nations than have the differences in material wealth. This flood of new knowledge makes it impossible for them to catch up and become self-sufficient, resulting in a new and more sinister form of colonialism. This perspective embitters relationships between us and the have-not nations and will increase in the future."[5]

Restatements

A restatement is a reiteration of an idea in different words or in a different way. It has a subconscious persuasive impact and can make a point memorable. Be clear and precise and avoid repetition that is boring.

Restatement was used well by Paul M. Weyrich, president of the Free Congress Research and Education Foundation, in an address to the Washington, D.C., University Club. Weyrich pointed out, "The computer cannot solve all of our problems for we must first define what our problems truly are." Then he used poetry to repeat the thought in a different way. "In 1928," Weyrich said, "before the computer age had dawned, American poet Archibald MacLeish wrote the following lines: 'We have learned the answers, all the answers: It is the question that we do not know.'"[6] And he reiterated his thought again using the following colorful analogy:

Yes, we do have the answers, lots of answers, more answers than we know what to do with. Our computers are crammed with answers. But what is the question that will endow those random facts with significance, and purpose? Like orphaned keys found in an attic drawer, facts by themselves are useless, however bright and shiny they may seem. Better to have a lock without a key, a puzzle in steel to solve, than keys to nothing.

I emphasize several times in my classes that you need to edit your words, since 20 percent of what you say makes 80 percent of the impact. I give examples of this idea and illustrate it with a visual. Several former students have told me they remember the 20/80 rule from my class and are motivated to edit their words in their communications. Repetition made the concept memorable years later. Telling, rephrasing, and expanding on an important idea will give your audience time to process the information and put it into long-term memory.

Quotations and Testimony

Prime Minister Winston Churchill studied quotations intently: "Quotations, when engraved upon the memory, give you good thoughts. They also make you anxious to read the author and look for more." Quotations can be a way of saying that you and a well-known person such as Einstein, the pope, or a Nobel Prize–winner think alike. The statement doesn't have to come from an expert if the person says precisely what you mean. Children, friends, parents, or the gas station attendant can be great sources. You can find hundreds of books full of quotations on every topic imaginable, but it is more important to start keeping your own notebook of favorite quotations.

Testimony refers to the opinions or conclusions expressed by others and can be used to support your points. Testimony is an opinion about facts and therefore is not as effective as the facts themselves. The person quoted should be qualified by training or experience as an authority respected by your audience and not be unduly biased. Use authorities your audience agrees with or respects. An environmental engineer who cites only other environmental engineers will not convince an audience who thinks the speaker's company is out to ravage the environment. Sometimes, reluctant testimony can be very influential. Lee A. Iacocca, chairman of the board of Chrysler Corporation, was adamantly against air bags in automobiles for several years. However, a TV commercial now has him saying that he is a believer in them. A highly respected person who has always advocated one position and then admits to a change of mind can convince others to examine their beliefs. Figure 4 contains a brief list of quotations.

Figure 4. Some famous quotations.

Woe be to him who tries to isolate one department of knowledge from the rest. All science is one. Language, literature and history, physics, math and philosophy— subjects which seem the most remote from one another—are in reality connected, or rather they all form a single system.

—Jules Michelet

If you can't convince them, confuse them.

—Harry S. Truman

The intellect has little to do on the road to discovery. There comes a leap in consciousness, call it intuition or what you will, and the solution comes to you and you don't know how or why.

—Albert Einstein

Whenever you fall, pick up something.

—Oswald Avery

Science has promised us truth. It has never promised us either peace or happiness.

—Gustave Le Bon

I've met a few people in my time who were enthusiastic about hard work. And it was just my luck that all of them happened to be men I was working for at the time.

—Bill Gold

Human history becomes more and more a race between education and catastrophe.

—H. G. Wells

We owe a lot to Thomas Edison—if it wasn't for him, we'd be watching television by candlelight.

—Milton Berle

Good design is intelligence made visible.

—Frank Pick

The universe is full of magical things patiently wating for our wits to grow sharper.

—Eden Philpotts

(continues)

Figure 4 *(continued)*.

The man who can think and does not know how to express what he thinks is at the level of him who cannot think.

—Pericles

If you do not know what you are doing, do it neatly.

—Arthur Bloch

Science is nothing but developed perception, integrated intent, common sense rounded out and minutely articulated.

—George Santayana

The great majority of men are bundles of beginnings.

—Ralph Waldo Emerson

We do not talk, we bludgeon one another with facts and theories gleaned from cursory readings in newspapers, magazines, and digests.

—Henry Miller

It is the time you have wasted on your rose that makes your rose so important.
—Antoine de Saint Exupéry

Science is facts; just as houses are made of stones, so is science made of facts; but a pile of stones is not a house, and a collection of facts is not necessarily science.
—Jules Henri Poincaré

Knowledge sharpens our vision. Skill makes us effective. But it is a consciousness of ignorance that can keep us alive. It is the spur of ignorance, the consciousness of not understanding and the curiosity about that which lies beyond that are essential to progress.

—John Pierce

You can't say that civilization don't advance, for in every war they kill you a new way.

—Will Rodgers

No amount of experimentation can ever prove me right; a single experiment can prove me wrong.

—Albert Einstein

Technological wizardry is not an end in itself, it is desirable only if it makes for human welfare, and this is the test that any tool ought to be made to pass.
—Arnold Toynbee

Never let your sense of morals prevent you from doing what is right.
—Isaac Asimov

Things in their original simplicity contain their own natural power, power that is easily spoiled or lost when that simplicity is changed.

—Benjamin Hoff

Human problem solving, from the most blundering to the most insightful, involves nothing more than varying mixtures of trial and error and selectivity.

—Herbert Simon

It's always your next move.

—Napoleon Hill

Emotional Appeals

"The world has kept sentimentalities simply because they are the most practical things in the world. They alone make men do things. The world does not encourage a perfectly rational lover, simply because a perfectly rational lover would never get married. The world does not encourage a perfectly rational army, because a perfectly rational army would run away."

—Gilbert K. Chesterton

As you choose your anecdotes, statistics, testimonies, and other supporting materials, always keep the emotional needs of your audience in mind. Model communicators in technical and scientific fields say that they do not hesitate to use emotional appeals in technical presentations. They are able to break up the constant flow of dry, complex information by using examples, anecdotes, explanations, and quotations. They are aware emotional appeals can be very seductive and persuasive. These supporting points give variety to the pace of the presentation and make it easier and more comfortable for the audience to follow the content. Good speakers, regardless of their subject matter, choose supporting points that are vivid and always directed toward the immediate needs of the audience.

Abraham Maslow's hierarchy of needs lists five levels. The first level includes the basic needs of survival and sex; the second level, the needs of safety and security; the third level, the need of belonging; the fourth level, the needs of self-esteem, recognition, and competence; and the fifth level, the needs of self-actualization, challenge, and realization of potential. A speaker must determine at what level the needs of the audience are unsatisfied, deal with those concerns, and only then advance to appeals at the next level.

A manager from an engineering firm was asked to talk to a high school class about achievement and leadership, which are qualities in the fourth level of Maslow's hierarchy of needs. He was savvy enough to recognize that most of the high school students were primarily concerned with the third level of belonging and being accepted by their peer group. Since all these needs were not being met, only the popular students or sports stars would be interested in the next level of leadership. So he cited examples of the football team, the drama club, and the school newspaper needing teamwork. He pointed out that a good leader was required to make each of these teams success-ful. The students could relate to these examples and listened to his talk because they wanted their school to be number one.

The best way to get someone to do something *you want them to do* is to *get them to want to do it*. People do what they do based on *their* values, not on yours. Why would this be important to them? Emotion-al appeals can be *positive* or *negative*. You can tell them they will forfeit peace, safety, or harmony unless they act in a certain way or they will obtain peace, safety, or harmony if they do act in a certain way.

My daughter told me that her friend who has a brain tumor surveyed hospitals to find the best brain surgeon. She narrowed down the field to three doctors and based her final decision on the one with the best "bedside manner." It seems totally illogical to me to be going under anesthesia for an extremely complicated operation and feeling reassured because the neurosurgeon will be warm and comforting if, and when, she wakes up. But even in this extreme case, emotional appeal was more important than logical reasoning.

Following are some emotional appeals to consider. How can you help your audiences to:

- Feel better about themselves?
- Avoid being boxed into a corner?
- Keep their present job or be promoted?
- Make their work easier, not harder?
- Be thought of as honest, fair, kind, and responsible?
- Finish this proposal, update, or negotiation, and move on to something else?
- Know the truth?
- Feel that they are doing something that matters?
- Avoid failure and preclude future risks and trouble?
- Meet personal goals without violating their integrity?

- Be listened to?
- Avoid surprises and abrupt changes?
- Be liked?
- Be challenged?
- Gain power?

A computer sales rep told me that initially his clients go through extensive logical analysis to determine if his product will meet their needs. But their final decision is a "gut level" emotional one based on many of the factors in the preceding list.

This sales rep recognizes his clients' fear of failure. They want to make a safe decision and avoid future trouble and risks. To answer this need, he stresses the successes that other clients with similar job responsibilities have had with his products. Another emotional appeal he uses is that purchasing his product will gain approval from management. His product is proven and has a track record of success.

He taps into the fifth level of Maslow's hierarchy of needs when closing a sale. He appeals to the clients' desire to achieve their potential. He compliments them on making an excellent decision. They have addressed a problem and answered the challenge in a competent, thorough way. The clients are left feeling good about themselves and their abilities.

Realize that superficial feelings displayed in public are rarely the real reasons a person will disagree with you. Most emotions are based on fear, and if you can discover that insecurity and resolve it in your presentation, you are more apt to get approval.

Commitment

Your emotional appeals will be accepted in relationship to your perceived credibility. Billy Graham can talk about hell and damnation and be very emotional because his credibility is extremely high with most of his audiences. A renowned scientist or engineer in his profession for thirty years can freely use emotional appeals. But if you are unknown and inexperienced, persuasive facts and statistics will be needed to support your points before you add many emotional appeals.

If you make an emotional appeal, your commitment should be heard in your words and voice. It is disconcerting to have presenters using emotional appeals who seem to have distanced themselves from the whole situation.

If you offer a solution, describe it in vivid terms and paint a picture of it. Recently I was told of a gentleman that came to the Northwest to raise funds for a project. He intended to create an island in the Bahamas and to build a luxurious gambling community on it. Now there was absolutely no such island except in his imagination. He had an architect draw renderings and create a three-dimensional model of the proposed island and gambling resort. This man was so convincing and painted such a clear, vivid picture that people were jumping on the bandwagon to invest money in this dream. A highly educated businessman that I spoke with said that although he had reservations, he was prepared to give the man a check when the man became ill and died. The clarity of this promoter's vision was hard to resist.

When you are gathering your supporting materials, remember the lion's, the tin woodsman's, and the scarecrow's quest for courage, emotions, and brains from the Wizard of Oz. You must be prepared to confidently supply both logical and emotional arguments in your presentation. All three elements must be present for you to successfully persuade your audience to accept your ideas.

KEY IDEAS

- Bring your main points into sharp focus with convincing supporting points.
- Be logical but also address emotional needs.
- Review your audience analysis to choose appropriate logical and emotional appeals.
- Start compiling your collection of quotes, interesting facts, and anecdotes for future presentations.
- Use a variety of types of supporting points such as statistics, examples, testimony, and quotations throughout your presentation.

Notes

1. Irving B. Harris, "Education—Does It Make Any Difference When You Start?" *Vital Speeches of the Day* (April 1, 1990).
2. Harold L. Adams, "Technology—Trap or Triumph?" *Vital Speeches of the Day* (November 15, 1987).

3. William Van Dusen Wishard, "What in the World Is Going On?" *Vital Speeches of the Day* (March 1, 1990).

4. Governor Booth Gardner, "Educational Change," *Vital Speeches of the Day* (August 15, 1990).

5. Professor David F. Linowes, "The Information Age," *Vital Speeches of the Day* (January 1, 1990).

6. Paul M. Weyrich, "A Conservative Vision for America's Future," *Vital Speeches of the Day* (October 1, 1990).

10

Saying It
With a Visual

"The task of the designer is to give visual access to the subtle
and the difficult—that is, the revelation of the complex."

—Edward Tufte
Visual Display of Quantitative Information

Overview

*Effective visuals can clarify and support your points and play a major
role in emotionally and intellectually persuading your listeners. They
can grab an audience's attention and can quickly convey abstract
concepts and complicated relationships. Visual aids will also increase
the audience's retention of your material. This chapter discusses the
design of visuals and lists advantages and disadvantages of different
types of visual media. Leading edge technology is making it easier to
create dazzling visuals. However, visuals should not upstage you or
your message.*

Soviet cosmonaut Yuri Romanenko and his American counter-
part, astronaut Rusty Schweickart, came to Seattle to present a slide
lecture program about their experiences in space: Romanenko spent
426 days in orbit around earth; Schweickart spent 10. Anticipating a
large turnout, the promoters booked a 2,500-seat theater. Their expectations must have come crashing down on the night of the program when only 250 showed up. Nevertheless, as they say in the
entertainment business, the show must go on.

Taking quick note of the situation, Schweickart, without revealing even a hint of disappointment, invited those of us in the audience—scattered throughout the enormous hall—to sit closer together near the stage. He told us, "I'd like to invite you to come with us and take a journey into outer space." Classical music began to play in the background, as he proceeded to show us breathtaking slides of a rocket launch, astronauts walking in the incredible brilliant blues and whites of space, and the overwhelming beauty of our small planet. We became a small intimate group totally involved in their mission. The dramatic visuals completely captivated our attention.

Romanenko and Schweickart followed the slide show by delivering spoken presentations that were every bit as dramatic. Romanenko's hesitant English only served to further charm the audience as he entertained us with his insights and humor. And Schweickart's talk touched home when he described how he felt an "awesome personal relationship, suddenly realized, with all life on this amazing planet." The visuals in their program could have dominated the entire presentation, but the strong personalities of the speakers managed to keep the audience's focus on the message of the program.

The space explorers' use of spectacular color slides of our planet to illustrate their talk is a far cry from the first drawings on cave walls made by our ancient forebears. Today, through the magic of high-tech wizardry, computer programs enable presenters to change dull numbers and dry reports into multihued graphs and pie charts. However, presenters should heed a word of caution. Special-effects visuals can be used to dazzle your audiences, but are they truly helping you to communicate your message?

Daniel P. Wiener in *U.S. News and World Report* offers this observation: "Fancy pictures and flashy colors can't compensate for superficiality and sloppy thinking. You can actually waste a lot of time creating presentations where gratuitous graphics overshadow information."[1] The primary purpose for visual aids is to clarify the meanings of your ideas. If they fail to enhance your ideas, don't allow them to clutter up your presentation.

Seeing Is Believing

We learn through our senses. It is a fact that audiences will remember what they see five times more readily than what they hear. If I were to read you a description of a panther, it might take you several seconds to identify what I was talking about. But if I were to show you a picture of a panther, your brain would be able to interpret the visual message instantaneously.

Kim Sturla, director of the San Mateo Peninsula Humane Society, built her antibreeding education campaigns around dry statistics. She has told audiences that a single fertile cat's offspring can produce 420,715 kittens in seven years. She has told them that 10 million domestic animals are destroyed each year in the United States. But numbers did not do the trick, Sturla said, so the agency bought advertising inserts, and 178,000 San Mateo families looked at pictures of trash barrels full of dead cats along with their morning coffee. "You have to see it," she explained, "to experience the immorality of it. We tried to tell the public with numbers, but it didn't work. It's time to take a two-by-four and hit them over the head."

We receive 1 percent of our information by taste, 1.5 percent by touch, 3.5 percent by smell, 11 percent by hearing, and 83 percent by sight. Eight hours after a presentation, audiences will have forgotten more than half of what they heard if the information received was not accompanied by visuals.

An independent research study sponsored by 3M concluded that presenters who used viewgraphs were "perceived as significantly better prepared, more professional, more persuasive, more highly credible, and more interesting than those who did not use them." They also tended to elicit more favorable responses from audiences and were able to conduct their meetings in less time than those without visual aids. The study also found that the use of viewgraphs enabled group decisions to be made more quickly in 79 percent of the cases.

Visuals can be especially helpful when addressing nontechnical audiences about technical subjects because illustrations allow complex ideas to be conveyed in a simple way. Have you ever struggled to understand an explanation and then had an "aha" when shown a flowchart? Visuals are especially valuable when speaking to audiences that have multiple levels of knowledge, low levels of literacy, or international members. Each speaker is responsible for using visuals that do not distort information or mislead the audience.

Engineers and scientists need to present large data sets, and visuals can display the data at several levels of detail in a more understandable way than statistical tables. Some information may have to be presented in a sequential manner. Visuals are a good way to display the component parts, the steps followed, or the entire process in one image. The listener will grasp the big picture and will not have as much ambiguity to cope with.

Visual aids are also helpful in revealing similarities or differences in processes or objects. Whereas audiences may have difficulty remembering multiple comparisons, visual aids can graphically depict the same data in a manner that allows for easier retention. Many engineers say they find visuals such as viewgraphs or slides useful during their presentations in helping them to remember the sequence of their material. Visuals can increase involvement in the sagging middle of a presentation, when audience attention is usually the lowest.

Illustrate and Illuminate Your Message

Now that you have targeted your objective, planned your message, and chosen your main points, decide what elements would benefit by being dramatized and reinforced by visuals. These might include the nature and scope of the material, your methodology, critical statistics and financial figures, the results of your research, and your conclusions or recommendations. Are there any other important comparisons or abstract ideas in your presentation that could be clarified by being translated into images?

For example, you may want to compare a new process with a current process. You could translate this information into text, a diagram, a table of statistics, a flowchart, a bar graph, photographs, or drawings. Experiment and choose the form that quickly clarifies your information. Try to include both text and images on your visuals. Words alone take time for the audience to read, process, and interpret. Strong images make data stand out. Images should be easily recognizable, provocative, unique, funny, or unusual to trigger associations and aid retention.

Prepare a Storyboard

Storyboarding is an excellent tool for you to get your ideas on paper, translate them into images, and decide on the best placement of visuals in the presentation. Capsulize your ideas into short statements and write them down. Use colored markers on sheets of 8½-by-11-inch paper and sketch graphs and illustrations to represent your key points. Jot down some titles. Arrange your sheets of paper on a table or tape them on a wall and begin adjusting and editing. Now you have a visual outline of your presentation. You may discover that you need another visual to help clarify a certain concept or that you can eliminate a visual and still convey the necessary information.

A commonly accepted guideline is to have one visual for every two minutes of your presentation. Keep in mind, however, that even though you could use fifteen visuals in a thirty-minute speech, you may only need five. Try not to have more than three visuals consisting only of text in succession. Storyboards are particularly useful to clarify objectives and to ensure continuity in team presentations and panel discussions.

Visual Design—ASAP

Now that you have your preliminary sketches for visuals and a plan for their use during your presentation, it is time to decide on a functional design for each visual. A good rule is: *As Simple As Possible* (ASAP). Here are some good design strategies that will aid your audience's speed of comprehension, recall, and understanding of the quantitative information on your visual:

- Use graphics to present dominant conclusions or features.
- Emphasize only one idea or closely related ideas on the visual.
- Choose simple typefaces.
- Make text legible and visible to your entire audience.
- Limit text to five words per line, four to six lines per visual.
- Position information on the top three-fourths of the visual so back rows will be able to see.
- Emphasize points with underlining, boldface, or color.
- Label the plot storyline clearly.
- Use upper- and lowercase type instead of all capitals, which are harder to read.
- Check carefully for grammatical or numerical errors and misspelled words.

Steve Jackson, a computer artist, said, "In drawing any graphic piece, I try to break down overall meaning and portray it as simply as possible, as with an icon. For example, in a flowchart, every single element represents a process or product and the overall procedure or product is represented by a series of icons. The icon can represent a vast amount of text."

Use action titles on your visual to make an informative or persuasive point. For instance, the title *Fuel Efficiency* for a graph indicates the subject, but the title *Fuel Efficiency Reduced 20 Percent* tells your audiences what conclusions they can draw from the visual.

Colors can be chosen to provide consistency or contrast in your color scheme. They can affect your audience emotionally. You might choose a background color of blue for the entire presentation and highlight good news in yellow and negative news in red or black. The fact that you have a choice of 16,000 color hues does not mean that you have to use them all. Choose colors that provide enough contrast so that your images and text are clearly visible.

If you have a PC or a Macintosh, a graphics software program, and a laser printer, you can create your own viewgraphs and slides. Many organizations have purchased film recorders or send out disks by modem to imaging service bureaus. If you have in-house facilities, presenters can make last-minute corrections and additions on slides and ensure that proprietary material remains confidential.

Desktop presentation software can automatically convert your presentation outline into slides or viewgraphs. Various software packages supply predesigned templates that can be used as is or customized. Be careful that you don't use or create a template where the logo and border design take up useful space on each slide or viewgraph. You can take the preliminary sketches from your storyboard and draw, import clip art, edit text, add color or bullets on the computer, and use the on-screen sorter to get an overall idea of the visuals. Scanners can reproduce photos, and software can add text to those photos for imaginative viewgraphs or slides.

Choices of Graphic Formats

You can choose from among many graphic formats to display statistics, relationships, patterns, processes, and images clearly and accurately.

- Tables can show a large amount of data and relationships between items (see Figure 5).
- Pie charts are "pies" or circles divided up into sections to show component parts such as proportions or percentages (see Figure 6).
- Bar charts are used to highlight similarities, contrasts, ranks,

Figure 5. An example of a table.

SOUND LEVELS AND HUMAN RESPONSE

Common Sounds	Noise Level (dB)	Effect
Jet Operation Carrier deck Air raid siren	140	Painfully loud
	130	
Jet takeoff (200 feet) Thunderclap Discotheque Auto horn (3 feet)	120	Maximum vocal effort
Pile drivers	110	
Garbage truck	100	
Heavy truck (50 feet) City traffic	90	Very annoying Hearing damage (8 hours)
Alarm clock (2 feet) Hair dryer	80	Annoying
Noisy restaurant Freeway traffic Man's voice (3 feet)	70	Telephone use difficult
Air conditioning unit (20 feet)	60	Intrusive
Light auto traffic (100 feet)	50	Quiet
Living room Bedroom Quiet office	40	
Library Soft whisper (15 feet)	30	Very quiet
Broadcasting studio	20	
	10	Just audible
	0	Hearing begins

This decibel (dB) table compares some common sounds and shows how they rank in potential harm to hearing. Note that 70 dB is the point at which noise begins to harm hearing. To the ear, each 10 dB increase seems twice as loud.

Source: Noise and Its Measurement, EPA.

Artwork courtesy of: GENIGRAPHICS Corp.

Figure 6. An example of a pie chart.

ELECTRICAL GENERATION IN THE UNITED STATES

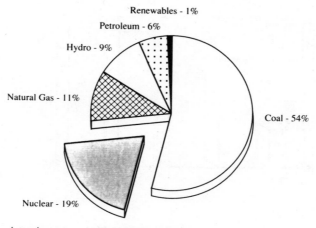

Artwork courtesy of: GENIGRAPHICS Corp.

proportions, and frequencies. They have a single common variable. They can have either vertical or horizontal bars (see Figure 7).

- Line graphs depict changes in one or more variables, trends, increases/decreases, or concentrations over a period of time (see Figure 8).
- Flowcharts (see Figure 9) and process charts can be used to show various stages of a process or to illustrate the line of command in an organization or relationships among parts of a structure.
- Diagrams simplify or emphasize important relationships. Cutaways are a common example (see Figure 10).
- Maps show spatial relationships and can be used to illustrate the geographical distribution of resources, products, sales figures, populations, warehouses, and so on.
- Photographs can show the actual details of objects, places, or persons.
- Cartoons can be used to simplify or exaggerate data in a humorous way.
- Drawings illustrate ideas with images.

Figure 7. An example of a bar chart.

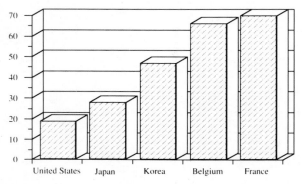

NUCLEAR ENERGY AROUND THE WORLD
(Percent of electricity from nuclear energy)

Artwork courtesy of: GENIGRAPHICS Corp.

Choosing the Best Medium for Your Message

Your choice of a visual medium will depend on your objective, audience size, physical site, equipment available, budget, time constraints, and what is appropriate for your profession. For instance, your approach might be to create an intimate "down-to-business" feeling. You could use a flip chart or whiteboard instead of video, which is often thought of as an entertainment medium. The size of your audience is one of your first considerations. An audience of 200 will require slides, several TV or computer monitors, or large screens. If you are doing a project update and want to convince an audience of 10 that you are in control, viewgraphs are better than slides because you can keep normal lighting and maintain rapport and better eye contact throughout the presentation. And, of course, your budget and lead time will affect your selection. Figure 11 lists some of the most common forms of visual media and discusses their advantages and disadvantages. Combine two different media to add variety and interest to your presentation.

Figure 8. An example of a line graph.

NET EARNINGS

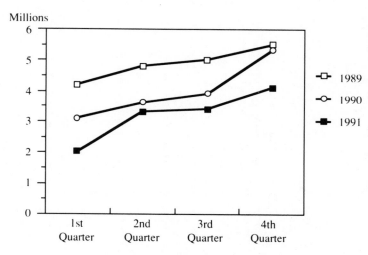

Artwork courtesy of: GENIGRAPHICS Corp.

Flip Charts

Flip chart pads can be purchased with faint blue grid lines that will help you keep your letters and diagrams aligned. Write in plain, large letters that are legible to everyone in the room. Make sure you know how to spell the terms that may be used. Important facts, figures, or major headings can be written on the flip chart in pencil before your presentation. If you plan to rip off the sheets as you finish them, start with a clean perforation; otherwise, flip them over carefully. Practice tearing or turning the sheets so you can devote your attention to your audience while you're making the change. Avoid embarrassment by checking to see that the pages in your flip chart have not been used before.

Figure 9. An example of a flow chart.

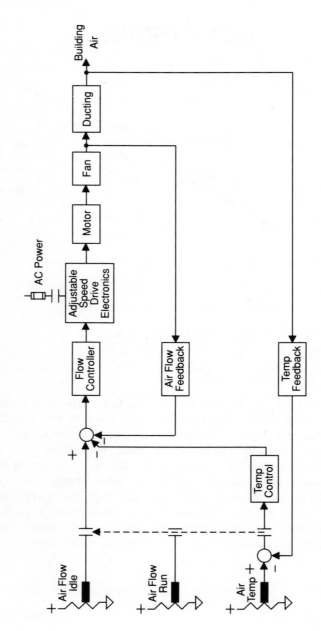

Figure 10. Examples of diagrams.

[Diagram 1]

Storm Drainage After Development

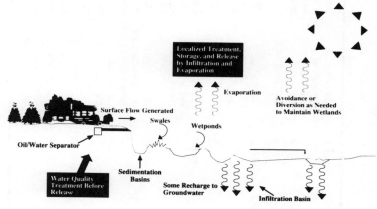

Source: Peninsula Partners, L.P.
Artwork courtesy of: GENIGRAPHICS Corp.

[Diagram 2]

Source: *The Mars Observer* Newsletter
Mars Observer Project Office
The Jet Propulsion Laboratory/NASA

Figure 11. Selecting the appropriate visual media.

Medium	Audience Size	Flexibility	Cost	Interaction	Lighting	Eye Contact	Advantages	Disadvantages
Flip chart	Up to 30	Yes	Inexpensive	High	Normal	Limited	Spontaneous; customized; no equipment problems; short lead time.	Limited visibility; limited eye contact; requires good handwriting.
Viewgraphs	Up to 125	Yes	Inexpensive	High	Low-Normal	Good	Quick; colorful; presenter has control.	Difficult to keep clean; glaring light; noisy.
Slides	Up to 1,000	No	Can be expensive	Limited	Low	Limited	Professional; easily portable; colorful.	Less flexibility for speaker; can detract from speaker.
Video	Depends on screen size	No	Expensive	Limited	Normal	Limited	Attention-getting; easily duplicated; shows real people, places, and objects.	Long lead time; may overshadow speaker; hard to transport equipment.
Computer	Depends on screen size	Yes	Expensive	High	Low-Normal	Limited	Can "massage" information; import data; animation; printouts available.	Needs projection system; equipment failure; learning curve.

Drawings can be made prior to the presentation, rolled up, and carried easily in a large mailing tube. New chart printers allow you to make instant color or black and white, flip-chart-size enlargements of your 8½-by-11-inch originals.

Individual pages from flip charts can be taped around the room for reinforcement of ideas and for later reference. Two charts are helpful if you wish to make comparisons. When writing down ideas from the audience, be careful about changing the wording or intent. Bring your own colored marking pens and use blue, red, and green to print, underline, and make arrows. Put the cap back on your pen when you're through. One speaker tapped her forehead as she paused to think about a question and spent the rest of the session walking around with several purple marks on her face.

Many rooms have stationary or electronic whiteboards that can be used in place of a flip chart. Whatever equipment you use, do not neglect your audience. Write or draw briefly, and then turn and reestablish eye contact.

Viewgraphs

Viewgraphs are sometimes referred to as viewfoils, overheads, foils, or transparencies and are shown on overhead projectors. New projectors on the market allow you to zoom in on small details of your viewgraph. Use plastic flip frames to protect viewgraphs; they will also give you a place for crib notes. Increase the timeliness and support of your presentation by clipping a relevant headline or picture from the newspaper or current industry magazine; create a viewgraph by enlarging and copying the item on a plain copier using transparency film.

Try using novel pens that create highlighting effects and give the effect of "burning" through special transparency film. Contact a company that sells viewgraph products; many give free workshops on how to create high-quality visuals. Don't overuse viewgraphs because they are easy to make. Be selective.

Slides

Slides will give your presentation a polished, professional look. Images and text are sharp and the color is intense. Dramatic effects can be created by using multiple projectors and combining them with sound effects or music.

Check the level of light necessary for good visibility. Rear projection (light projected from behind the screen) will allow you to have low-level light in the room. Group your visuals to avoid switching the lights on and off frequently. For example, begin your presentation by speaking directly to the audience, show several slides, then turn up the lights for further discussion. Repeat the process two or three times; then finish with the lights up and be ready to go into the question and answer portion. Appoint someone to manage the light switches during the discussion segments. Have a light focused on you to avoid being a disembodied voice.

Check that your slides are inserted properly in the slide tray and then secure the cover. Run a colored marker along the top edge of the slides when they are loaded to indicate they are right-side-up. Always do a trial run with your remote control and preview *every* slide. Check the focus and center the image on the screen. Avoid seating people next to the slide projector if they will have difficulty hearing over the fan. To really wow your audience, anticipate questions and have slides prepared for your answers!

Video

Audiences are conditioned to pay attention to video. If monitors or a large screen is present, indicate in your introduction when the video will be shown. This will minimize lack of attention to the rest of your presentation. Tell the audience key points or images they are to look for during the tape. Video is especially useful for on-location filming of equipment, processes, or people. If you have more than twenty people in your audience, you will need a video projection system and a large screen.

Computer

Computers allow you to present your visuals directly on a PC monitor or a larger screen and eliminate slide and viewgraph production. They enable the presenter to manipulate images on the screen as your audience questions, offers opinions, and makes suggestions. You can have access to screens on file and show side-by-side comparisons of data with fancy wipes and fades. You can also produce hard copy of your visuals. Bigger audiences will require a data projection system to transmit the images to a large screen.

Handouts—Diversion or Direction?

One engineer told me that he prepared exact duplicates of his viewgraphs as handouts and passed them out prior to his presentation. The key decision maker at his meeting flipped through the handouts and, tossing them aside, said, "Okay, this defines the problem. Now, what are you going to do about it?" The engineer's entire presentation had been reviewed and dismissed, and he had prepared nothing further. Although this is a pitfall of giving handouts prior to a presentation, the presenter should have found out earlier if he was expected to offer solutions as well as presenting the problem.

Handouts, which are commonly duplicates of viewgraphs, are expected in some organizations. It may be necessary to include complicated charts, schematics, and statistics in handouts for you to convince key decision makers. Well-prepared handouts provide structure and organizational pattern for both the audience and you to follow. They can explain in detail, give additional reference material, and be a record of the presentation. However, your audience can also look ahead to financial figures or conclusions before you get to them.

James Baltusnik, a programs officer for the U.S. Federal Park System, says, "Since the material in my presentation is complex and the group knows that they must try to understand, they are ill at ease. I tell them that I will give them a handout at the end with a summary. I find there is too much confusion if I give handouts during a meeting, but if they know they're getting a handout at the end, they aren't so obsessed with taking notes."

If you are energized, have a strong voice, and have reasonable pacing, it is possible to keep control and focus the audience's attention on you, a visual, or a prop. It is only when the sense of progression is lost that the audience wants to read ahead. The appearance of your handouts should be in keeping with the high quality of your visuals and the rest of your presentation. Always carry a master copy that can be duplicated if necessary.

Props Will Support Your Message

Displaying a real object can explain an abstract concept and lend credibility and drama to your message. John Imlay, CEO of Dun and Bradstreet Software Services, Inc., used a sword during a presentation to make a story about a Japanese martial artist more vivid. Imlay says he likes to use props that produce memorable analogies.

During that same presentation, he had a well-known violinist come on stage and play while he recited the poem "The Master's Hand." Imlay's point was that a computer chip is nothing without software. It takes a master programmer to develop the software to make the computer sing just as it takes a master violinist to bring the violin to life.

Every year during his employee and customer updates, Imlay brings a live animal on stage with him to set a theme for the coming year. For example, one year he featured a tiger to emphasize aggressiveness in the marketplace. Another year was symbolized by an eagle and another year by a lion. When someone refers to the year of the tiger, everyone immediately understands that was 1985.

Keep your props out of sight until you need them to illustrate a point. When you use them, make sure they are clearly visible to everyone in the audience. If you have a small group, you may want to pass objects around so that the audience can experience properties such as weight, smoothness, or hardness. Put them away when they have served their purpose so they don't distract the audience. If they are detailed, you can invite your audience to view them after the presentation.

Complement Your Visuals With Your Delivery Style

The information and mood of the visual should match your words, facial expressions, body language, and tone of voice. This way your audience receives the same information through many channels. Don't make an important point while you are doing something physical, such as changing viewgraphs or turning flip charts, because the audience will give more attention to watching you than to listening to you.

The normal tendency when showing visuals is for the speaker to stand next to the projector. If you have an assistant to change your viewgraphs or a remote control for slides, it is preferable to have the screen on your left as you face the audience. People read from left to right and their eyes will return to you on their left. Give the audience a moment to absorb the information on a visual, then repeat the key ideas and talk briefly about the subject. You shouldn't have to look at the visual again unless you need to point to something. Keep your eyes and attention focused on the audience, not on the visual aid!

One way to have the audience follow your train of thought is to progressively disclose your ideas by creating a sequence of viewgraphs or slides that gradually reveal information. You can also block out light on a viewgraph with an opaque sheet and slide it down as you address each point. A series of sheets can be taped to your flip chart and removed one by one to disclose information. These techniques are purposeless if your conclusions are already printed in handouts. Use overlays for complicated information or divide the information into several slides or viewgraphs. If you need to enlarge a portion of a schematic, do so on a second slide.

Ask for a white matte screen with a keystone eliminator (a steel bar that pulls out of the extension tube and flips forward), which will allow you to hang the screen at a slant and get a good square image. The screen should be placed in the corner at a forty-five-degree angle to the audience so that the presenter won't be walking in front of the screen and obstructing their view. However, many technical facilities place the screen squarely in the middle of the room and the presenter needs to avoid walking through the light beam of the projector. Don't use the overhead projector as your companion throughout the entire presentation. Step away from the projector and speak directly to the audience several times. And turn it off when you aren't using it. Remember that when the lights come on after each group of slides is shown, your rapport with the audience will be diluted and will need to be reestablished. A pointer can be useful but don't allow it to become a distracting toy. Laser pointers require a steady hand.

Technical Rehearsal—Be Prepared

Since visuals are often completed at the last minute, many presenters have no opportunity to rehearse with them. They forfeit the value of rehearsal and the opportunity to review and revise. Rehearsal also allows one to properly focus projectors and check each visual's legibility, look for spelling errors, see that the viewgraphs are clean, and check that the slides are inserted properly. Rehearse manipulation of computer files and software. Become familiar with your equipment and your sequence of visuals, using a computer printout or storyboard, so that you can concentrate on interacting with the audience.

During preparation and rehearsal, keep your objective in mind. Visuals can be a crutch, and many people hide behind them. You are not incidental to the presentation—you are your own best visual.

Visuals Can Enhance—
They Can't Substitute for Your Message

John Carter, the president and CEO of Equitable Life Financial, remarked, "Futurism for the sake of futurism isn't really what business communications are all about. You can develop all the gizmos and gadgets imaginable but if they don't promote better and more efficient communication, they're worthless."

At a recent conference, several presenters struggled with state-of-the-art computers and software that failed to work properly. The audience waited impatiently. Attendees remarked that the best presenter had no visuals and no handouts. He was compelling and memorable, and his material was of value. You can fall into the trap of becoming a technician operating complicated equipment instead of a speaker showing visuals to support your main points. You should be paying as much attention to your listeners as you want paid to your material. Sometimes you don't need a sophisticated computer graphic to explain your points. Your audience should be intrigued by useful data, not by how you were able to produce flashy animation and a series of fancy diagrams.

Several years ago I was teaching government personnel in Anchorage, Alaska, how to prepare their presentations. A CIA administrator walked to the front of the room with a stack of viewgraphs. He began by looking at the empty screen. "My first picture would have clarified my starting point," he said, "but I can't show it to you because it's classified." He held up a second viewgraph without revealing its content and said, "You would be able to see how this graph sharply illustrates the difference, but you'll have to use your imagination."

He then picked up the next viewgraph, saying, "This picture shows vivid details of the project, but it's classified too." The audience waited in anticipation and uncertainty as he proceeded to refer to imaginary images on the screen throughout the rest of his presentation. The substance of his talk had vanished with the visuals.

Your visuals may not be classified, but if your equipment broke down, would your audience still be able to get the necessary information from your words? Would you still be able to achieve your objective?

Emerging Techniques for Visual Presentations

New and emerging presentation tools are making it easier to create exciting visuals. Recent technology has contributed to making the exchange of information more interactive. A liquid crystal display (LCD) panel, for example, placed on an overhead projector's surface will project images from the computer screen in real time. The presenter can make changes to the computer visuals on the spot, if necessary, and respond to requests from audience members to show specific graphics. New LCD panels allow color computer graphics to be displayed.

Creative uses of other types of equipment are also facilitating interactive meetings. Meeting rooms equipped with computer stations at each seat, for instance, allow members to electronically converse with the presenter, who can access their responses through a control panel (usually with a touchscreen) built into the lectern. Auditoriums and lecture halls with remote keypads in the arms of the chairs allow members to interact with the presenter, with the aid of a lectern with a control panel and computer. The computer also provides the presenter with audience responses to questions, both for the whole group and individually.

Bernie DeKoven, in his book *Connected Executives,* foresees that the presenter in the future will be simply another participant in computer-enhanced communications. "Everybody—fellow participants, the person playing emcee, the person playing technographer (controlling computer and data)—will control the pace and the focus of the presentation. The 'live' environment of the shared computer screen allows speakers to make very powerful, responsive presentations."[2] Several companies are already conducting these highly interactive meetings.

Another emerging technology is the multimedia presentation that blends full-motion video with audio, graphics, and text created on a desktop computer and displayed on a screen. In short, it combines the impact of television with the power of a PC, making for dramatic presentations. Several computer manufacturers have announced plans to introduce specially designed multimedia PCs with built-in CD-ROM (compact disc read only memory) drives for large storage needs, as well as built-in audio capabilities. Software manufacturers are introducing programs that allow sophisticated three-dimensional animations and photo-realistic graphics to be created by novice users. Experts predict that video may one day be compressed to the point where it can be stored on CDs like music and computer graphics. Although multimedia is able to produce dazzling visual and audio effects at a fraction of the cost of doing it traditionally, it is not always a cost-effective solution for everyday presentation needs. In that respect, it is comparable to the early beginnings of desktop publishing. However, you will benefit from exploring developments in the field, so that you will know when your use justifies the investment.

Today we are dealing with more information than we can comfortably absorb. Visuals are a way to condense and pace that information. Effective visuals help you present complex information in a logical, planned sequence to influence and facilitate problem solving and decision making. The visually sophisticated audiences of today are accustomed to high-quality visuals. A presentation with well-planned and well-executed visuals can reflect favorably upon your expertise within your organization.

No matter what set of techniques and high-tech tools you choose to use, you should not forget the original purpose of your presentation—to deliver a message to your audience in the clearest, most easily understood manner. Think in images and use the visual channel as an exciting means of communicating your ideas!

KEY IDEAS

- Remember, you are your own best visual.
- Choose and design visuals that will influence the audience emotionally as well as intellectually.
- Use a variety of image graphics as well as text.
- Rehearse with all equipment and have Plan B.
- Support and enhance your message with visuals, but don't let them dominate the presentation.

Notes

1. Daniel P. Wiener, "Dazzling Artwork From Dull Numbers," *U.S. News and World Report* (January 9, 1989).
2. Bernie DeKoven, *Connected Executives* (Palo Alto: Institute for Better Meetings, 1990).

11

Organizing
Your Content

"A forest of facts unordered by concepts and constructive relations may be cherished for its existential appeal, its vividness, its pleasure, or its nausea, yet it is meaningless, insignificant, and usually uninteresting unless it is organized by reason."

—Henry Margenau

Overview

Your listeners need to be able to relate the facts and data you present to a frame of reference. A strong organizational pattern will provide that structure and bring order and clarity to your presentation. This chapter discusses several patterns that will enable your audience to follow your reasoning and reach the same conclusion that you do. Structure can serve as a memory device for you to anchor your thoughts. This chapter also emphasizes the need for transitional words and phrases to signal important relationships between key points.

You have defined your objective, analyzed your audience, and gathered your main points and supporting points. You have decided on your conclusion and your start. Now how do you arrange the key points in the body of your presentation in an order that will effectively lead your audience by easy stages toward acceptance of your ideas? If you are going to Chicago from Los Angeles, would it be better to travel by hot air balloon, skateboard, train, jet plane, or horse and buggy? Your answer depends not on your destination but on the purpose of your trip, your objective. Your objective may be to get there as quickly as possible, to have a leisurely trip, to travel in the least expensive manner, or to visit all the tourist attractions in between. You select the way to go according to what you want to accomplish. All of the transportation methods mentioned will get you to Chicago, but not all will necessarily accomplish your objective.

In a presentation, your choice of organizational pattern should be based on your subject matter; the needs, values, and knowledge of your audience, and your perceived credibility with the audience. Whatever the organizational pattern you choose, it should clarify your message, lend interest to your topic, emphasize those points that you want your audience to focus on, and exhibit your creativity and grasp of the topic.

Imposing Order on Chaos

Why be organized? By developing the structure of your presentation, you and your audience will be able to remember key ideas. You lighten the strain on the listeners, for they will be able to immediately grasp the relationship of your points and the meaning or relevance of your ideas. In addition, you will be more credible. Studies show that audiences perceive very quickly when a speaker is organized and, based on that perception, grant a degree of credibility to a speaker. Organization also provides you with a scheme that will propel you forward and give your presentation a feeling of momentum.

The president of the local International Association of Business Communicators gave a presentation at the group's monthly meeting. Her objective was to inform newcomers of the association and to encourage people to join. Her message was that membership in the IABC could be a valuable career boost. She began by saying, "I could give you the usual facts about our organization, but I think you can get a better picture if I tell you what it has meant to me." She outlined her career history and described how the IABC had been an important factor in each of her career moves. The way in which she arranged her information showed the connection between IABC membership and career advancement. Instead of giving the audience a dry list of salient points, she engaged the listeners with a personal story and won them over.

Good News, Bad News

If you need to present negative information, the audience probably will not listen closely until you deal with the controversial topic. One speaker used humor to lessen the impact of a negative quarterly report. He began:

> I have some good news to relate from research and develop-
> ment but first I want to deal with the financial setback this
> last quarter. I don't believe in the rationale of a scientist
> who had been unjustly accused and convicted of treason in
> a Near Eastern country and found himself forgotten in a
> prison in the midst of the desert. He was given a cellmate
> who tried to convince him to make an escape attempt, but
> he refused. The cellmate went ahead with his plans on his
> own and made his escape. However, he ran out of food and
> water and nearly succumbed to the intense heat. Despon-
> dently he returned to the prison and related his traumatic
> ordeal to the scientist, who astonished him by agreeing,
> "Yes, it was horrible. When I tried it, I also failed." The
> cellmate indignantly demanded, "For heaven's sake, man,
> when you knew I was going to make a break for it, why
> didn't you tell me what it was like out there?" The scientist
> shrugged his shoulders and replied, "Who publishes nega-
> tive results?"

The speaker's approach relaxed the audience and they knew they would be getting the full story on the status of the company.

Abraham Lincoln remarked, "My way of opening and winning an argument is first to find common ground or agreement." Establishing commonality, an agreement of ideas, in the beginning will lead to rapport and trust. If you start to threaten deep-seated values and strongly held beliefs, your audience will not listen to your persuasive argument but will start thinking of why you are wrong. A thorough audience analysis should uncover those beliefs.

Many of my clients ask if they should present an opposing view. A speaker addressing an educated and intelligent issue-oriented audience will be more effective if she presents both sides of an argument and meets the principal opposition head-on. If your audi-ence is hostile to your view, it is also preferable to present both sides, so you look fair. When an audience is in agreement with you, almost anything you say will reinforce beliefs. The best evidence points to the general principle that if the audience agrees with you and knows little of the opposing position, stronger temporary effects will be produced by showing only your side of the controversy. However, in most situations it is better to meet the principal opposition argu-ments. Your listeners will read about them or hear about them in any case, and if you expect to be persuasive in the long run, you may choose to deal openly and frankly with the material contrary to your message. You need to decide this on a case-by-case basis.

If you have high credibility, your listeners may be more patient with the way you parcel out good or bad news. If you do not have seniority or authority, they will probably demand you address their concerns immediately.

Organizational Patterns

Normal sequence of product design:

1. Management announces the product.
2. Technical writing publishes the manual.
3. Engineering begins designing it.

—Horton's Law
William Horton

The presentation is often promised and publicized long before the speaker has any idea of what he is going to say. As a result, the sequence of materials in presentations is often organized haphazardly. No organizational structure is right for every topic or every audience. Which plan will take into consideration the different levels of knowledge within your audience, their most pressing needs, the hidden agendas? Which plan will illuminate your subject? Which plan will automatically feed into a persuasive finale? Your finish should have a major influence on your choice of pattern. Here are some examples to consider.

Chronological Order

This pattern organizes your ideas by time such as the past, present, and future. It has a built-in sense of forward movement. Your topic may dictate this organizational pattern. In a scientific or technical presentation, for example, speakers may need to describe the steps in an assembly process or an operational cycle. Complex, technical instructions should be presented in the proper sequential order so as not to leave out critical steps.

Rather than give dull minute-by-minute or year-by-year accounting, try to cover periods of time and make them more vivid. For example, your main points could be that sales were slow from 1982 to 1985, peaked during 1986 to 1990, and held steady until the present. Former chairman Robert M. Price from Control Data Corporation imaginatively discussed generations of computers by their role in society rather than by technological progression. He said a societal view of computers showed three generations, each one roughly equivalent to a twenty-year human generation. He compared the first computers to the immigrants to America from Europe. Then he took his audience through the second and third generations and said of the third generation, "They will be better educated and more affluent than their predecessors, based on a spectrum of technology their grandparents couldn't imagine. They will be literate, articulate, and completely integrated with their human partners."[1]

Topical Order

Discover interesting ways to divide your subject into different parts. It is quite common for project managers to divide their progress reports into categories of personnel, equipment, time, and budget. Rick Chappell, assistant director of science for NASA at Huntsville, Alabama, spoke about the proposed cooperative venture between the United States and Russia for exploring Mars, and divided the information into its social, political, economical, and cultural aspects.

Topical divisions shouldn't be a random list of items. The divisions used should relate to one another and be of approximately equal importance. If you are presenting four results of research, ask yourself what order would be most logical and natural considering your audience's level of knowledge, the information most valuable to them, and the easiest way for them to understand the information. Take into consideration the memory curve that exists during any presentation. Attention will usually be highest in the beginning and toward the end. Your most important division should be positioned up front and reviewed toward the end. Maintain a sense of forward movement to that irresistible conclusion.

Escalating Pattern

Speakers who use this pattern can organize their material smallest to largest, easiest to hardest, inexpensive to costly. A pilot told me that it was critical in his training program to learn the first level of information and practice it before he progressed to the next level. Similarly, if you are showing a person a new software program, you must progress through its applications from the most basic to the more complex. Each application must be learned before advancing to the next one. An overload of information at the beginning is useless.

A hospital equipment company may present plans to distribute its products on a local, regional, national, and international level. This progression could be combined with a chronological analysis of past accounts, present sales figures, and future outlook.

SAFW

How many times have you been in a meeting and the chairperson has asked you to "say a few words" about the topic under discussion? SAFW stands for "statement, amplification, a few examples, and windup." This formula will help you organize your thoughts so that you sound intelligent and poised. Begin with a strong statement that encapsulates your feelings, insight, and belief about the subject. Then amplify that statement. Transitional phrases could begin with "that means," "therefore," "however," or "for that reason." Cite one or two examples, depending on your time constraints, and wind up by making a recommendation or offering a solution and circling back to your original statement. Try using the SAFW formula the next time someone asks you a question.

Experiential Order

Experiential order reveals how we came to an understanding or developed a belief. This arrangement of ideas can be very effective if you are talking about a certain methodology or experiment that you disbelieved and now agree with. For example, a person might tell how he doubted citizen garbage recycling efforts would work. He reports that after reexamining the evidence, and personally participating in recycling, he now believes in allocating more funds to support recycling projects. If the speaker's credentials are highly regarded, this can be a convincing way to organize material.

Pro and Con

This pattern gives all the points in favor, all the points against, and then concludes which side is best. You may also give the advantages or disadvantages of two sides of an issue and end up offering a compromise. If you are talking to your peers, you may be able to jump into the heart of a technical discussion on advantages and disadvantages. However, general audiences may require more background material to bring them up to a basic understanding of your main points.

Cause-Effect

This pattern points out that one thing can lead to another. Of course, you have to prove your thesis is true. Many presenters will find a cause-effect organizational pattern ideal for discussing environmental concerns, occupational hazards, or results of research.

One presenter was trying to convince his audience of the dangers of mercury-amalgam dental fillings. To prove that mercury was harmful, he cited the classic example involving the felt hatmakers in the nineteenth century. At that time, felt hats were dipped in mercuric nitrate solution to make the felt easier to shape. The workers were subject to severe mercury poisoning after inhaling mercury vapors and absorbing mercury through the skin. This caused tremors, incoherent speech, muscular dysfunction, and even feeblemindedness. The author Lewis Carroll portrayed these effects with his memorable character the Mad Hatter in *Alice in Wonderland*.

The presenter went on to describe how current research had turned up many patients with various health problems who also had mercury in their dental fillings. When the fillings were removed, the patients reported amazing relief. In this case, as with any presentation using a cause-effect organizational pattern, the audience had to decide whether the causal relationship was effectively demonstrated.

Scientific Method

This organizational pattern gives the background of the problem and purpose of the research, lists the materials used, explains the experimental methodology, gives results, and enumerates implications or makes recommendations. David Suzuki, in his book *Inventing the Future*, questions the rote, passionless way that students learn to communicate their research. He tells of screening more than a quarter million flies carrying chromosomes exposed to powerful chemical mutagens and recovering a temperature-sensitive paralytic mutation:

> At 22 degrees Celsius, the flies could fly, walk, and mate. They seemed normal. But when shifted to 29 degrees Cen-

tigrade, they instantly fell down, completely paralyzed. When they were placed in a container kept at 22 degrees Centigrade, they started flying again before they hit the bottom! It was a spectacular mutant, and, when we found it, we screamed and danced and celebrated. We soon discovered that our mutation was a defect in nerves, rather than muscle.

And how did we write up our results? We riffled through all our records, selected the ones that said what we wanted and then wrote the experiment up in the proper way: purpose, methods and materials, results, and so forth. The report was making "sense" of our discovery, putting our results into a context that our colleagues could understand and repeat. But it conveyed nothing of the excitement, hard work, frustration, disappointment, and exhilaration of the search; or the original reason we started the search for paralytic mutants.[2]

Problem-Solution

Many of your presentations will lend themselves to a problem-solution organizational pattern. Sales presentations, including TV commercials, often use this pattern. First, focus the attention of the audience on a particular problem, sometimes making the audience aware there *is* a problem. The next step is offering a solution or satisfying a need. Then take your audience through the visualization step or what will happen by implementing the solution, and finally ask for action.

One aerospace company was wrestling with communication problems between its manufacturing and engineering departments. It was up to selected team leaders to talk candidly to their departments. During one presentation, the team leader focused *attention* on the company's need to deliver a quality product on time while keeping costs down. He explained that costly mistakes were showing up and time was lost when work had to be redone. Some of the engineering designs were difficult to implement, because manufacturing wasn't involved early on in the design process. He went to great lengths to make sure that the *problems* were clearly understood before he moved into possible *solutions*.

The administration proposed training workshops for both engineers and manufacturing workers so each group would learn the other's roles. In these training sessions, they would discuss what happens when you design a product and what processes manufacturing has to go through. They would also talk about maintenance and customer needs. These teams would be brought together for weekly or monthly meetings. The team leader went on to show how this preventive method of team counterchecks would save rework time, improve the quality of the product, and eliminate the need for extra inspectors. He asked them to *visualize* the time and extra work they would save, the frustrations that would be minimized, and the possibility of innovative ideas that could result from the meetings. The team leader finished by asking for *action*. He wanted the team's acceptance and support. This thorough problem-solution presentation successfully launched an improved communications program.

Experiment to Find the Best Pattern

These are a few of the different patterns you can use. The most efficient and appropriate pattern may not be apparent at first glance. Outline and condense your information into six minutes and experiment by putting this information into different organizational patterns. By trial and elimination, you will discover that one pattern seems to simplify and illuminate the material better than the others. As you restructure the ideas, the different arrangement may also suggest new ways to clarify your information. You many find that you lack evidence in one part or another, or that your supporting points are not of equal weight. You might choose to reverse the order of main points because your audience needs to be aware of specific information before they can grasp your last point.

Your organizational pattern should be flexible, so that you can adapt to unexpected audience reactions or situations. Just as you may have to make a long detour on your journey because a bridge is out, you may have to spend extra time explaining a concept and then condense another part of your speech to stay within your scheduled time limit.

Many speakers hesitate to preview or review points, because they think the reiteration will be boring. However, audiences usually welcome the repetition if the point is important for them to remember. References to points previously made should relate to the single purpose the speaker hopes to achieve. Several model communicators have told me that they follow the old adage that you tell them what you're going to tell them, tell them, and then tell them what you've told them. This format helps their audiences remember the essential information.

Model communicators emphasize that most listeners appreciate smooth transitions that tie sections of a speech together with a ribbon of relevancy. Use words and phrases to help the listener connect one point with the next and see their relationship to the whole message. Verbal signals will help even the distracted audience member to eventually catch up.

You can ask listeners to shift from the general to the specific by saying "for example" or "one instance." Alert them to a change of direction and guide your audience along by saying "nevertheless," "but," or "on the other hand." Summarize what you have said and forecast what is coming up by saying, "We have looked at the recent research on termites, and now we are going to examine how the principles of this experiment relate to our present insect population."

If you have a clear organizational pattern, the audience can mentally check off points as you make them. Don't jump abruptly from one point to another. You may have everything clearly worked out in your mind, but the audience needs to be prompted so that they can discover the continuity within your presentation.

In the same way, clearly signal to your audience the interrelationships among your points. When you need to establish a sequence, use such terms as "subsequently," "after," "next," or "now we come to the third step in the process." Connect statistics with something you said earlier and relate each section of your presentation to your overall thesis. Use such phrases as "another viewpoint," "and yet," "a final relationship," "however," or "it is equally important." If you wish to report implications of research, you could use phrases such as "in the future," "we predict," or "the outlook in the years ahead." Look back over your presentation to see where you might insert connecting statements that not only help the audience keep up with you, but also lead toward the acceptance of your ideas.

Keep Everyone—Including Yourself—On Track

Model communicators will choose an organizational pattern that emphasizes certain points and de-emphasizes others. Most audiences that have to absorb and remember scientific and technical information appreciate a road map. They're most comfortable with speakers who tell them what's coming: "I would like to discuss how this affects the environment locally, statewide, and nationally" or "I would like to state the results and then note how I've proceeded with our project."

A clear design will help you, the speaker, remember the order of your points, even if you should lose your place. The road map not only makes your audience feel comfortable and secure, but also reminds you, as a leader, of your direction.

One of my clients was asked to speak to two different audiences on the same topic. He was given thirty minutes for his first presentation and two hours for the second one. When he told me he would cut his two-hour speech to fit into thirty minutes, I cautioned him against this method because each presentation and audience demands a different strategy. He ended up using a topical approach for the two-hour speech and a simple problem-solution approach for the shorter presentation.

Each issue of the British magazine *Structural Engineer* carries the following quote on its masthead: "Structural Engineering is the science and art of designing and making, with economy and elegance, buildings, bridges, frameworks and other similar structures so that they can safely resist the forces to which they may be subjected." If you can give your speech an economical and elegant structure, you will find that it, too, can withstand unforeseen circumstances. You will also find that you look at your material in a fresh new way. Examine the logical sequence of your material and judge its probable effectiveness as a whole. It doesn't matter which pattern or combination of patterns you choose as long as the information is presented in a way that promotes understanding.

KEY IDEAS

- Choose an appropriate organizational pattern that clarifies your message and helps the audience remember it.
- Experiment with different patterns to find the best fit.
- Practice using formulas (SAFW) to organize your ideas when you answer questions or make brief comments.
- Create a feeling of forward movement in your presentation.
- Move your audience from point to point with transitional phrases and highlight the interrelationships of your ideas.

Notes

1. Robert M. Price, "The Coming of the Third Generation," *The Executive Speaker* (newsletter) (Dayton, Ohio: The Executive Speaker Co., June 1990).
2. David Suzuki, *Inventing the Future* (Toronto: Stoddart, 1989). Used with permission of the author.

12

Adding Variety

"The spectator forgives everything except dreariness."

—Voltaire

Overview

The only thing worse than sitting through a boring presentation is giving one! This chapter encourages you to lift your presentation out of the mundane by adding variety to your material, voice, and style and the way you interact with your listeners. You must capture and keep the attention of your audience to communicate your message and accomplish your objective. Retain the listener's attention by using contrasts, changing stimuli, and alternating the mood within your presentation.

Bill Nye, who calls himself "The Science Guy," is an example of a model communicator who consciously orchestrates his presentations. He considers teaching to be a performance and uses stories, analogies, props, visual aids, and demonstrations to communicate principles of science to his audiences:

> First of all, I try to think of innovative analogies for the ideas I am teaching. For instance, I wanted to answer a popular question: "If you are in an elevator that starts falling, can you save yourself by jumping up at the last moment?" I realized this was an opportunity to explain potential and kinetic energy. I designed a Barbie and Ken–size wooden elevator about 9 inches tall in an 8-foot-high elevator shaft. My passenger was an egg. I reeled the egg up to the top of the elevator shaft and explained that this

was potential energy. This potential energy was converted to kinetic or moving energy when I cut the rope and let the egg go. A spring mechanism caused the egg to "jump" a second before impact. The smashed egg clearly answered the initial question. If you fall 500 feet in an elevator and are able to jump up 12 inches, you still fall 499 feet!

A local physics professor told me he tries to stimulate his students' thinking and look for ways to move his classes beyond the theoretical. For example, he illustrated magnetic levitation by using a new high-temperature superconductor. The students watched him demonstrate this extraordinary phenomenon and wanted to know exactly how it worked. His advice to speakers is to "play your audience and fan a small interest into a fire."

Just as you would become bored listening to a repetitious melody for an hour, an audience's attention will wander if your material, pacing, and interaction do not vary. In today's electronic environment, our focus is on speed and hyperefficiency. Audiences have gotten used to the computer's nanosecond time frame and your information must now compete with, and triumph over, other stimuli. Usually an audience will listen attentively for the first ten to twelve minutes of a speech. Thirty minutes into an hour-long speech, the audience's attention is at its lowest ebb. After fifty minutes, it is difficult for an impatient audience to concentrate on any material, no matter how fascinating the subject is for the presenter. And keep in mind that according to one study, an executive's attention span is six minutes.

An audience listening to scientific and technical information doesn't possess a miraculous trait that improves their concentration. In fact, when you present complex information, unfamiliar concepts, extensive background material, statistics, and a myriad of dry details, it takes more energy for your audience to focus, search for associations, and store the information in long-term memory. It is important that you give the audience periods within your speech to relax and absorb complex information.

Keep in mind that time seems to pass more slowly for the audience than it does for the presenter. A model communicator takes responsibility for keeping the audience alert and consciously adds variety to enliven the presentation. A preacher had a reputation throughout the countryside of being a dynamic speaker. An aspiring young clergyman sought him out and asked for his advice. "I understand that you keep everyone's attention during your sermons," he said. "How do you do it?" "Well," replied the preacher, "it's quite simple. I have a young man with a long, pointed stick who stands on the platform with me. Whenever anyone in the congregation starts to fall asleep, he pokes *me*."

Now that you have prepared and organized your material, review it to see where you can add some variety. Look at your material and your choice of words. Do you have an abundance of words at your disposal to precisely and vividly describe your thoughts? How can you add variety to your delivery, especially your voice? Can you increase the interaction with your audience?

The Ultimate Word Processor—You

A golfer selects the appropriate putter, a fisherman the right gear, a carpenter the proper tool. If you select vivid, descriptive words and use them precisely, you will have more control over the visual images that others call up in their minds. An excellent style cannot be achieved with a small vocabulary. Your words should be concrete, unambiguous, economical, and specific. Eliminate clichés and tired, overused words.

Model communicators are known for their originality and individuality of expression, accurate vocabulary, and command of grammar. Do your words obscure or enhance your meaning? Do your words have spirit and energy? Will they call up vivid associations and fire off the neurons in the minds of your listeners? The average person's speaking vocabulary is very small. Researchers recorded telephone conversations of approximately 80,000 words and found that speakers had a working vocabulary of only 2,040 words. Elevate your speaking vocabulary to the level of your reading vocabulary. Keep a copy of *Rodale's Synonym Finder* or *Roget's Thesaurus* on your desk at all times. Several computer software programs include a thesaurus to help you find that perfect word. Increasing your vocabulary is tantamount to increasing your thinking capacity.

Have you considered the connotations as well as the denotations of your words? The denotation is the explicit meaning, and connotations are what the word suggests. The name of the Patriot antimissile used by the coalition forces during the war in the Middle East connotes freedom, the flag, and loyalty. The mere thought of the word "SCUD" for the missiles from the Iraqi forces suggests the "bad guys." Use words that evoke rich and favorable imagery.

Usually technical speeches are impersonal, and presenters use third-person pronouns. Because the research is seen as separate and distinct from the researcher, the speaker slips into the passive voice: "The bridge was determined to be unstable..." or "The cultures were subjected to heat." The impersonal voice is also overused: "It should be noted that..." or "The research demonstrates...." The sentence structure, as you can see in these examples, becomes cautious, circumspect, and loses its forcefulness. The verb can be your strongest element in a statement. Active verbs require concrete, interesting nouns. Make them specific, bright, lively, and vigorous. Streamline your prose and choose active rather than passive verbs. "The engineers noted that the bridge..." or "We heated the cultures...." Identify who is doing what with first- and second-person pronouns: "To analyze the data, I fed the samples through..." or "You should note...."

If you speak in abstract generalities, you are giving your audiences more leeway to think about other things. If your audiences have to stop and figure out what you're saying, they lose contact with your message. Help them avoid blind alleys and running into walls by using a colorful vocabulary that illuminates your ideas. If your words are vague, they may be open to several interpretations and may weaken your message. Be specific; take responsibility for what you say.

Words should not be used to gratuitously demonstrate your knowledge or to impress people. Yeats cautioned, "Think like a wise man but communicate in the language of the people." Sometimes the professional buzzwords and jargon are equated with the elitist aspects and complexity of a profession, and members of that profession are reluctant to relinquish this mystique and in-talk. Empower your audiences by giving them new word choices. They won't be alarmed or confused if you introduce new words, define them carefully, and emphasize the words as you use them.

Replace unnecessary technical words with a word familiar to your specific audience. For example, a physicist might talk about coherent superposition, whereas a chemist refers to synergy, but a general audience would understand that the whole is greater than the sum of the parts.

Choose emotionally powerful words. As author and science editor Edward Tenner points out in his book, *Tech Speak*:

> Most dictators are direct. They use simple, honest words like home, children, blood, soil, work, fate, strength, youth and, of course, victory.
>
> Scientists from the seventeenth century have retained a profound suspicion of eloquent argument. Where lawyers

see no injustice in having a case decided for the party with the more articulate champion, scientists believe that evidence, not persuasion, must prevail. Of course, this leads some of them to a kind of reverse rhetoric that uses needless complexity to imply an absence of verbal tricks. Language reform has led to what is denounced as language abuse.[1]

Publishing consultant Wendell Forbes reminded an audience that in the age of scientific approaches, "the gentle art of communication is of paramount import. Nothing cuts through the information clutter better than a well-turned phrase." Your choice of words should bridge the familiar to the unfamiliar. Your words should unify rather than separate people.

Variety in Delivery and Interaction With Listeners

How can you add variety and contrast to your delivery? If you remain behind the lectern, your lack of activity will lull the audience to sleep. Very few immobile people can keep the attention of their audience. James Burke, host of the British Broadcasting Company programs *Connections* and *The Day the Earth Changed*, is one exception. His eye contact, humor, drama, and rapid-fire eloquence make each person feel that Burke is talking individually to him or her, even when there are 2,500 people present! A speaker needs a commanding voice if he is riveted to one spot. When there is no discrimination with the voice, the audience is forced to make their own interpretation of what is important and what needs to be remembered. Vary your voice by speaking loudly and softly, changing pitch, and using pauses.

Moving into the audience can get their attention. Wait until you sense you have achieved rapport and it is okay to invade the audience's space. Cross the invisible barrier two or three times during the presentation and for the question and answer period. If you are on a platform and need the height to be seen, you can still go down the steps into the audience briefly. Practice these moves so that they go smoothly.

The speaker sends information to the audience, gets back information, and adapts or modifies her material and delivery. If you aren't receiving information back from your listeners, communication, in essence, has broken down and won't work to its maximum efficiency.

One engineer confided to me, "The audience distracts me and, if I get too involved with them, I lose my place." I encouraged him to pay attention to reactions from his audience, for they will forgive lapses of memory before they forgive being bored or ignored.

Ask your listeners rhetorical questions or ask questions that require them to raise their hands. In some situations, you can have your audience write down answers to questions and then share them with a partner or within a small group. Find out the names of your audience, put them on tent cards, or have people wear name tags. Announce early in your presentation that you will be looking for feedback later on, then walk into the audience and call people by name. "Dave, have you ever had the problem of . . . ?" or "Sarah, how do you feel about . . . ?" Asking your listeners about their feelings is nonthreatening because there is no right or wrong answer. The activity will keep them alert.

Your audience understands and learns not only by seeing and hearing, but by feeling, smelling, tasting, and touching. Use tactile images and words such as "wet," "ice-cold," "slippery," or "rough" to describe physical objects. A pilot described what g-force felt like by telling his audience to imagine that they had to make every movement with sixty-pound weights on each arm. Some presenters play upbeat music as their audience files in for an association meeting or use background music to enhance the mood of slides or a video. All of these add interest to presentations.

Jack Vallentyne, a Canadian ecologist who performs for children under the name of Johnny Biosphere, demonstrates to his audience how everyone is a part of the ecosystem. He asks his listeners to hold their breath. He then tells them that the gas molecules now in their lungs have been in the lungs of everyone else in the room. He further emphasizes that we are linked with every other human being from Jesus Christ to Michael Jackson by shared molecules in the air, water, and soil. Sometimes the audience tries to stop breathing because they are shocked and even disgusted by the idea that they are sharing the air with others. This graphic demonstration involves the children mentally, physically, and emotionally. They will always remember we are all part of the same ecosystem.

To Read or Not to Read...

It is a rare speaker who can read from a manuscript and still be successful at injecting variety into his voice, style, and audience interaction. However, some technical audiences prefer that you stick to a manuscript, especially when there are complex formulas and critical information.

Before reading from a manuscript, you should plan several rehearsals so that you become so familiar with the script that you can concentrate on the audience. Double- or triple-space your manuscript so that you can read the words easily. Underline key words and draw wavy lines over important phrases where you should change your inflection, add emphasis, or pause. As you read aloud, you will find sentences that are unwieldy, too long, or complicated. Break them into manageable segments and create a more conversational style. Think the thoughts as if you were saying them for the first time. Speech writer Jerry Tarver says, "When spoken words lack a proper beat, listeners smell the odor of ink."

Style—More Than the Sum of Its Parts

In *Wind in the Willows*, Toad's egotistical style of speaking forced his friends into blunt honesty:

> "Now, look here, Toad," said the Rat. "It's about this Banquet, and very sorry I am to have to speak to you like this. But we want you to understand clearly, once and for all, that there are going to be no speeches and no songs. Try and grasp the fact that on this occasion we're not arguing with you; we're just telling you...."
>
> "Mayn't I sing them just one *little* song?" Toad pleaded piteously.
>
> "No, not *one* little song," replied the Rat firmly.... "It's no good, Toady; you know well that your songs are all conceit and boasting and vanity; and your speeches are all self-praise and—and—well, and gross exaggeration and—and—"
>
> "And gas," put in the Badger in his common way.
>
> "It's for your own good, Toady," went on the Rat....
>
> "It was, to be sure [Toad said], but a small thing that I asked, merely leave to blossom and expand for yet one more evening, to let myself go and hear the tumultuous applause that always seems to me—somehow—to bring out my best qualities. However, you are right, I know, and I am wrong....But, O dear, O dear, this is a hard world!"

And, pressing his handkerchief to his face, he left the room with faltering footsteps.[2]

Toad had to face the fact that style wouldn't lift his speeches out of mediocrity if there was no substance. But style and substance are not mutually exclusive. The mistaken perception in many scientific and technical arenas is that to have substance, you have to give up style, and vice versa. Layne A. Longfellow, a dynamic model communicator, emphatically states that the "more profound and intellectual your message, the more you need to emphasize style."

Everyone has a personal style of delivery. Your style is a composite of the words you select, your gestures and movements, appearance, voice, and the way you make your ideas available to others. A columnist once wrote of President Kennedy: "It is no use trying to say what I mean by the Kennedy style. Style is not something one can define exactly or prescribe for another. It has something to do with taste, something to do with restraint and control and something to do, finally, with grace and gallantry."

Stanford University professor and author John W. Gardner said, "The image makers encourage the individual to fashion yourself into a smooth coin, negotiable in any market." Rather than fading into the woodwork in your organization, you can—and should—insist on expressing your unique personality in your presentations. What sets you apart? Think of small creative ways in which you can add interest to your style, and remember that rarely will anyone protest if you present a dry subject in an entertaining and informative way.

Be innovative. Increase the frequency of your eye contact with people in the audience, and add more intensity to your voice. Smile. Be more open and vulnerable. Use humor and crispness. The tempo of music changes—so should the pacing of your presentation.

Your style should change to suit the situation, your material, and the audience. A lighthearted after-dinner speech for your local engineering association will require a more casual style than a formal budget request. Your language, delivery, pacing, and appearance may all change.

Your ideas may be beneficial and your facts accurate, but if you lose the attention of your audience, you will not get the response you want. Go back over your material and examine where you can vary material, its pacing, and your delivery. Think of ways to present your information vividly, forcefully, and economically in your own inimitable style.

KEY IDEAS

- Keep the audience's attention by introducing change throughout your presentation.
- Help your audience make associations by using descriptive, concrete words.
- Develop and trust your own unique style.
- Do not fear that a strong personal style is incompatible with substance.
- Adapt your style to your audience and the situation.

Notes

1. Edward Tenner, *Tech Speak* (New York: Crown Publishers, Inc., 1986).
2. Kenneth Grahame, *Wind in the Willows* (New York: Charles Scribner's Sons [an imprint of Macmillan Books], 1961). Used with permission of the publisher.

13

Rehearsing

"You did say you wanted to be out of the mob, didn't you?"
"Yes, but how did you ... ?"
"Like everything else, Fletcher. Practice."

—Richard Bach
Jonathan Livingston Seagull

Overview

Rehearsal, both physical and mental, frees you from internal critiques and allows you to concentrate on your words and feedback from the audience. This chapter describes how practice will improve your delivery, make you feel secure, and help you adapt to unexpected circumstances. It also suggests what should be included in your rehearsal and criteria to evaluate rehearsals.

Rehearsal is an important final step in the process of mastering your material and developing a sense of timing. If you feel comfortable, you won't panic should something go awry. Most people know they should prepare and rehearse presentations, but many speakers tend to emphasize the accuracy of their material and postpone attention to delivery until the last minute. One engineer said, "It is always on the fly around here. Often I am told that I'll be giving a report the next morning. I don't have the opportunity to do anything more than a few simple graphics on my computer. I'm lucky if I have time to review the material in my head while I'm on my way to work."

Information changes so rapidly that speakers often feel uncomfortable trying to explain it to others because they haven't had the time to become thoroughly versed with the latest data themselves. It requires extra effort on the part of the technical professional to find the time to prepare thoroughly and to do a run-through. The speaker's reward for preparation and rehearsal is feeling more comfortable during the presentation and eliciting genuine applause at the conclusion.

Physical Rehearsal

Why rehearse out loud? Because it is an efficient and powerful way to edit and revise. The German word for rehearsal is *die Probe*, and indeed it provides an opportunity for the speaker to probe and examine, to check out his material and delivery.

Set up the imagined area and walk through the speech. I was videotaping one client and asked her to present her material exactly as she would give it the next day. She began, "And here I do this, and then I'll show a picture, and then I'll go through the next example." I stopped her. "Don't talk about what you'll do; do it. If you get under pressure, you will revert back to how you rehearsed it." "You're right," she agreed. "In my last presentation, I actually said, 'And then I'll walk over to the flip chart.'"

If at all possible, visit the actual speech site. Sit on the chairs, touch the tables, and count the number of steps from your seat to the front of the room. Notice how the paint is worn thin on the lectern where previous speakers have gripped it with white knuckles. Look everywhere. Walk around the room making large gestures. Keep your body in comfortable alignment. Because of your practice and mastery of your ideas, your gestures and body language will come easily and spontaneously.

You may encounter problems that you can't resolve. Feedback from other speakers who have appeared before the same audience can be a valuable resource. Call and ask them about the general attitude, knowledge level, types of questions, and any problems that they experienced at the site of the speech.

Graphics are usually finished at the last minute. You will integrate them more successfully into your presentation if you practice with preliminary sketches and check the time necessary for the audience to read and interpret your slides or viewgraphs. Practice the sequence of visuals while directing your attention toward the audience. If computers are a part of your program, it is mandatory to practice and anticipate any problems.

If you will use a lectern, rehearse with one, or stack some books on a table and put your notes on top. It makes a difference in your eye contact with the audience. If you intend to use a pointer, rehearse with it; and practice putting it away!

If you are the third or fourth presenter, practice walking to the front with your materials and changing the audiovisual equipment. Even if your meeting is a regular in-house presentation, rehearse getting up from your chair and going to the front of the room, smoothly setting down your viewgraphs, reaching for the proper switch to turn on the projector or the computer, and distributing handouts.

Rehearse that humorous story or anecdote in the actual room or one that is the same size. It may go over well in an intimate boardroom but fall flat in a large auditorium. One of my clients had to speak at Radio City Music Hall after the Rockettes had performed. I reserved Seattle's Fifth Avenue Theater, which seats 2,500, so that my client could get acclimatized to a big space. He reported later that this hour-long rehearsal was a major factor in his ability to "own his space" in Radio City Music Hall.

Notes

When someone says that he will speak "off the cuff," we know that he will be speaking impromptu, with no preparation. Originally, "off the cuff" meant that the speaker wrote notes on his shirt cuff that could be read easily without giving the appearance of having notes. Experienced speakers have always known that a good ad-lib takes hours of preparation.

Memorize the first few lines of your speech for an impressive opening. Practice directing your attention and energy toward the audience. Know the route you are traveling onstage and where you will be during each part of your presentation. Memorize the final few lines.

Read through your speech again and concentrate not only on the main points but on the details supporting each main point. You can use 5-by-8 note cards to help you organize your information, but make sure to number them. Give your speech using whatever words happen to come to mind. Get through the whole speech, even if you have to gloss over certain parts. Note how long it takes. When are you at the halfway point? When are you five minutes from the end? Take into account that during your actual speech you may talk faster if you are nervous.

The night before your speech, list the main headings of your presentation and read them aloud several times. One model communicator told me that he tape-records his speech and listens to the tape on his Walkman during his flight to the city where he'll be speaking. Another client told me that she has a precise routine she follows on the day of a presentation. She always gets up at 5:00 A.M., dresses, and does a complete run-through. She is motivated to practice, she explained, by the memory of how confident she felt the last time she gave a rehearsed presentation.

Mental Rehearsal

Visualization is simply mental practice, the process of forming a mental image of your presentation. The mind does not distinguish between imagining a situation in detail and actually doing it. Many athletes who compete at the international level recognize the value of mental practice.

Doug Reynolds, an Olympic pistol marksman, says that he imagines himself going through each step of his three-minute preparation period, in which he methodically lays out everything he will need during his performance. The process allows him to enter each match with an automatic rhythm and allows him a better chance to adapt to the things that inevitably go wrong.

Some people find it difficult to visualize. If this seems foreign to you, give it a try, because it does work successfully for many people. Take some quiet time. Close your eyes, sit back, and visualize the entire situation, placing yourself in the scheme. Use all your senses. What will you hear, see, smell, touch? See yourself being successful giving the presentation. Visualize the audience responding favorably to your material. The mental image of success must be implanted firmly in your mind before it can occur in reality.

In *Cerebral Symphony*, William Calvin observes:

> As you become highly practiced in a skill, it no longer qualifies as novel. It does move from conscious control to less-than-conscious. In Zen archery, the object is to become so practiced that no conscious will is required to release the arrow at the right moment. You can simply watch the arrow being released, as if someone else were doing it.[1]

Rehearsal Schedule

When basics become habit, a speaker can concentrate on the audience, adapting to the feedback he receives or to any unexpected circumstance. If you are worried about your content or about appearing nervous, you could find yourself overwhelmed if a senior executive arrives unannounced or if extra chairs and handouts are needed for additional attendees. You can win points with the audience by smoothly handling interruptions or adverse conditions. Experience, of course, will make you feel more at ease. But rehearsal is the next best thing. Following is a suggested rehearsal schedule. The evaluation checklist in Figure 12 can also be used to critique a videotaped rehearsal.

Preparation

1. Create a mind map or brainstorm for the essential points to cover.
2. Research your important facts, statistics, and evidence.
3. Make a rough outline.
4. Write a first draft.
5. Decide which main points should be made into visuals. Do rough sketches. Create a storyboard.

First Rehearsal

1. Walk and talk through your presentation.
2. Include sketches of visuals.
3. Double-check the accuracy of all statistics, facts, and technical data.

Second Rehearsal

1. Give the presentation. Check times, props, and visuals.
2. Get feedback on your content, organization, and visuals. Modify as needed.
3. Review your presentation. Add variety through examples, analogies, and humor.
4. Decide on the best seating arrangement, if you have any control.

Third Rehearsal

1. Videotape or tape-record (audio) your presentation. Use a minimum of notes and stay within the time allotted. Check or rehearse with others if it is a joint presentation.

Figure 12. Evaluation checklist (video observation sheet).

Mark each statement with an X for "excellent," an S for "satisfactory," or an N for "needs improvement."

A. Organization and Development of Content

Opening statement gained immediate attention? _____

Purpose of presentation made clear? _____

Previewed content of speech? _____

Main ideas stated clearly and logically? _____

Organizational pattern easy to follow? _____

Main points explained or proved by supporting points? _____

(testimony, statistics, etc.)? _____

Variety of supporting points (testimony, statics, etc.)? _____

Conclusion adequately summed up main points, purpose? _____

Audiovisuals clear and visible to entire audience? _____

Audiovisuals emphasized main points? _____

B. Delivery

Presenter "owned the space" and was in control? _____

Rapport with the audience throughout the speech? _____

Eye contact with everyone in the audience? _____

Posture and gestures appropriate? _____

Voice rate. _____

Voice pitch. _____

Voice volume. _____

Voice quality. _____

Comments:

_____

_____

_____

_____

2. Have someone evaluate your presentation. Use the evaluation checklist in Figure 12 to help critique your performance.
3. Prepare your handouts; get necessary clearances.
4. Visit the site of your presentation; become familiar with the space. Check audio-visual equipment and practice with the microphone.
5. Memorize the opening and ending of your speech.

Speech Presentation

1. Choose clothing that is comfortable, professional, and unobtrusive.
2. Warm up your voice; do some physical exercises to get rid of tension.
3. Eat and drink lightly.
4. Have some quiet time by yourself to focus your energy.
5. Concentrate on your audience.
6. Enjoy yourself and give a dynamite presentation!

Try to cover as many of the preceding points as possible, even when you don't have much lead time. Expect that each situation will be different. Be flexible so that you can adapt the subject and your style to the particular audience and situation. Eventually everyone does rehearse. Make sure your rehearsal is not before an audience!

KEY IDEAS

- Start rehearsing early, as it is a method of editing and will allow you to focus on the audience.
- Prepare to speak "extemporaneously."
- Memorize the opening and closing lines of your speech.
- Rehearse at the actual site of your speech.
- Visualize a successful presentation.

Note

1. William H. Calvin, *Cerebral Symphony* (New York: Bantam Books, 1990).

Part III
Making a Compelling Delivery

14

Communicating With Effective Body Language

"There was speech in their dumbness, language in their very gesture."

—Shakespeare
The Winter's Tale

Overview

Many times a person will spend a great deal of time doing in-depth research, gathering facts, and preparing elaborate visuals, but won't think about the importance of the delivery of this material. This chapter will help increase your awareness of your own nonverbal messages and suggest techniques to make your gestures enhance the words you are saying, rather than diluting or detracting from your content. Your delivery and body language cannot improve the ideas in your presentation, but they will determine how well your ideas are received and remembered by the audience.

There are two parts to a speech: the content and the delivery. In scientific and technical fields, audiences have been conditioned to believe that if information is important, with some semblance of organization and logic, the speaker's delivery can be haphazard. Realistically, if two engineers present essentially the same message to the same audience, the one with the more congruent, effective body language, voice, and presence will be more successful in eliciting the response she wants.

The breakthroughs in technology that were intended to make communication simpler and effortless have actually created the opposite effect. Too much information has had an anesthetizing effect. Now that everybody uses new technology to scream for attention, audiences try to escape and shut down to avoid the overload. The demands on their time and attention prompt them to ignore or filter out what is not immediately relevant to them. The communicator has to search for ways to break through these barriers.

The answer is not to scream louder or to overuse additional high-technology stimuli. Your message must be clear, concise, brief, and relevant. By developing your nonverbal skills, your most important message will be heard and understood.

It Is a Performance

Before you even open your mouth, you need to show your audience that you deserve their attention. Much of the time, communication takes place without speech, by your body language and presence. If people do not like what they see in a speaker's appearance and what they hear in her voice, they will not care about the words they hear. If your delivery is forceful, brief, and dramatic, the listener is more likely to receive your intended message, and you are more apt to get results.

Model communicators are very concerned with how they present their material. They know that their delivery can be a deciding factor in whether they are perceived as credible and whether others are willing to accept what they say.

Many people tell me that they are excellent communicators in one-on-one situations; they have problems only when speaking in front of a group. That is because public speaking involves performing as much as it does presenting information. You need to have a sense of theater, a sense of style to get your message across to your employees, customers, peers, superiors, or subordinates.

Let's compare content to food, and delivery to the way that it is served. Take a lowly hot dog on a bun that has been carefully arranged on Dresden china. The waiter deftly serves it to you and silently waits to do your bidding. Add candlelight, an exquisite white linen tablecloth, aromatic roses, and beautiful soft music playing in the background. It can be quite pleasant.

Now have someone carefully prepare you a delicate Swiss chocolate soufflé. The waiter throws it on a paper plate and slides the plate across to you on a greasy plastic tablecloth with such a shove that the soufflé slops over the side. The waiter turns on some heavy metal rock, tosses you a broken plastic fork, and grunts, "Eat!" It can be quite unpleasant. Delivery makes a difference!

What Are Your Gestures, Mannerisms, and Posture Saying?

Communication is a transfer of ideas and energy. That energy is demonstrated through your body language, which includes eye contact, facial expressions, gestures, posture, and presence. Body language is the manifestation of internal feelings. It is usually more accurate than your words, which can be manipulated much more successfully.

Although "body language" is a universal term, it really is a misnomer. To call something a language is to say that each component has three or four accepted meanings and those meanings can be catalogued and listed in a dictionary. Gestures have a multitude of meanings, depending on the context, your cultural background, expectations, and previous experience.

Your audience receives over half of their information from your body language. Are your gestures adding to the meaning of what you're saying or are they telling the audience that you lack confidence, are nervous, or are unprepared? Before key decision makers give you control over people, resources, or money, you must convince them that you are indeed in control of yourself and in control of your circumstances.

Most of us, when we're sitting in an audience, can pick up the nonverbal cues that alert us to the fact that a speaker is not entirely comfortable. Is he uncomfortable because he fears speaking in public or is he not really prepared to discuss the subject? Confident speakers make no apologies, have a strong, confident posture, and possess a relaxed, alert manner. They calmly recover from mistakes, use few notes, and make good use of their personal space. They have animated faces, pleasant voices, strong eye contact, and warm smiles. The speakers who are uncomfortable have nervous gestures, have bland or tense facial expressions, clench their hands or play with objects, and may hunch over or slouch. Their eyes are unfocused and squinting, they shift their pace and their weight, and they appear devoid of energy. What is your nonverbal language saying?

Going Beyond Yourself and the Material

There are three stages in the development of presenters. In the first stage, people are involved with themselves and concerned about how they look and how people are judging them. In the second stage, people are involved with their material. Is it accurate? Are there enough statistics, proof, and visuals? Is it logical and well organized? Most technical professionals are in this stage.

Presenters in the third stage are involved with their audience. Is the audience profiting from the message? Am I using words and images that mean something to them? Am I starting from where they are? Am I really communicating with them? Am I getting the response I want?

Space engineer and science-fiction author Gentry Lee is an excellent example of a model communicator. He is involved with the audience from the moment he steps in front of them. He asks rhetorical and actual questions to get interaction and stimulate his audience. His gestures are spontaneous and punctuate his words. It is apparent that he is enjoying himself, and his contagious enthusiasm pulls in even the most resistant listener to discover what is so fascinating about science.

Your Body Language Reflects Your Mental Attitude

Recently I attended a recital at the Northwest Suzuki School of Music. The children were having a group lesson and the headmaster gave a short critique after each child played. One child was having trouble with a series of fast notes. The headmaster told him that he was not playing the runs crisply enough. The child laboriously placed each finger on the piano keys. The headmaster stood up and solemnly declared, "You don't play the piano with your fingers, you play it with your mind!"

The headmaster was trying to teach the child that you will be more successful working on the mental causes of your errors than dwelling exclusively on the physical. What is going on inside your mind? How do you feel about yourself, your material, the audience, and the situation? Our thoughts trigger our emotions, which trigger our body language and vocal tone. What you are thinking will determine how you feel, and that, in turn, will influence your gestures, posture, and enthusiasm. Anxieties, personal problems, health, and ego all affect your ability to influence your audience. Your inner emotions can conflict with and destroy your real ability to sell your ideas.

Your body language grows out of your self-image. If you start to think that you will be a failure, you might feel depressed about the whole situation and your facial expressions and body language will reflect your uneasiness. If you have decided that you will do a good job, your emotions will be upbeat and confident, and your enthusiasm will be evident in your posture, your eagerness to be understood, and the smile that is on your face when you begin.

All of us have days, of course, when we don't feel terrific about ourselves. You can always ask yourself what you would do if you were confident, self-assured, and in control. Psychologist William James said, "Outward physical confidence, even though feigned, actually increases internal, psychological confidence." If you aren't feeling in top form, act as though you are, and your performance will convince everyone, including yourself.

Psychologist Paul Ekman of the University of California, San Francisco, has shown that when Americans are asked to make faces corresponding with different emotions, their heartbeat, blood pressure, and other physical responses change to match the feigned emotions. For example, if you make faces corresponding to fear, anger, sadness, and disgust, actual chemical changes occur in your body. If you imagine that you are happy and confident, your body's chemistry changes to correspond to those emotions. Your body language can actually influence what happens to you biologically.

Which Animal Are You?

One client was having trouble running his weekly sales meetings and had been advised that he would lose his job if he could not take control. Although he was quite capable in many areas, he did not project an authoritative image. He was short and rather overweight.

At our meeting I noticed a soft, pliable Smurf doll sitting on his desk. I asked him which animal projected the characteristics that would help him reach his objective in meetings. He thought for a moment and then declared, "An eagle. It has a commanding presence. It's majestic and bold. And it soars to great heights and can get perspective on situations." I suggested that he get rid of the Smurf doll and replace it with his new image. Last Christmas his wife bought him a brass eagle with a three-foot wingspread that soars on his wall. He reports that it reminds him of the strength he wants to convey and results in stronger body language.

Look around your office to see what your brain is constantly absorbing. What images are reinforcing themselves? Which animal are you now and which would you like to be? Some answers have been revealing. One company president said that he was a snake because he liked to stay hidden but wanted to be deadly when he struck. He wasn't interested in changing his image, but for his presentations I helped him communicate his qualities of alertness and cunning.

I asked a systems engineer if he could think of an animal that had similar body language to his. He answered, "A rabbit." Indeed, he rarely spoke and was timid. He decided that he should be something stronger, such as a dog, and his choice made a difference in his body language. I suggested that he purchase a statue of a Great Dane and put it on his desk. Now, every time he picks up the phone, he thinks of the characteristics of a powerful dog and it affects the quality of his voice.

This isn't a parlor game. You can actually remind your body to act in a different way when you are delivering your material.

Own Your Space

"The Soviet leader President Mikhail Gorbachev can command a room like no one else in the world today, and he knows it," reports author Gail Sheehy. "He invades your space. He's a master of small-room charisma."

"He's a very gifted performer," remarked actor Paul Newman, after meeting Gorbachev. "He'd make a good actor because he's loose and you don't see the machinery of that looseness. He's not working to be loose and easy. He is, naturally."

Model communicators are at ease with themselves and with their space. Their presence expands until it takes up the entire room, and they are clearly comfortable with their space, their turf.

Here is an exercise to help you own your space: Pretend that you are very unsure of yourself. Hang your head. Act apologetic. Pull your body together so that you take up the smallest amount of space possible. Then stand tall, stretch your arms wide open, breathe deeply, and take up the entire room. Go back and forth from withdrawal to expansiveness. Feel the difference. The next time you walk to the front of the room to give a presentation, recapture that same feeling of owning the whole room. You can practice at your next cocktail party.

Once you are visible to the audience, your body language can establish or destroy your credibility. Most speakers don't establish their presence until about five minutes into the presentation and they may have already lost the audience. During your first few moments at the front of the room, take your time, pause. Let your audience become focused on you. Stand erect, and breathe deeply. Walk around (if it's possible and appropriate) to dissipate your tension. Smile, have fun, and enjoy the opportunity of having the attention of the audience. Let your attitude tell them that you would rather be here than anyplace else in the world.

Posture, Gestures, and Facial Expressions

Queen Victoria of England, who was only five feet one inch tall, often tied a garland of holly under her neck to remind her to keep her chin up. Good body alignment conveys confidence and authority. Poor posture projects defensiveness, rigidity, awkwardness, and aggressiveness. During rehearsals and before you begin each presentation, go through a posture check.

Stand with your feet about six inches apart and with your weight balanced on the balls of your feet. Bend your knees slightly. Tuck your buttocks under and pull your waist up out of your hips. Shrug your shoulders and practice feeling comfortable with your hands down at your sides. Keep your chin parallel to the floor. Now, pretend to grow two inches taller. Imagine that your head, like that of a marionette, is being pulled up by a headstring that rises from your skull and goes up into the clouds.

If your body is in alignment, it will feel easy and natural for you to use your hands to make gestures. The old practice of walking around with a book on your head will force you to stand up straight. Try it! You will find that your hands fall comfortably to your sides. Avoid clasping your hands in front of or behind you, and don't fold your arms across your chest. These gestures keep the energy around you. You want your energy to flow to your audience. Your audience will mirror your body language. If you lean heavily on the lectern and talk in a monotone, your audience will go to sleep. If you are alert and energetic, your audience will be alert and energetic.

The futurist David Pearce Snyder uses strong, animated gestures that add to the meaning of his words. If you turn off the sound on one of his videos, you can see the vitality in his movement. If I turned off the sound on one of *your* presentations, would I be able to tell if you're enthusiastic about your subject? What are you saying with your nonverbal language?

Be careful about rocking back and forth or aimlessly wandering around. If you are using a pointer, magic marker, or other tool or prop, put it down as soon as you have used it. An audience can become

distracted when you play with toys. Much of this behavior is uncon-
scious, but remember that small gestures can be distracting and often
make you appear weak or nervous.

Your listeners receive a large percentage of information from
your facial expressions. If your facial muscles never move or reflect
what you are saying, are you enhancing your words? No one expects
you to be an animated clown, but enthusiastic facial expressions will
not detract from a serious presentation.

Eye Contact

Your eyes will immediately signal your degree of confidence to everyone when you get up to give a presentation. Studies show that eye
contact increases the audience's attention, interests, understanding,
and satisfaction with the speaker.

You can either take in the participants and send out a message
that says, "We both count," or you can dismiss everyone in one sweep
of your eyes. It is not a good idea to focus your attention on an object
in the back of the room or on one or two people in the audience. Learn
to have private conversations with the people throughout the audience. Acknowledge the eye contact of those who seem interested in
your message and learn to grab and hold those who need to be
brought into your presentation. Hold eye contact for a short duration;
don't make someone uncomfortable by staring at him or her. Show the
listeners that they are valued and accepted.

Author Ralph Waldo Emerson said, "The eyes of men converse as
much as their tongues with the advantage that the ocular dialect
needs no dictionary, but is understood the world over." Although we
can mask our facial expressions, rarely can we mask what we say
with our eyes.

If it is imperative that you read some lengthy statistics, be sure
to glance up frequently and reestablish eye contact with your audience. Focused, direct eye contact will play a large part in establishing
your authoritative presence in a room and increase your rapport with
the audience.

Charisma Is Energy

Your delivery should be crisp and relaxed and reach out to the minds
of the audience. The prolific science writer and speaker Isaac Asimov
is an example of someone who combines an expressive voice and body

language to convey the passion he feels for his subject. Model communicators are enthusiastic about their work and feel a need to communicate their excitement to others. The key is radiating positive energy and enthusiasm even when you don't feel it. Author James Winans noted that "an audience will forgive a speaker almost any lack if he is manifestly earnest about his proposal. Earnestness moves our emotions, thaws our indifference, and gives us faith, which a leader must create."

Before you make a presentation, walk around briskly, shrug your shoulders, do knee bends, and feel the energy come from your toes. Let's see the enthusiasm in your facial expressions and hear it in your voice.

I often ask my clients to draw a stick figure of themselves and then draw arrows from the parts that radiate energy. Most people are puzzled and then draw an arrow from the eyes or hands. One woman said, "I never thought about energy below my neck." What parts of your body do you dislike? Some men and women are self-conscious about their weight or wrinkles or other parts of their body, so they withdraw to protect themselves. You block your energy when you try to hide parts of your body. So start liking yourself, in spite of any shortcomings. Say, "Hips, I love you!" "Receding hairline, I'm proud of you!" "Wrinkles, you're a sign of wisdom!" Energy must come from all over the body, but particularly from the solar plexus. Pretend that a beacon of light emanates from your waistline. It will make an amazing difference!

If you are serious and steady and not given to shows of emotion, there is no need for you to be effervescent. One of the most charismatic people I ever met was a tiny nun who went about her work without noise or commotion, but who spoke and listened with intensity and concentration. Your style may be quiet and serious, but it is certainly salable. Radiate competency, personal warmth, and credibility from your entire body.

Speaking in public implies a certain amount of effort and degree of tension. Relaxed alertness is impossible if you are physically exhausted. Flying coast to coast and dealing with jet lag presents a problem. If you are feeling fragmented, it will add to your nervousness. The body and voice must be rested. Get in training several days prior to your presentation by exercising and eating and sleeping well.

Flexibility is important because you will be facing different audiences and trying to influence those audiences. It is difficult when you have spent time and preparation on your report and then have the person ahead of you speak too long, have people arrive late, or have an overhead projector stop working. If you are rested, it will be easier to adjust to inconveniences or distractions. You can focus on your main concern of getting into the minds of your listeners.

Practicing Nonverbal Communication

Spend some time observing other people's nonverbal communication. What do they do that's positive, that enhances their communication? Then ask a mentor, a supervisor you respect, or a friend for feedback on your body language. Listen objectively, not defensively, and resolve to make whatever changes you can while being comfortable with who you are.

Model communicators say that their delivery skills suffer most when they are inadequately prepared or not sure of their material. Obviously, your first consideration should be the content of your message. In everyday conversation, sensitize yourself to the muscles in your face and feel what you are doing when you are expressing an emotion, qualifying a statement, or answering a difficult question. Do you squint or frown on a regular basis? Some people have a habit of looking angry no matter what emotion they are trying to express. Videotape yourself to find out if your perceived image actually comes across to others the way you think it does. Eliminate annoying mannerisms such as jingling pocket change, pushing up your eyeglasses, or drumming your fingers on a lectern. Observe what is going on in the audience and capitalize on what is happening. Make people comfortable, and use the energy of the audience. Don't get caught up in being perfect. A creative, informative presentation needn't be flawless.

Frog or Prince?

Do you consider the people in your audience to be your superiors or your subordinates or your peers? In other words, are they frogs or princes? Whether we like to admit it or not, we unconsciously make an immediate decision about our relationship to other people based on their authority, social status, educational status, material possessions, or even physical appearance. That decision affects our body language and tone of voice.

Many speakers deny that they react to some people differently, but if you walked into a room and found a group of subordinates, wouldn't your body language and voice be different than if you discovered you were facing the chairman of the board and senior administration? Monitor what changes occur in your body language when you attempt to persuade superiors or subordinates. Give others respect because of age, experience, or position but talk to them as equals.

Effective Delivery Skills

In my experiences with scientists and technologists, it has been a pleasant and refreshing experience to find the organization and logic of speeches exemplary. I salute them for their emphasis on substance but also know that they could increase their influence if they would pay more attention to the delivery of their information. You may have a better story than your competition, but you may lose a contract if they tell their story better. You will find that enthusiasm and openness to the audience will make you more persuasive.

Even if you don't have initial credibility, you can gain it during the presentation. Nonverbal signals can support and enhance the simplest statements. Believe in yourself, your ideas, and the value they have for other people. The audience will hear and see this. The unspoken word may have the most lasting impact of all!

KEY IDEAS

- Be pleased with yourself because your self-image is the most important factor affecting how you communicate.
- Spend time watching other people's body language and get feedback on your own postures, gestures, and mannerisms.
- Make your body language congruent with your words and tone of voice.
- Own your space.
- Communicate your enthusiasm about your subject through your delivery.

15

Developing a Colorful, Expressive Voice

"For his voice could search the heart, and that was his gift and his strength."

—Stephen Vincent Benét
The Devil and Daniel Webster

Overview

The voice is an instrument to be used by the speaker to convey the total meaning of a message. You should be able to control and use your voice adequately but always in an unobtrusive way. The effectiveness of your voice will be a critical factor in whether your opinions, insights, and instructions will be listened to and acted upon. This chapter will give you techniques for developing an expressive voice to successfully enhance your image and to effectively convey your information.

Pat Moneymaker, commander of the U.S. Navy's Blue Angels team, told me:

> I say the exact same 4,000 words every time we fly. There is no time to embellish the commands or comment, "It's bumpy out here," so I change the inflection in my voice to indicate the conditions, anticipation, and degree. For instance I may say, "Addd powerrrr" and stretch out the words. It's almost a second language for my pilots, and they understand if I mean to add power faster or slower. They only hear my voice, and they have to have absolute trust in what I am saying.

You may not be giving life and death commands in your next presentation, but your voice will either add to the understanding of your material or dilute your authority and your ability to persuade others. It will have a pronounced effect, good or bad, on your audience.

On several occasions, companies have asked me to work with their engineers on presentation skills saying, "You can skip the part about voice. They don't need that." What they don't realize, however, is that a third of the information that your audience receives will be from your voice. A clear, pleasing, expressive voice with precise articulation can accurately communicate your ideas and keep your listeners' attention. They will remember what you say and respond in the way you want.

I was fortunate to be a student of the legendary voice-over actor Daws Butler, who created the voices of Yogi Bear, Captain Crunch, Snaggle Puss, and more than fifty other characters. One evening, three of us met for a workshop at Daws' home. Usually we rehearsed scripts, perfected our timing, or worked on dialects. But on this evening Daws asked us to be seated, and for three hours he played selections of beautiful instrumental music that elicited very different emotions. At the end of class, he summed up the lesson, "Never forget your voice is a powerful instrument. Good night."

Voice makes the image whole. Other people define who we are by our voice and the words we use. Feelings, attitudes, physical state, and self-image are revealed by your body language and voice. Your voice should accurately reveal your emotions. Develop the instrument of your voice so that you are able to communicate the many fascinating dimensions of your personality.

Analyzing Your Voice

Have you ever felt that your audience isn't really listening, even though your information should capture their attention? Does your voice detract from the perception that you are an authority on your subject? Can your voice energize the audience? Do people frequently interrupt you or ask you to repeat your words? Does your voice add to the meaning of your words? You can increase the emotional and mental involvement of your listeners by having more resonance, variety, warmth, and vitality in your voice.

We acquired our voices by hearing and imitating family and relatives as we grew up. Sometimes we rebel against a loud voice that we've heard and adopt a very soft voice. But in any case, the voice we use on a daily basis is not always our natural voice. Fears and anxieties, tensions, and negative habits distort our voices and prevent us from using our natural voices. The best way to produce a strong, pleasant voice is to allow the body to do what it naturally and efficiently wants to do. Voice production should be effortless, and your vocal chords should not become strained or fatigued.

To improve your voice, you must refine your listening skills to know when you're speaking correctly. You may be surprised when you listen to yourself in a taped conversation. You may discover that your voice is higher-pitched than you thought, or you may find you talk too rapidly or slur your words.

If you want to tone and firm your body, you outline a strategy of diet, weight lifting, and exercise. It is equally necessary to analyze your voice to determine which qualities are working well for you now and to become aware of the flaws in your voice that should be minimized. By setting goals, you can train your voice to function efficiently and well. A fantastic body is not an overnight achievement. Developing a compelling voice will also take time, self-discipline, and practice.

Diaphragmatic Breathing

Do not underestimate the value of proper breathing. Almost every problem of the voice—harshness, shrillness, a pitch that is too high or too low, speech patterns that are too choppy or annoying—can be traced to improper breath control. Your speaking style, rate, quality, and resonance are affected by tension, which affects your breathing. The muscles of breathing should be exercised in the same way that we lift weights to exercise other muscles in our body or stretch to become flexible.

The diaphragm is a dome-shaped muscle that divides the chest cavity from the abdominal cavity, and it is the single most important element in voice production (see Figure 13). When air is inhaled, the diaphragm contracts, lowers, and flattens. This action creates a vacuum, and air rushes into the lungs to restore the balance. You may think that your throat is the primary source of your voice, but actually you should avoid using your throat as much as possible.

Join your hands over your stomach above your waist. Find the diaphragm by saying "whoa!" or "halt!" To feel your diaphragm moving, pant like a dog twenty times. Try this exercise. Extend your arms toward the corners of the room. Take a deep breath and pretend

Figure 13. Abdominal cavity and diaphragm (contracted and relaxed).

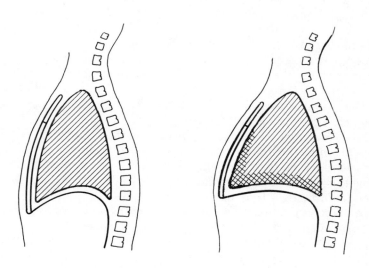

your lungs are a balloon you are filling from the bottom up. Then slowly, evenly, exhale. Release all the air until the balloon becomes flat and empty. Make sure you exhale every ounce of air. Keep relaxing all your muscles. Do not allow your upper chest or shoulders to move when you inhale or exhale. Feel your abdominal muscles, lower ribs, the rib muscles on the side, and back muscles expand slightly upon inhalation, like a bellows, and relax upon exhalation. Practice until it feels comfortable and normal for you to breathe from your midsection. If you have trouble breathing diaphragmatically, lean over a table or bend over from the waist or lie down. You will automatically breathe correctly.

Sound is produced when we exhale. Air is sent from the lungs through the trachea to the vocal folds in the larynx, which vibrate at different speeds and produce a variety of pitches. This vibration is given its unique resonance by the chest and lower throat and the nasal and sinus cavities. Sound is shaped by the hard and soft palates, teeth, jawbone, cheekbones, and nose. The consonants are formed by the lips, teeth, and tongue.

Imagine a long, white, plastic pipe that extends from the middle of your diaphragm through the middle of your lungs, and up through your throat. Tilt your head backward and open your mouth, so that the pipe can come out your mouth and head straight to the ceiling. But since you cannot walk around with your chin tilted upward all the time, you need to relax your chin so that it's parallel to the floor. Thus, we have to insert a white, plastic pipe elbow that curves and directs the airflow out of the mouth. What we want is an unrestricted, unimpeded stream of air and sound passing through that channel. It's that curve in our throat, however, where there is usually a traffic jam. Any muscle tension in the throat, chest, jaw, or tongue will adversely affect the sounds we produce. Relaxation during exhalation should be consciously induced and controlled.

Have you ever seen the drawing for the lottery on TV? The lottery machine keeps all the numbered balls bouncing in the air. When the machine is turned off, the balls fall. Picture that stream of air keeping your words bouncing into the audience effortlessly. Send the sound through a free, open channel.

An erect but relaxed posture is important when you speak. This is not so much a matter of relaxing the muscles as releasing the joints. Attach an imaginary string to the top of your head. Imagine your head floating up from your body like a balloon. Your neck should be free from tension and your spine should lengthen. Keep your body in alignment.

A phony voice cannot truly express your feelings. It is not necessary to use one voice for every day happenings and another voice for public speaking. You play many different roles, and your speaking style should be adaptable. If you were asked to explain engineering basics to a high school class, you might use a different speaking style from that you would use when addressing an international association of your peers, but the sound of your voice should remain the same.

A seventy-four-year-old widow began studying with me when she discovered at her fiftieth college reunion that a fellow classmate had never liked her because of her high-pitched voice. Her greatest moment came when the maitre d' at her country club refused to give her a table for Saturday night because he did not recognize her voice and admonished her for pretending to be a member. Another client told me that he had always been rather quiet and faded into the woodwork during meetings. His new assertive voice earned him greater respect from his colleagues and his views were now accepted as authoritative.

The Five Characteristics of Voice

Rate

Rate refers to how slow or how fast you speak and is unconsciously influenced by your temperament and personality characteristics. If you talk extremely fast, people may perceive you to be very nervous. If you talk slowly and hesitate, you may be thought of as introverted or unsure of your material. Your rate is also affected by your attitude toward what you are saying and your purpose with respect to your audience.

Often a speaker has a tendency to race through his material. You'll be misunderstood if you talk too rapidly, especially if you are trying to convey complex technical information. Slow down to deliver technical data or statistics, particularly when your audience doesn't have reference material. If you're reading material, vary the pace; speak slowly and deliberately when you want to emphasize a point. This will give those words more importance. Slow down when you refer to information in your handouts. If you are too slow and ponderous, however, the audience will tune you out. Be careful not to ramble, for it will dilute your authority. Put periods at the ends of your sentences. Make a powerful statement, then leave it alone.

Creating pauses can provide a pleasant and interesting variety of tempo. The great pianist Vladimir Horowitz remarked that he played the notes, but the beautiful music was between the notes. A presenter can communicate volumes to her audience with skillful pauses between the lines.

Pauses provide you with a means of emphasis, a kind of oral punctuation that points out the significant information you want the listener to remember. A meaningful pause will tell your audience to reflect on what you have just said or to listen carefully to what's coming next. You can alter the pace of your information by talking at normal speed and then slowing down and pausing before a critical point to emphasize and draw attention to it.

Pauses can be powerful. You can ask rhetorical questions and then pause while the audience thinks about what you have asked. Pauses can set up a line of an anecdote or add the twist in a humorous story.

Most people are shocked to discover when they listen to a tape of themselves that they use fillers such as "um" or "you know" during their pauses. These vocal interferences make the speaker appear nervous and they diminish credibility. Ask a friend for feedback. If you have this habit, try to talk for sixty seconds without using fillers. Be silent at the end of each sentence. In your everyday speaking, consciously strive to avoid the use of such distracting vocal mannerisms.

Practice standing comfortably during a pause. It will add authority to your presence. Pause a moment before you begin to speak, and you will show that you are in control of the situation. You can pause when you conclude your presentation and let the audience digest your final words. Stand there for a moment and then return to your seat.

Volume

Volume is the loudness or softness of sounds. The same volume, whether loud or soft, can become monotonous. Don't overuse loudness to emphasize your points; decreasing volume may also lend intensity to a special point. Maintain adequate breath control so that your sentence endings don't fade away.

Adjust your volume to the size of your audience, the physical characteristics of the room, and your proximity to the microphone. Arrive early at your speech site to check out the best volume level, but realize that when the room fills up with people, you may need to speak louder.

A Vietnamese engineer in one of my classes was very shy and barely spoke above a whisper. He had difficulty putting more enthusiasm and volume into his voice. I had him come to the front of the room with another client and pretend that he was selling fish at Seattle's famous Pike Place Market, where the merchants keep up a steady, boisterous patter to entice customers to their stalls. The engineer was transformed in an instant as he persuaded a prospective customer to buy his fish. I told him to keep that same attitude and asked him to go into his presentation. The class applauded when he finished his lively project update. He told me later that he had once been a fish seller in Vietnam before he escaped to the United States.

Don't confuse volume with projection. Projection is the art of directing your voice to a specific target. Your first requirement for adequate projection is sufficient volume so that the sound will carry as far as the situation demands. Second, you need the right mental attitude. Projection is a product not only of breath control, but also of the speaker's awareness of the audience. Reach out to the entire audience and share your message.

Pitch

Pitch refers to how high or how low your voice registers on the musical scale. One of the easiest ways to make your voice expressive is to add pitch variety. Pitch is determined by your attitude toward your audience, your material, and yourself. A good way to determine your natural pitch is to hum quietly and then say your name and birth date. That pitch is the middle of your natural range. From there, you can go both up and down the scale.

Inflection is a variation of tone and is illustrated on a piano keyboard. Sound engineers will tell you that middle C on a piano keyboard has 256 vibrations per second. No matter how heavily or lightly you touch middle C, you will not vary the number of these vibrations. Every other note also has a specific vibration rate. If you have only one tone of voice, your voice always has the same number of vibrations. It will be monotonous and tiresome to others.

If you play a melody of only three notes, it won't be very interesting. The same is true of your speech. Speak in rainbows of notes instead of a somber monotone. High-pitched voices are frequently shrill and thin and do not convey strength. If you want to lower the pitch of your voice, care must be taken to avoid strain. Do not force the voice down. Merely let it drop to its natural landing place. Support the voice by breathing from the diaphragm. The pitch level will gradually become lower. Think low.

Here is a good exercise to help you find your low-pitched, natural voice. Gradually bend over from the waist toward the floor and say, "The rock fell down, down, down." When you are in this position, you have to breathe correctly. And you will find that switching to diaphragmatic breathing will lower your pitch.

Develop pitch variety by reading your morning newspaper and making extreme changes up and down your vocal range. I suggested to one engineer that he read fairy tales to his four-year-old daughter. The child wouldn't stay interested in the witch and the dragon unless he used variety in his voice.

Develop a physical responsiveness to words. Say the word *soft*. Now picture soft white cotton, soft puffy pillows, soft white clouds. Now say the word *soft*. One of my clients, who was describing research on wind tunnels, was able to picture them vividly and add variety to his pitch as he described the variables and results of his work.

Daws Butler, my teacher, reminded his students to touch their pronouns "like dust on a moth's wings." It is amazing what a slight inflection on the pronouns of "you," "we," and "us" will add to the intimacy of the talk and to your ability to draw the audience in. Say, "We want *you* to be satisfied with our service," or "I am glad that *we* decided to sit down and talk about the problem."

If you end your sentences with an upward inflection, your audience will not feel that you have confidence in your statements. Ask, "Are there any questions?" while thinking, "I certainly hope so." Now ask, "Are there any questions?" while thinking, "I hope not!" Notice the difference in the vocal pitch.

A monotonous voice will be perceived as less credible. Exercise your voice by reading some of your material aloud. Visualize someone you're always happy to talk with. See what happens to the expressiveness in your voice! By visualizing what you're saying and by using vivid language, you'll help the audiences form a similar image in their minds. Your reality will become their reality, and you will be more persuasive.

If you are speaking for forty-five minutes and have a 10,000-word speech, all 10,000 words do not deserve equal emphasis. Your audience cannot possibly remember every one of them. Emphasize important thoughts by putting them in "italics" with your voice to create a vocal signal that the information is critical. Disneyland tour directors do this well: "On the right, we have an *alligator* and—*watch out!*—in front of the boat is a *hippo!*" Pretend you're a tour director, and direct your audience to certain key points. Be in control, but be lively.

A voice lacking in pitch variety often reveals tension in the speaker. The exercises in Figure 14 will help you achieve relaxed alertness.

Quality

Quality is the distinctive sound of your voice. It enables someone else to identify you merely by hearing your "hello" on the telephone. The quality of your voice is affected by your emotional state: Happiness, relief, stress, fatigue, and anxiety are all apparent. Since voice quality is closely associated with mood and feeling, it will be influenced by your attitude toward your material, your empathy with the audience, and your desire to communicate. The audience can tell from your first words if you are confident and believe in your information.

In my classes, I ask clients to give a five-minute talk about a favorite cause such as better education, the environment, or the use of animals in research. Invariably, their voices have color, expressiveness, and variety in pitch. Then I ask them to talk about a work project, and their voices usually flatten into a monotone. Sometimes there is a "Well, you probably already know this" attitude. There is a direct relationship between their enthusiasm for a subject and the quality of their voices.

A theater actor must memorize two hours of dialogue and then repeat the same lines for every matinee and evening performance as if they had never been spoken before. It is difficult to keep that freshness, that spontaneity in the voice night after night, month after month, and, for some actors, year after year.

The Mousetrap has been playing on the London stage for twenty-five years with some actors from the original cast. The actors know the murderer's identity, they know all of everyone's words, and yet they must react in believable ways. How does an actor do it? How does a speaker do it? By concentrating and focusing all their energy on the present moment. Internalize your ideas. The quality of your voice will be governed by what is going on in your mind. Lift the words out of your notes and make them come alive. Think the thought before you say it. Smile with the mind before you use your mouth, and your voice will smile.

Although you want a confident tone of voice, it must not sound arrogant. While an audience can truly admire intelligence, if it is wrapped in arrogance, they will be suspicious and uncomfortable. One of my friends has a superior tone of voice even when he talks about such mundane things as the weather. I am sure his audiences must feel intimidated when he speaks about his aerospace projects. On the other hand, a young man from Microsoft solved my computer problem over the phone and had such a reassuring voice that I didn't feel stupid asking a basic question. Your voice should sound sincere and balanced and should add to the overall impression that after carefully examining all the facts, you have arrived at well-founded conclusions.

The quality of your voice is also determined by the resonance. As air passes through your chest, throat, and head, it can acquire richness and fullness. Imagine your body vibrating like a tuning fork as sounds reverberate through your body. If you string a piece of catgut between two chairs and draw a violin bow across it, what kind of sound would you get? You would hear a very high and squeaky sound. But put that violin string on a Stradivarius and a bow produces a wonderful, rich, mellow tone. Blowing through the mouthpiece of a French horn produces a high-pitched sound. Place it back on the instrument and you will have a wonderful, rich sound. In the same way, resonance cavities in your body contribute to the quality of the sounds you make. Don't be a talking head. Talk from your toes. Breathing exercises will help.

Articulation

Speech must be not only audible but also articulate, distinct, and accurate. Your listeners cannot be attentive if they constantly have to guess at your words. Remember that English may be a second language for many of those in your workplace or at conferences. It is even difficult for southerners and northerners to "translate" each other's language. If your information is technical and complex, it is even more critical that your listeners be able to follow your words easily.

Every speaker should be careful not to omit endings or otherwise mispronounce words. An actor will purposely drop endings from words or substitute "jest" for "just" and "fer" for "far" to indicate a poorly educated person. If you say "comin'," "goin'," "wanna," or "tryin'," it will detract from an image of professionalism. Articulation exercises will help improve the clarity of your voice. Reading tongue twisters out loud as fast as you can will loosen stiff jaws, lazy lips, and a sleepy tongue. I've included some exercises along with a voice analysis checklist in Figure 14.

Figure 14.   Voice analysis checklist and exercises.

Voice Analysis

Rate

1.   Could be slower. _____
2.   Could be faster. _____
3.   Phrasing could be improved. _____
4.   Choppy, need to smooth out. _____
5.   Too many hesitations without meaning. _____
6.   Can use more variety. _____

Volume

1.   Could be more expansive and full. _____
2.   Could be softer. _____
3.   Need more variety. _____

4. Force (punch) overused as a form of emphasis. _____
5. Need to project more directly to the listeners. _____

Pitch

1. General level could be lower. _____ Higher. _____
2. Need to eliminate repetive pitch pattern. _____
3. Need more variety _____

Quality

1. Too flat—need more richness and resonance. _____
2. Too harsh. _____
3. Need to relax throat—strained, strident, shrill. _____
4. Too timid _____
5. Need more variety _____

Articulation
1. Articulation of consonants needs to be more distince. _____
2. Ending of words omitted or slurred. _____
3. Lips, tongue, jaw can be used more effectively. _____
Body Warm-Up Exercises

Body Warm-Up Exercises

1. Yawn deeply and fully several times; sigh with a fully vocalized "ah."
2. Stand as tall as you can; stretch your arms over your head; reach up with one hand and then the other.
3. Bend over gradually until your hands touch the floor.
4. Bend your knees, squat, lower your head, and relax.
5. Slowly stand up, rollong up your spine, vertebra by vertebra, until you are standing.
6. Roll your head side to side. Rubbermouth your face: Purse your lips and then pull them back into a smile.
7. Shrug your shoulders, shake your hands and wrists, and shake all over like a rag doll.

Vocal Warm-Up Exercises

1. Hum through your nose. Try to feel the vibration on the inside of your head, bring it around to the sides, bring it around to the front. Create a buzzing hum

(continues)

Figure 14 *(continued)*.

> around your head like a helmet. Feel the vibration on the bridge of your nose and sides of the head. Open your mouth slowly and go into an "ah" sound. Do this several times.

2. Place one hand on your diaphragm and the other on your back. Say the following phrases slowly, exaggerating the vowel sounds and running the words together. Make the tones rich, round and full. You should feel your hands vibrate.
   a. In her tomb by thesounding sea.
   b. A time to love, and a time to hate.
   c. One by one, they went away.
3. Say the consonants precisely. Use the front of the mouth, and lips, teeth, and tongue.

   b, c, d, f, g, h, j, k, l, m, n, p, q, r, s, t, v, w, y, z.
4. Relax your lips. Say: buh bay, buh bee, buh bye, buh bow, buh boo, buh say, buh see, buh sigh, buh sew, buh sue, buh fay, buh fee, buh dee, buh dough, buh do.
5. Relax the jaw. Repeat "chew-chaw" ten times. Pronounce the following words: choose, chip, chill, cheap, latch, pitch, peach, scratch, shop, tot, guard, not, hot.

Tongue Twisters for Precise Articulation

1. She selld short shirts and shells in the shop near the shore.
2. Big brown bumblebees were buried beside the bulbs in Bobby Brook's bulb bowls, baskets and boxes.
3. The duke dragged the dizzy dragon down into the deep, dark, dank dungeon.
4. Matthew Mather's mother munches mashed marmalade muffins muttering about a multitude of misguided memories.
5. Rich rajahs ride reindeer with rakish red rope reins around their regal necks.
6. Susan ceaseth shining shoes and socks, for socks and shoes silly Susan.
7. Great crushing crates create great crumbling craters.
8. Terrific Tilda with thin, tawny hair tumbling to her toes was a tremendously talented typist for Teeper, Teeder, and Teeber on Tuesdays.
9. Lazy lizards sizzle in a drizzle, prize lizards are wizards with scissors.
10. Victor vowed vengeance and the valuable velvet vanished from the veranda.

Suggestions for Improving Your Voice

A tape recorder is indispensable for voice improvement. Record every one of your presentations. Listen to the playback and work on one characteristic at a time. Identify your strengths and pinpoint areas that need to be improved. This time, you might want to work on eliminating fillers and slowing down your rate of speech. Next time, concentrate on increasing the variety in your pitch. Illuminate every shade of meaning in the words.

Read poetry or good literature out loud and make it emotionally expressive. Experiment with different vocal qualities or rates of delivery. Repeat the consonants (b, c, d, f, g) emphasizing different emotions. Be happy, pleading, seductive, conspiratorial, angry, sad, domineering, playful, or threatening.

Your personal life-style will affect your voice. Drinking alcohol or caffeinated drinks dehydrates the body and can alter your voice. Irregular sleep and inadequate exercise will cause fatigue, which will be evident in your voice. Emotional stress will prevent your voice from sounding balanced and in control. Shouting or straining your voice can produce hoarseness. Sipping honey and lemon in warm water is soothing, or add a teaspoon of salt to a half cup of warm water and gargle a full five minutes.

Think of the range of notes, rhythms, and intensities in intriguing music. Work on the exercises in Figure 14 to help make your voice a powerful instrument. Your voice should be unpretentious and unobtrusive. A compelling voice will help you present a more forceful image. You will enjoy hearing yourself speak and so will others.

KEY IDEAS

- Play your voice like an instrument.
- Use variety in rate, volume, pitch, and quality to keep your audience attentive.
- Talk from your toes and use your whole body to resonate or resound your voice.
- Use creative pauses to call attention to your words and to demonstrate your confidence.
- Use your voice to call attention to your message, not to the voice itself.

16

Using Humor

Overview

Humor enhances your credibility because it shows you are confident and in control. If you use humor appropriately, your audience will listen attentively and positively; they will remember your message. Humor gives your ideas perspective and illustrates them succinctly. Although the use of humor can be risky, speakers who choose relevant stories or one-liners that are appropriate to specific audiences, topics, and situations can be very successful. This chapter will show you how to incorporate humor into your presentation.

Dick Lantz, a design engineer with NASA, began his presentation to a group of engineers with a humorous anecdote using the familiar "rule of three" or triad device:

A group of aerospace engineers were developing a new airplane design. During the first trial run, the wings came off—so it was back to the drawing board. At the beginning of the second test, everyone was convinced the errors had been corrected. The plane started down the runway with a roar, and both wings began to vibrate and snapped off.

Everyone was perplexed, but a janitor was watching the tests and offered a suggestion. "Drill a hole every two inches along the line where you join the wing to the plane," he said. The engineers followed his advice, and on the third trial, the plane went down the runway, became airborne, and had a successful flight. The designer was flabbergasted. He went back to the janitor and asked him how he knew so much about stress concentration factors. "That's easy," the janitor said. "Everyone knows that perforated paper never tears on the holes."

[Lantz then stated his principle:] Frequently in design work, it is easy to overlook the obvious.

People look forward to being amused. Humor in the form of personal stories or jokes can ease tension, build better relationships, gain the audience's attention, revive interest, wipe out hostility, and help clarify your ideas. Personal anecdotes can be a useful communication tool and effectively create a bond with the audience. Your objective is not to be "guffaw funny" in a presentation. If the story elicits a chuckle or smile from an audience recognizing a truth or acknowledging a point, you've been successful.

When I ask company executives to name their favorite model communicators in science and technology, invariably they mention a speaker who uses humor. A person who successfully handles humor demonstrates to an audience that he or she is confident and in control. And it has been shown that an audience will be more receptive to a suggestion immediately after they have laughed.

Some people think that humor has no place in technical presentations, that it detracts from the seriousness of a topic. The reverse is true: Because the topics are often dry, humor is a wonderful tool that can help a speaker gain and keep rapport with the audience. Many people confronted with technical information wonder if they will be able to understand and absorb the material. They may resist both the speaker and the subject. Laughter helps break down such obstacles and makes the speaker seem more approachable and the material less forbidding. When you laugh, both you and your audience let go of anger, frustration, and anxiety. And remember, for the speaker, humor is one of the best remedies to counteract the fear of public speaking.

The Benefits of Using Humor

I once attended an extremely technical videoconferencing seminar. A presenter from a nontechnical profession remarked that although he was pleased to be invited, he didn't know how much he could contribute to the meeting. "I feel like the farmer who entered his mule in the Kentucky Derby," he said. "He knew that his mule couldn't win, but he felt the association would do it good." The audience laughed and relaxed. With those two sentences, the speaker established the parameters of his expertise and therefore prepared his audience. His humor had purpose, it was brief, and it won their attention.

Let your humor clarify the point you are making. Visiting Rotarian scholar Seiichi Kanise told the following story:

> As a frequent visitor to your country, I understand the American frustration over Japan's recent economic success. When a revolution occurred in a country which will remain unnamed, the heads of all branches of foreign companies were arrested and sentenced to death as anti-revolutionaries. Prior to their execution, they were asked if they had any last wishes. The French businessman said that he wanted to sing the French national anthem, *La Marseillaise*, before he died and his wish was granted. The next, a Japanese businessman, said, "I want to give my last lecture on Japanese management." Upon hearing this, the American businessman shouted, "You'd better shoot me first, I'm sick of it."[1]

Professor Marvin Minsky points out in *Society of Mind* that "laughter focuses attention on the present state of mind." If an audience laughs together, they become focused on the speaker and you have broken through the preoccupation barrier. Since the mind can only have one dominant thought at a time, if your audience laughs, you immediately know that they are with you. This is also true with one-on-one communication. If your superior can laugh with you, a bond is established.

Many speakers can relate horror stories of presentations that went wrong, microphones that stopped working, workers who started banging, or groups of people who trooped into the room. One woman told me about a situation in a hotel conference room when the temperature dipped into the fifties and everyone sat huddled in coats. The handouts were lost between the mail room and the conference room. Rock music was piped into the room at odd intervals. When management failed to respond to her pleas, the speaker moved the thirty attendees into the sunny lobby of the hotel next to a sign advertising the cocktail lounge. She quipped, "If this is what they mean by happy hour, can you imagine what we can expect later on this morning?" She got everyone to laugh about the inconveniences by developing a camaraderie with the audience and helping them to gain a different perspective on the situation.

Some Words of Caution

The flip side of attempted humor is that if it fails you can lose dignity. If humor is pointless and falls flat, it will be a definite setback and you will need to work twice as hard to establish your desired image. One engineer told me that the risk of standing up in front of everyone and looking like a "fool" is a definite deterrent to his use of humorous stories in technical presentations. Sometimes he attempts a one-liner, but nothing longer. "It's a defense mechanism," he replied thoughtfully. "If I tell a joke or a story, I'm announcing my intention to be funny. It's easier to toss off a line or two. If no one laughs, I'm already on to something else, as if I hadn't really tried to be funny. I haven't invested time or my self-esteem."

He mentioned trying to explain that a processor his company was designing was too powerful for the client's needs. He thought it would strike a negative chord to simply say it was overkill, so he stated, "It's like driving a Ferrari in a thirty-five-mile-an-hour speed zone." Everyone laughed, and he was able to get a sensitive point across.

Are you comfortable with being humorous? Stay with the one-liners if you are successful with them. But in addition, begin to try some personal stories. Audiences respond favorably to stories with a ring of truth. You need not abandon your own personality to be humorous. Many excellent speakers use cartoons or funny visuals to make a point when they don't feel as comfortable telling stories.

Never tell a joke merely for the sake of getting a laugh from your audience. Of course, there are always exceptions to the rule. When passing by a hotel banquet room where an Institute of Electrical and Electronics Engineers dinner meeting was taking place, I overheard the president's opening remark: "Somebody said I should be funny and tell a joke when I got up here." I winced inwardly but remained to listen, expecting to hear him fall flat on his face. But he told the joke with enthusiasm. It was hilarious and I started laughing with everyone else. The audience settled into a warm receptive mood for the president's rather dry material.

I have learned never to say "never." There are few things worse than an inappropriate story at an inopportune time. However, if you have a story that is tasteful and will survive under most circumstances, try it!

William D. Ruckelshaus, a model communicator who deftly uses humor in serious presentations, says that over the years, he has collected several thousand quotations and anecdotes. "They aren't really filed under special topics, but I have gone over them so many times that I know where to find the funny ones and the ones that will work for a specific occasion." After several presentations, you will learn which stories invariably succeed and which ones to eliminate.

A story that doesn't work at all for one audience may bring howls of laughter from another. Different cultures have different ideas about what is funny. If your comedy is dependent on subtleties of the English language and English is not the first language for most of your audience, you stand a good chance of failing with your humor. Inside jokes about your profession may be appropriate within your organization or association but probably won't get a positive response from the general public.

Understand your audience and why they are present. If your listeners take themselves seriously, then perhaps you will gain more rapport by being serious and skipping attempts at humor. That same serious audience, however, might expect to be entertained during an after-dinner speech.

A pickup truck pulled up to the barn and the driver hailed the farmer. "How much is that old bull out by the road worth to you?" he asked. "Depends," drawled the farmer after a moment's hesitation. "Are you the tax assessor? Do you want to buy him? Or did you run him down with your truck?" As with humor, sometimes it just depends on your audience.

Finding Humor in Ordinary Occurrences, Our Frailties, Our Professions

Often, the ordinary things that happen to us in our daily lives tickle our funny bones. Our flaws make us laughable. Humor can be a painfully honest comment about ourselves, both individually and as a species.

Garrison Keillor, the author of *Lake Wobegon Days*, and columnist Dave Barry are people who see the humor of everyday situations. One of Dave Barry's columns began:

Recently, I ran out of clean underwear in Los Angeles. So I wandered into the men's clothing department of an upscale department store, the kind of store where the sales clerks all have sharp haircuts and perfectly tailored suits that are far nicer than anything you own, and, although they act very deferential, you know they're secretly watching to see which clothes you touch so they can have them burned later as a precaution against vermin. And I came across this regular white T-shirt by Ralph Lauren. The price was $57.50. I once bought an entire *suit* for less than that. I wound up having to go elsewhere and purchase another famous designer underwear brand. A French one. Le Mart du K.[2]

Comic Stephen Wright emphasizes:

You must know how something works to find humor in it. We all know the normal angle at which you are supposed to see things. But there are loopholes in logic, because there are other logics. For instance, I went down to a store where the sign read: OPEN 24 HOURS, but the guy was closing. I said, "I thought that you were open 24 hours." "Not in a row," he responded.

Wright's "logical" observations are made in a monotone voice: "A lot of people are afraid of heights: I'm afraid of widths." "If I melt dry ice, can I swim without getting wet?"

Examine your profession for humor. It requires insight to joke about your specialty. Russell Morash, the director of Julia Child's TV cooking show, said that although Child's sense of humor is acclaimed, "it would be wrong to think of her as a clown. The woman is an incredible scholar and understands her subject so completely that she's able to impose humor on top of it."

A function of humor is to shake up our perceptions, expose frailty and ambiguity, and ultimately assure ourselves that it's really okay just the way things are. People like the unusual and unexpected twist. When Neil Armstrong was asked on the anniversary of his moon walk how the astronauts' lives had been changed by their adventure, he responded, "Before 1969, press conferences were much smaller."

Contrast is the essence of comedy, to see incongruities in normal, everyday events. If we say that sense is the normal order of things, then incongruity makes nonsense. For example, Albert Einstein played the violin and was once playing in a string quartet with Gregor Piatigorsky, William Primrose, and Jascha Heifetz. Einstein was not in the same class as these masters but was allowed to play second violin. During one passage, Einstein repeatedly came in at the wrong time. Finally an exasperated Piatigorsky stopped and blurted out, "Mr. Einstein, can't you count?"

The key to creativity is looking at one thing and seeing another. Watch for the inconsistencies in everyday logic. It could be an observation made by your child or the strange way the waitress served you in a coffee shop. Can you relate some amusing or clever everyday happening to a point in your speech?

A telephone company spokesperson began his talk to a public gathering about a rate increase by saying, "It's true that long-distance rates may go up. That's the bad news. The good news is that the continents are drifting closer together." The potentially hostile audience was so surprised by the unexpected humor that they laughed. Then the spokesperson acknowledged the audience's concern about rate increases so that they knew he wasn't being flippant about the situation. When emotions are running high, it is mandatory to lighten things up if you want your message to be heard at all. Humor can show that you aren't rigid when everyone else is uptight.

Knowing the Beat

Timing is a critical factor when telling a story. Timing dictates how long you pause before, between, or after words or sentences. It is knowing when to pounce on words, to hold them, to start again, to throw them away, or to aim them precisely. Bob Hope has said that "perfect timing is the meshing of your brain with the audience's brain."

Several years ago when I was playing opposite Shelley Berman in the play *Don't Drink the Water*, Shelley told me to walk on stage, say the first part of my line, set down my suitcase, finish the line, and then look at him. I wondered how he could dissect the line so minutely. I decided instead to do it my own way. The result failed to provoke even a chuckle from the audience.

The next night I did as Shelley told me. The result was uproarious laughter. He gave me an "I told you so" look. Setting down the suitcase provided a pause that added an extra beat to the rhythm of the line.

Timing also includes the use of body language. We usually pay attention to the delivery of our words in a story, but the audience gets most of their information from our gestures, our facial expressions, and what isn't said. This is why it is so necessary to be totally involved when you tell a story. Don't be tentative; jump in with both feet!

If you have a funny story that hasn't worked well in the past, think of it in terms of a song. You may have to add another word to make the beat of the line come out right. Adding a pause, a look, or a gesture before the punch line can highlight the words that follow. Watch and listen to your favorite comedians and comediennes. Observe their body language, the way they become totally involved in what they are saying, and, especially, their timing.

Timing also means being prepared to change or eliminate your story depending on the circumstances. One speaker was adept at incorporating humor into the first few moments of his speeches. However, prior to his introduction to a local organization, the president called for a moment of silence in memory of a member who had died that week. The speaker knew that he couldn't possibly begin with a joke, and it was not until the middle of his presentation that he felt he could introduce a humorous tone.

Humor Is an Attitude

We are all born with the potential for being amusing. If you have suppressed your sense of humor as an adult, it can be revived. Humor is more than telling a joke; it is the ability to be delighted with life. Do not allow a poor response to your attempt at humor to keep you from trying again. Humor is subjective, and if it doesn't go over well the first time, it's not always a reflection on you or your choice of stories. Often there are other factors affecting the audience's response. It can be difficult to "read" technical and scientific audiences. One presenter said, "Your timing and confidence can go haywire if you assume from the silence that your first story is a dud. I've found some audiences may be laughing inside while displaying a stoic attitude outside."

Tips on Using Humor

1. Check your audience analysis again, evaluating this particular situation, audience, and topic. What type of humor might appeal to this audience? What image will work best for you in this situation to obtain your objective?

2. Make your story relevant to your message.

3. Be clean and lean. Write out your story and edit it to take out the "padding," the extra words and unnecessary details. Don't give it more than a minute unless the point it makes warrants taking time from the main body of your speech.

4. Provide a transition from your story to your topic and blend in the edges. Make the story sound as spontaneous as possible.

5. Avoid off-color stories or jokes about minorities, women, the disabled, or ethnic groups. Remember that the purpose of humor is to enhance your message.

6. Display your modesty and humility by telling a story that reveals an embarrassment or a minor failing. This allows the audience to feel superior. But don't humble yourself to excess. Such stories and put-downs can work only if the speaker is clearly very confident.

7. Use the "rule of three." Humorous stories often contain three elements.

8. Use descriptive words to call up vivid images. A humorous story is like a balloon: Pump it up with details and then puncture it with a punch line.

9. Make sure everyone hears the punch line, but don't dilute it by explaining its meaning.

10. Be precise. There are no uhs, ifs, or maybes in humor.

11. Summarize your message with a witty or humorous quote and leave the audience with a warm feeling.

12. Be totally involved in the story as you tell it. Believe in it. Take risks.

13. Rehearse, rehearse! Repeat it over and over again to anyone who will listen so that you are comfortable with the words. Then practice telling your story under conditions similar to those you will face, in front of people who are representative of your audience. The actor Don Ameche related a story about the legendary comic Jack Benny, who accompanied him to a charity luncheon in Hollywood. Benny knew that someone would recognize him, and he spent an hour trying out several surprised looks and quips for Ameche's approval. Later, at the luncheon, Benny was recognized and introduced. He feigned amazement, as he rose to applause. Ameche said that Benny used the exact "ad-libs" and body language that he had rehearsed.

14. Start keeping a notebook of humorous stories and arrange them topically. Joke books and anthologies are only the beginning. Clip and save amusing quotations, funny newspaper stories, cartoons,

or stories from magazines. Good stories sweep the country and can lose their punch because everyone has heard them. On the other hand, a personal anecdote is uniquely yours and can be even more appealing than a "joke," creating a bond between you and the audience. It can be edited, embellished, and adapted and often gets better with repetition.

When you have the substance of your presentation's main points and supporting points outlined and written down, review your material. How can humor support your points? How can you use humor to illustrate, give perspective, or clarify images? Can you add a personal story, anecdote, or humorous quotation or plan a quick "ad-lib"? Humor will strengthen any presentation if it is relevant, appropriate, tasteful, and properly timed.

KEY IDEAS

- Use humor in your presentation to add to your credibility.
- Share personal stories to create a bond between you and the audience.
- Collect humorous anecdotes and quotations.
- Sharpen your delivery and timing by rehearsal.
- Cultivate your sense of humor by looking for the nonsense in daily life.

Notes

1. Seiichi Kanise, "U.S. and Japan Relationship," *Vital Speeches of the Day* (July 15, 1988). Kanise was a 1987–1988 Rotary scholar.
2. Dave Barry's syndicated column (week of July 29, 1990). Reprinted by permission: Tribune Media Services.

17

Handling Questions With Ease

"He who asks questions cannot avoid the answers."

—Cameroonian proverb

Overview

The question and answer period should be thought of as an extension of your presentation. Welcome this opportunity to clarify your ideas and fortify your message. The audience will be able to see your mastery of the subject and how well you think on your feet. This dialogue can also provide valuable feedback, with a clearer understanding of how the audience has examined and accepted your ideas. This chapter gives you ideas on how to make your Q&A session the most lively, thought-provoking, and successful part of your presentation.

Few people invest in an expensive suit without trying it on, and most people need to try on your ideas before they buy them. Encourage your listeners to participate in the Q&A period and involve them mentally and emotionally. If they can question, explore, discuss, challenge, dispute, or probe your subject matter and have their uncertainties satisfied, they will be more likely to accept your ideas.

Many times a question will reveal a controversial point that you neglected to cover in your presentation. A convincing answer may mean the difference between the audience's acceptance or rejection of your entire presentation. Realize there are no "canned" answers. Different audiences or situations will require different responses to the same question.

To prepare for a question and answer session, decide how you can reinforce your message and advance your objective to inform, instruct, report, or persuade during the Q&A period. Anticipate which questions might be asked and prepare answers for the most difficult or controversial. Review your audience analysis checklist. Who are the people in your audience and what is their background? Can you expect them to accept your ideas or to challenge you? For each possible question, decide how you will finish and start, state your main point, support that point, present an additional visual aid, and choose the best organizational pattern. Can you add variety to the Q&A session? If you anticipate controversial questions, rehearse with your peers and go through some "what if" scenarios.

An aerospace engineer told me that he spent weeks preparing for a presentation to a former Boeing chairman. There was only one question for which he said that he had no answer, but he felt that he covered all of the other information so well that it might not matter. When he finished his presentation, the chairman asked him the one question he dreaded. And he wasn't able to answer it!

Colonel Milton Hunter, of the Army Corps of Engineers, says that he prepares periodic updates on his region for the Corps office in Washington, D.C. He asks his staff to play the devil's advocate and grill him on the information in his presentation. These sessions clarify which topics still need work and help eliminate surprises in the Q&A.

Tone of the Q&A

Your attitude during the question and answer period can demonstrate your control and further your credibility. The audience will usually go along with any approach to the Q&A session as long as the speaker shows confidence and leadership. If listeners sense you are weak, uncertain, capricious, or quarrelsome, they will consider their time wasted and resist taking part in the session. Select words that define your image; you might want to come across as calm, concerned, in control, or helpful. Remind yourself that your body language and tone of voice should reflect the image you have chosen.

One engineer who was experienced in answering mediation questions or acting as an expert witness in a courtroom said that he is usually part of a design team. "The team can include representatives from an architectural firm, a structural firm, a mechanical firm, and depending on the site of work, a civil engineering firm. We meet beforehand to go over the specific claims so that we can put on a united front. It would be folly to have disagreement within the team."

He continued to explain, "When you are in court, you have to be careful what you say and how you say it. It's not productive to be anything but calm or at least exhibit calmness, even though you may be really mad inside. If there's a claim that you believe is false, you want the opportunity to explain and defend your work."

If you ask for questions while standing behind a lectern, chances are that this barrier will discourage a response from the audience. Get out from behind overhead projectors or tables. By being open and vulnerable, you will encourage your audience to risk a question or comment. Stand in close proximity to your audience, raise your hand, and ask, "Would anyone like to start?" Or you might ask, "Are there any comments?" or "I would like to hear any remarks that can add to our discussion." Your vocal tone will indicate your attitude. Avoid sending your audience a message that says, "I hope not!" or "Let's get out of here."

Motives of the Questioner

Pay special attention to the first question you hear, since several people may want that same point clarified. If there is a large audience, restate the question so that everyone can hear it and feel included in the discussion. Concentrate on the questioner and listen intently. The audience will sense immediately that you value what is being said. Try to catch the intent of the questioner, as well as the content of the query. You will find that the members of your audience usually ask questions for one of the following reasons:

1. They are interested in obtaining additional information from you, a clarification, or an interpretation.
2. They want your personal insight, recommendation, or judgment.
3. They want to show you or the rest of the audience how smart they are.
4. They want to embarrass or intimidate you. They may draw attention to what they consider to be incorrect statements, try to invalidate your thesis, challenge your sources, or attempt to anger you.

If you are making an in-house presentation and know the styles and motives of the principal players, you may be able to anticipate the types of questions (and questioners) and prepare accordingly.

Tips for Your Q&A Session

■ *Reinforce and expand on your objective.* A question and answer period gives you a second chance to plant a message and to expand and reinforce your point of view. When your audience leaves, what main idea do you want them to walk away with? To be persuasive, note how your plan, proposal, or request will produce a beneficial effect for each of the different members of the audience. Then during the question and answer period, take every opportunity to build your case by outlining the benefits.

■ *Think about the question before you think about the answer.* Time can be used to your advantage. A pause can give value to the question and give you enough time to search for the most concise way to answer the question. Don't overuse expressions such as "Glad you asked that question," or the audience may believe that you are stalling.

■ *Establish strong eye contact.* One researcher had a habit of looking down at the floor when she was asked a question. This gave the impression that she didn't know the answer. In reality, she was assessing the question and preparing her response. Whenever possible, you should make eye contact with the questioner. Since we receive most of our information from body language, try to absorb as much information as you can this way and discern why he or she is asking the question. You will also be able to check the reaction to your response.

■ *Watch filler words.* Too many "uhs," "ahs," and "you knows" not only are distracting but will make you appear nervous. It's better to say nothing.

■ *Be direct and concise.* Give a clear answer up front. Then you can expand your response if you feel that a longer explanation is necessary. The SAFW organizational pattern (statement, amplification, few examples, and windup) works well for answering questions concisely. Be wary of answering the unasked question.

■ *Don't ramble.* Your objective is to answer the question and move on to the next point. Rambling can dilute your message and authority.

■ *Use humor if appropriate.* If a humorous answer will make a point, use it! Some of the best model communicators are known for their wit. Humor makes you appear relaxed and confident.

■ *"Bookend" your answers.* Sometimes, you can make a direct answer at the beginning and, after expanding on the point, make it again at your conclusion. "So as you can see, we have taken the necessary steps...."

■ *Use rich imagery.* The audience is able to visualize your answer much better if your language is vivid. When Neil Armstrong was questioned about the use of robots to explore space, a technique favored by many scientists, he replied, "Man can be amused and amazed, and a robot can be neither."

■ *Choose several personal anecdotes and examples beforehand that can add interest during a Q&A period.* They can rarely be made up on the spot. Governor Dixy Lee Ray told me she was frequently asked, "Why can't a nuclear power plant explode?" Her answer was, "Radioactive material can be compared to flour. Flour in its dry state can blow up. There have been explosions in silos and flour mills. Mix the flour with water and you form dough; you have changed the physical state. Dough doesn't explode. Add other ingredients and bake it and you produce a loaf of bread. Bread doesn't explode. It is the same with radioactive material—it exists in a different physical state in the power plant and can't explode."

■ *Adapt your body language and tone of voice.* Adjust your rate of speech to the questioner's speech, and mirror her body language. One client told me that he went toe to toe with a hostile questioner and then slowly relaxed his body. He lowered his voice and slowed his speech. He was amazed that the other person began to mirror his response and they parted as friends.

Avoiding the Land Mines

■ *Wait until the questioner finishes.* Don't assume that you know what the person is asking and how you are going to answer before the question has been completed.

■ *Clarify the question.* With a large audience, you may want to repeat the question to make sure that everyone has heard it. Divide long or complex questions into parts. Ask for clarification if you are unsure what the person is asking or if the question can be interpreted in several ways. Listen carefully to general terms that crop up in questions and ask for specifics. "Who are 'they'?" "Can you give an example of what you mean by 'most objects'?" "'Better' as compared to...?" If you aren't sure what the person is asking, you will be at risk answering the question.

■ *Acknowledge the questioner's feelings.* Never deny the person's feelings. Don't say, "I understand how you feel" unless you have been in the same position.

■ *Avoid "yes" or "no" answers.* Even if it is the correct answer, use the opportunity to elaborate or explain. Direct the question toward an issue you want to cover, or change the subject. "Yes, we do expect to reduce staff this year, but I want to point out. . . ." "No, but it is more important to consider. . . ."

■ *Clear up assumptions in the question.* Be careful when answering questions such as "Why are you raising your rates and overcharging us again?" If you don't challenge the assumptive language or the negative points in a question, some people will accept them as fact. Rick Chappell, NASA's associate director of science in Huntsville, Alabama, was asked, "Why are we spending money in space when we have the homeless to take care of?" Chappell answered, "Money isn't spent in space, it is spent here on earth." Then he went on to tell about the medical advances and benefits for the ordinary citizen from space research, such as generating the new technology that will keep America competitive and will strengthen the economy and hence our quality of life.

■ *Watch out for unfamiliar statistics.* If a questioner gives statistics unknown to you, ask for the source before giving your answer or opinion. You have as much right to question sources as the questioner does.

■ *Listen for illogical reasoning.* One woman confronted a representative from a company that was voluntarily cleaning up toxic waste. "I have constant headaches and have been ill all winter," she said. "People who drink contaminated water have headaches. Isn't your plant contaminating my drinking water?" The man replied, "I can understand your concern about your health. Your headaches and other health problems may be attributed to other reasons. Your drinking water is not contaminated at the present time. Our company will have the cleanup completed in eight months, and we will keep in touch until it is done satisfactorily."

■ *Control irrelevant questions.* If someone asks a question that has no real bearing on the subject, acknowledge the person and the concern, but diplomatically get the discussion back on the subject matter.

■ *Admit when you don't know.* There will be times when you are not able to come up with an appropriate answer. Tell your audience that you don't know in a strong, confident manner, and say, "I will get back to you with the information"—and then be sure you do! Another possibility would be to say, "I don't feel that I should comment on that because I don't have the latest test results. However I can say, . . ." and go on to make a brief, positive point.

If there is someone else present who has the expertise to answer the question, you can request his comment. If you sense that the questioner wants to show off his knowledge, you can direct the comment back to him and ask how he sees the situation or what his information reveals.

Representative John Miller used that strategy when a student asked him what he thought of a new federal law that makes it more difficult for some college students to get government financial aid. The question was unexpected, but Miller didn't show it. "Tell me more about how this affects you," he encouraged the woman. Miller listened intently to her explanation and replied, "I appreciate your raising this issue. After this meeting is over, give your name to Bruce," indicating his top aide.

■ *Find out if the news media will be present.* Know whom you can trust if there are media representatives present. Always remember there are no such things as "off-the-record" remarks!

■ *Avoid questions you don't want to answer.* You might respond, "That is an important consideration, but we feel our customers are more concerned about . . ." and bridge to something else.

■ *Narrow down nonspecific questions.* You may also have to curb the participant who talks on and on without getting around to a question by politely interrupting and asking him or her, "Did you have a specific question?" Or you can dissect from the person's general commentary one or two points that most people can relate to and expand on them.

■ *Handle the person who dominates the question and answer period firmly but courteously.* Sometimes a participant won't let you finish your answer. Be polite. Ask to finish answering one question before going to another. Be in control. If it is obvious that one person is trying to monopolize the discussion, invite him to speak with you at a later time. Say that you want to give others a chance to get into the discussion, then quickly turn away and make eye contact with someone else who has a question. Never yield to the temptation to ridicule anyone.

One engineer cited an instance when a person on his review board demanded the engineer produce more data to back up his findings. The board member would not accept the answer that data were not immediately available. The engineer could see that the reviewer's motivation was to demonstrate his power in the group.

The engineer calmly replied that he would be happy to collect some substantiating data and deliver them in a day or two. If that was not satisfactory, he said, he would need additional resources to fulfill the request completely.

At this point, another board member asked if it was worthwhile to spend extra money and time to find the data and asked how the information would influence the decision they were supposed to make that day. The group decided the effect would be minimal. The engineer's controlled and cooperative manner of handling the questioning alerted the other board members to a power-play digression and they acted to bring the discussion back in line.

■ *Acknowledge that others may hold contrary viewpoints.* One engineer began his Q&A session by saying, "I don't expect everyone to agree with everything I have said here tonight, but I think that we are all in agreement that safety is the paramount consideration. I would like to hear your responses or questions in regard to my proposal." He thus reminded them of their common ground and that their opposition would have to be weighed against higher principles.

■ *Avoid answering a hypothetical question that lures you into a negative scenario.* When asked, "But what if you can't meet the production schedule?" you can confidently state, "We have completed this and this. The schedule is workable."

■ *Own up to your previous statements.* One of my clients had a sudden and complete turnabout in his beliefs on a certain subject. At his next presentation, a questioner produced an old newspaper clipping and demanded to know the reasons for the apparent change of heart. "Yes, those were my words a year ago," he replied, "but certain facts have been brought to my attention and they have convinced me to change my mind."

■ *Be calm and objective in a hostile situation.* You can depersonalize a question by rephrasing it in a neutral way; do not repeat a negative phrase. Your answer need not be an exact response to the query as long as it is true to your interpretation of the question. Recognize that some people wish to hold on to their beliefs regardless of the facts and statistics you have to back up your contention.

Expand and Contract

Keep in mind that the technical language level for the question and answer session must meet the needs of the entire audience. You may need to translate acronyms, define terms, or clarify exactly what a person is asking. You set the technical parameters for how complicated the questions will be. If there is a particularly complex question that would interest only a few members of the audience, invite the questioner to meet you afterward to discuss details. Don't waste audience time on answers that have no bearing on your objectives for the session.

No Questions Means No Applause!

If there are no questions, pause a moment and then say, "One question I am often asked is...," which may nudge others into taking a risk. If you spoke with members of the audience prior to your presentation, you can say, "I was asked earlier why..." or, simply close with, "I would like to leave you with..." and restate your main idea or request.

If possible, you might interview members of the audience before your presentation and ask them about their major concerns and questions. You can also ask your audience to write down questions as they come into the room. This is particularly helpful if the queries will be technical ones that might require extra data or visual aids.

Videotaping or audiotaping your responses to questions can be very revealing and will help you work toward a clear, crisp delivery in answering questions.

Compliments

An audience can learn a great deal about a presenter by the way he handles compliments. General H. Norman Schwarzkopf, commander of Operation Desert Storm in the Middle East following Iraq's 1990 invasion of Kuwait, was being interviewed on television. A reporter mentioned the colorful array of medals on the general's uniform. He asked, "Isn't that more medals than any man should carry around?" Schwarzkopf deftly responded, "This is a tribute to the poor marksmanship of the enemy."

Your Second Ending

Always end your Q&A periods on a positive note, before the audience tires. If you say, "I will take one more question," it may be a difficult, negative one, and the whole session could wind down unenthusiastically. Instead, if you feel you have answered a question well, say, "That's all for now, but I will be glad to answer further questions privately after we conclude."

Take a minute or so to summarize your main point. This short summary after the question and answer session is a vital part of your speech. Prepare it well. You may need to refine it slightly in view of the questions you've fielded, but get back to your main objective. Your audience will remember the points they hear last.

KEY IDEAS

- Gear your Q&A session toward the objectives you want to accomplish.
- Prepare possible questions and practice your responses.
- Decipher the motives of the questioner and acknowledge his or her beliefs or feelings in your response.
- Use hostile questions as an opportunity to clarify your points.
- Summarize your main point at the end of the Q&A session and end on a high note.

Part IV
Controlling Your Environment

18
Setting the Stage

"Any wire cut to length will be too short.
If a project requires n components, there will be (*n*-1) units in stock. The more innocuous a design change appears, the further its influence will extend."

—Contribution of Edsel Murphy to
"Understanding of Behavior in Inanimate Objects" in
EEE: The Magazine of Circuit Design (August 1967)

Overview

This chapter gives ideas, insights, and practical solutions for controlling your environment so that the audience's attention is focused on you and your presentation. Creating an atmosphere conducive to your audience's listening, responding, and remembering will make your goal easier to achieve. Maintain your professional image and be ready to adapt your material and your style if the site of your presentation is less than perfect.

You have prepared well for this presentation and have even had time to rehearse with your visuals. You feel in tip-top shape, and your audience is enthusiastic to hear what you have to say. Unfortunately, you didn't anticipate the retirement party next door. The smell of fresh-brewed coffee, baked beans, and hot dogs wafts down the hallway, and you have to raise your voice to be heard over the noise, laughter, and steady background beat of "Rock Around the Clock." And when your computer-aided visuals shut down in the middle of the presentation because of an electrical overload from the party next door, it's time to postpone the meeting and join the fun.

The ill-fated engineer who endured this scenario was thoroughly prepared for his presentation but had neglected to check out his environment in advance. And it proved to be his downfall. If you have encountered problems getting the response you want from your audience, have you considered that the site may be partially responsible? Perhaps the reason people are distracted, irritable, or sleepy has something to do with the physical surroundings.

Julie Swor, board member of the International Association of Conference Centers, asserts that "the physical environment sets a psychological mood, and research has shown the tremendous effect of the total atmosphere on learning. Light, colors, climate, and physical comfort combine to affect the brain's concentration and receptivity to information."

An audience's first impression of a speaker can influence their acceptance of his or her ideas; so can the audience's first impression of the site strongly affect their reaction to what follows. Each room has certain dynamics, and there are friendly rooms and rooms that work against the speaker. Windows, carpeting, acoustics, wall colors, tables, the seating arrangement, the placement of the lectern, and other factors can either add to the participants' comfort and responsiveness or distract them to the extent that you and your message are lost.

What Is Your Objective?

The environment should match the purpose of your meeting. If you are conducting a daylong training session, the seating arrangements will be different than that for a forty-five-minute project update, a panel discussion, or a series of single speakers.

Will your presentation be highly structured and formal? Do you want the focus to be on you at the front of the room? Will there be much audience involvement? Do people have to twist around in their seats if someone in the back row is talking? Will it be such a small room that some people may have to stand? Is the room so large that your audience will have difficulty hearing and seeing your material?

Sometimes conference centers and resorts send mixed messages with their plush facilities and task-oriented meeting spaces. The rooms in some companies are cold and impersonal with tile floors, bare tables, and hard chairs. In such environments, it will be difficult for the speaker to keep everyone's attention focused on the message.

One presenter told me that her association held a luncheon for 400 in a ballroom with music and an entertaining speaker. Immediately following the gala, she was responsible for presenting material to a group of 25 in a corner of the ballroom. It was extremely difficult for her and her listeners to make the transition and overcome the feeling that they were all lost in a huge, cold space. Her best defense would have been to get the audience focused at once by asking questions, having them interact with each other, and involving them intellectually and emotionally with her material.

Tom Zimmerman, a well-known researcher in integrated circuitry from TRW, says that he arrives early at the speech site and walks around the room. He sits in the back row of chairs to get the same feeling his audience will have. He puts on a viewgraph or inserts a slide in the projector and walks back to the most distant row of seats to see if the participants will have a clear line of sight or if the visual is legible.

If you will be speaking in an unfamiliar environment, discuss the size of the room and planned room arrangements with your host beforehand. Be firm about your requests and submit them in writing.

There are several seating arrangements that are suitable for different types of meetings and presentations. The best configuration will depend on the number of attendees, the interaction you want from the audience, and how you feel most comfortable. These arrangements are listed here and depicted in Figure 15.

■ *U-shape.* If you want your audience members to participate with each other and discuss issues, this is ideal. The speaker or facilitator can move around within the center and encourage involvement. This arrangement is useful for up to twenty-four people.

■ *Classroom.* For small or large groups or longer sessions, worktables can be set up in front of chairs. Arrange the tables herringbone-style so that the participants can see and interact with each other. Avoid having chairs directly behind one another.

■ *Conference room.* When there is no primary leader, this configuration is useful for audience interaction and idea exchange. The speaker should stand to deliver the presentation. Allow at least two feet or more per person for elbow space and comfort. The conference room arrangement is useful for four to twenty people, depending on the size of the room and table.

■ *Theater style.* This is sometimes referred to as auditorium style because the rows of chairs are placed much like those in a movie theater. A stage or platform is positioned in front, and the chairs are staggered so that no seat is directly behind another. This configuration can be used for large groups, but seats lacking armrests inhibit

Figure 15. Seating arrangements for meetings and presentations.

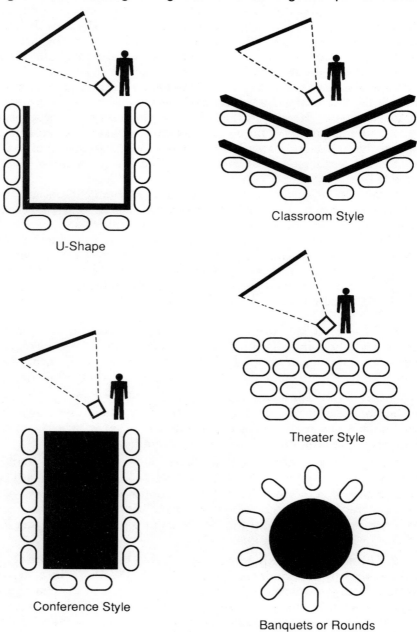

U-Shape

Classroom Style

Conference Style

Theater Style

Banquets or Rounds

note taking. Be aware of sight lines for visuals and realize that a microphone will probably be necessary. Eliminate the center aisle to capitalize on the energy between the audience and the speaker.

■ *Banquet or rounds.* This is a good arrangement for the exchange of ideas in small discussion groups. Position six to ten people around six-to-eight-foot tables. This pattern will sometimes be uncomfortable for participants if they frequently need to return their attention to the speaker at the head table.

If you walk into a room that has been used for another event, change the seating arrangement so that it will be comfortable for your audience to listen. If the stage were set for the Shakespearean tragedy *Macbeth*, you wouldn't want to use it to perform the TV comedy *Cheers*. The proper setting can provide a background that will at least be neutral, instead of detracting from your message.

Take into account wheelchair access and seating for the visually and hearing impaired. Realize that comfortable chairs may relax an audience too much, but if chairs are hard and stationary, the audience will have a tendency to fidget. Your listeners will be more alert if they are sitting in cushioned chairs that move.

If you have a choice of rooms, there may be trade-offs. A movable screen placed at an angle to the audience may be more important to your presentation than a room with windows. If you want a more intimate circle, arrange the chairs differently. One presenter had an audience of 250 people in a very large room. Many people sat in the back, and he couldn't coax them forward. If you run into this situation, stack the chairs in the back so that the early arrivals are forced to sit closer. As additional people arrive, chairs will still be available.

Emotions travel quickly through an audience. If you feel that your meeting will be a positive one, try to get everyone grouped together. If you have to announce bad news, it may be better to have the audience scattered.

Enhancing the Situation

The realities of the situation, of course, may leave you with little choice or flexibility regarding your meeting site. You may have to make do with whatever is available. Don't let inconveniences upset you. Concentrate on doing what you can to improve the situation and getting your audience focused on you and your message.

■ *Keep a clean house.* Arrive neat and with as few materials as possible. You can scare people by dumping folders of materials or a stack of viewgraphs in full view. Keep material out of sight or people will concentrate their energy on estimating the time it will take you to get through it. Keep your stage free of too many tables, paper cups, electrical cords, and nonessentials. If someone has left a used flip chart, turn it to a fresh sheet.

■ *Protect yourself.* One of my clients rehearsed for an interview on the six o'clock news. He called me later and was upset because a sound man had crossed two microphones directly over his notes. "Couldn't you move them or ask someone to fix the mikes differently?" I asked. "Everything happened so quickly that I went along with what the crew told me to do," he answered. In such situations, remember to protect yourself. The TV crew may only be doing their job, but it is your responsibility to request and insist on changes that will enhance your appearance.

You will find that some staff are reluctant to change arrangements in conference rooms or hotel meeting sites. One speaker asked to have a lectern moved to the side, but was told that was not possible because the microphone wires had been taped down. She got down on her hands and knees and started pulling up tape. The service staff then decided to take care of it. If a call to the management fails, it will be up to you to rearrange chairs, overhead projectors, and other equipment.

■ *Don't hide behind the lectern.* Podiums are objects you stand on; lecterns are objects you can place your notes on. I suggest you avoid lecterns if possible, for they can create a barrier between you and the audience. If you are using notes in a conference room, a short tabletop lectern will allow you to have better eye contact with the audience.

■ *Know your competition.* Check on events scheduled at the same time in rooms nearby. I will never forget addressing a group of managers in a hotel room during the Christmas season. In the midst of my talk, a deep, resounding "ho, ho, ho!" came booming over the loudspeaker. I tried to continue, but we were then interrupted with "Little girl, what would you like for Christmas?" This was followed by whispering, squeals, giggles, and a recurring "ho, ho, ho!" I dispatched someone to ask the management to fix the sound system, which alternately became louder, softer, then fell silent. I went back to my presentation, but five minutes later "ho, ho, ho!" rang out again. I was able to get my audience focused by asking them to do a two-minute communication exercise with a partner. I copied their comments onto a viewgraph and brought their attention back to the projected image in front of the room.

■ *Thank you for not smoking.* It is important to establish smoking or no smoking rules before a meeting starts. There is nothing worse than having a presenter gasp and cough or having to ask the key decision maker to snuff out his cigarette. One company placed this sign on the conference room door: IF YOU SMOKE, WE WILL ASSUME YOU ARE ON FIRE AND PUT YOU OUT.

■ *Keep the spotlight on you.* Hotel lighting is notorious for making the presenter look like a visitor from Transylvania. If you find the lighting less than flattering, move the lectern or table. You will be starting at a disadvantage if your audience sees only luminescent pools instead of your eyes.

Group your slides or viewgraphs so that the lights can be turned up between series of visuals. Know where the room's light switches are located and appoint someone to turn them on or off at your cue.

■ *Work with windows.* If the scene outside is distracting, draw the curtains or blinds. Windows generally have a positive effect on meetings, but there are exceptions to the rule. One speaker told me she checked the meeting room the night before her presentation and discovered it was a school cafeteria. Her voice bounced off the bare walls and tile floor. What she neglected to note was a wall of glass windows two stories high. The next day, the glare at noon made it impossible for the audience to see her viewgraphs. She had to change her whole approach and eliminate the visuals, which she felt weakened her message. "I learned a valuable lesson," she ruefully acknowledged. "Now I either visit or visualize a facility at the *same time of day* as my presentation to appraise the effect of the lighting."

■ *Make sure you can be heard.* The first requirement of a good speech is that it is comfortably heard by everyone. Have someone check to ensure that you can be heard in the back of the room. If there is the slightest chance of a problem, ask the group if they can hear you before you begin. Audiences are reluctant to stop a speaker to ask him to speak louder.

■ *Make your mike work for you.* Avoid using microphones if you can be comfortably heard in the back of the room. However, if a small room is darkened for slides or viewgraphs, a microphone will emphasize your presence in the room. Be selective in your choice of microphone. Wireless mikes are easiest to use because you need not worry about tripping over a cord and you are free to walk into the audience. Women might want to wear a jacket to conceal the transmitter.

Always test the microphone before you use it because batteries frequently run down. Since most wireless mikes use mixed frequencies, there is a chance they will pick up interference from taxis, rock bands, or radio signals. Be prepared with a backup mike.

A lavaliere microphone goes around the speaker's neck on a cord, which may need adjustment. Small clip-on mikes are also erroneously referred to as lavaliere mikes, so be exact when you request equipment. Avoid mikes that are affixed to the lectern unless they are attached to an adjustable gooseneck. Prior to your speech, position the mike the distance of your outstretched hand from your mouth. Hand-held mikes are trickier to use, since the volume of your voice can fluctuate as you move the mike. They can also present a problem if you are adjusting viewgraphs and need both hands.

Microphone cords should not be twisted or bent. Avoid touching the mike or tapping it in any way. Slip the cord through your belt and sweep the cord behind you. Try to arrive at the room early and establish a volume level that can be heard by everyone in the room but doesn't overwhelm the audience.

Don't make sudden bursts of breath or surprising changes in volume. Cover your mouth to the side if you must cough or clear your throat. Talk conversationally. Once you have the microphone in place and turned on, be careful about casual remarks unless you want them broadcast to the entire group. If you experience microphone feedback, the microphone is picking up the sound coming from the loudspeaker and may need to be moved or the volume adjusted.

In panel discussions, the participants are usually seated at a head table with one or more microphones on short stands. You don't have to lean awkwardly over the microphone because other people do. During an Oceanic Engineering Society/IEEE Association meeting, one presenter took the microphone out of the stand, got up, and placed a viewgraph on the projector. He discussed it briefly, then turned the projector off and continued to stand for the remainder of his talk. It was a smart tactic since his body language, voice, and energy were much stronger when he was standing.

■ *Respect time limits.* Position a clock with large numerals within your range of vision and adhere to your allotted time. Some speakers wear their watch facing inward so they can unobtrusively check the time. It is useless to go beyond your time limit. You will only lose listeners and annoy other presenters. Even if members of your audience have their hands raised for questions, conclude the session on time and offer to answer them afterward.

Remember the consequences of going overtime. Our ninth president, William Henry Harrison, was sixty-eight at his swearing-in ceremony. He gave the longest inaugural address (one hour and forty-five minutes) on record, caught pneumonia, and died on April 4, 1841, after only about a month in office.

■ *Control the temperature.* Try to have the room temperature between 68 degrees F and 70 degrees F. If it is any warmer, the audience will have a difficult time staying alert. Fluctuating room temperatures disturb the audience and physical discomfort will be foremost in their minds. Find out who is in charge of the temperature control before you begin to have trouble with it.

One of my clients was the last speaker on the second day of an international conference in New York. He had rehearsed his hour-long speech and we had videotaped and evaluated the presentation. By 2:00 P.M., the audience of 500 had begun to drift in and out of the ballroom. Others were sleeping or engaged in small group conversations. The air conditioning was not working and the room began to get warmer. Noise drifted in from the hall. Many of the speakers had heavy accents and were difficult to understand; several of them deferred controversial questions to my client.

By 3:45 P.M., the room was unbearably hot, and the audience was anticipating a break at 4:00. I walked up to my client and said, "Capsulize your speech into fifteen minutes. Give your introduction and the first anecdote, hit the three main points, and tell everyone you will meet them in the bar to answer their questions. The audience has a press release of your speech and can read it in its entirety if they want to."

When my client was introduced, he began, "I'm going to make my remarks brief and have you all out of here in fifteen minutes." The audience became alert and attentive and, when he finished and announced he would meet them in the bar, they cheered. There, he fielded questions brilliantly for an hour and was the hit of the conference.

■ *Take charge in emergencies.* I was finishing my closing remarks during a breakfast meeting when a man suddenly stood up in front of me, gasped for breath, grabbed his throat, and fell to the floor. Everyone was so startled that no one reacted for a few seconds. I was waiting for someone to do something when I realized that I was the one in charge at that moment. Using my microphone, I asked if there were any doctors or nurses in the room, directed a person by the door to call 911, announced that the meeting was concluded, and asked everyone to leave at once. The medics arrived within minutes and revived the man with oxygen. It was a frightening situation.

As a presenter, you may find yourself faced with an emergency and discover that it is up to you to take charge. Always locate emergency exits and know where and how help can be obtained.

■ *Create the mood.* Even before the presentation begins, a speaker can divert attention from site problems and warm up a room by exhibiting interpersonal communication skills. Greet and talk to audience members as they arrive. It is a mistake to be fiddling with papers or audio-visual equipment. Introduce yourself and shake hands. Make introductions between other audience members. Offer small talk or discuss the purpose of the meeting. Then excuse yourself to make any final physical or mental preparations before you begin.

If you have any control over the presentation's start, begin on time even if there are only a few people present. Of course, if the key decision maker has not arrived, you may need to delay your speech.

Plan A, Plan B, Plan C

"The mediocre person is ruled by his environment, whereas the successful man uses the pressure of adversity as an assist in obtaining his final objective."

—Clifton Burke

Murphy's Law will, at some time, go into effect before or during one of your presentations. Anticipating problems and having a back-up plan will give you more control, but every contingency cannot be predicted.

Your level of preparation and comfort with the site arrangements will have a critical effect on how you feel about yourself and, consequently, on your delivery. Do what you can to improve or maintain the temperament and attention of the audience, but realize that you may need to change your style of speaking in response to the environment. Figure 16 is a checklist that will help with site preparations.

Figure 16. Speech site checklist.

1. Best seating arrangement

    _____ U-shaped   _____ Placement of aisles

    _____ Conference style   _____ Classroom style

    _____ Banquets or rounds   _____ Theater style

2. Audiovisual equipment

    _____ Flip chart and colored pens   _____ 35mm slide projector (remote control)

    _____ Dry erase board

    _____ Overhead projector (spare lamp)   _____ Screen on raised platform

    _____ Blank viewgraph sheets or roll   _____ TV monitor(s) for computer or video

    _____ Table for projector and viewgraphs   _____ VCR

    _____ Computer   _____ Computer

    _____ LCD panel   _____ Extension cord(s)

    Who will deliver the audiovisual equipment? _____

    Time of setup? _____

    Location of electrical outlets, extension cord _____

    Adequate lighting on speaker _____

    Who will dim lights for slides? _____

    Location of light switches _____

    _____ Handouts _____ Number needed _____ Table for handouts at rear of room

3. Room equipment

    _____ Clip-on microphone

    _____ Stationary microphone

    _____ Lavalier microphone with 20-foot cord

Figure 16 *(continued)*.

_____ Lectern. Placement _____

_____ Wireless microphone

_____Hand-held microphone

4. Supplies

_____ Clock or watch

_____ Masking tape

_____ Pencils

_____ Note paper

_____ Name tags or cards

_____ Ash trays or "No Smoking" sign

_____ Water for speaker

_____ Refreshments: What? When? Where? _____

_____

How will telephone messages be handled? _____

_____ Room temperature at 68°F

_____ Emergency exits

KEY IDEAS

- Take responsibility for your presentation site; don't depend on anyone else to "set the stage" for you.
- Triple-check all equipment, supplies, and room arrangements. Have backup plans in mind.
- Arrive early so that you can change seating arrangements if necessary or reposition the audio-visual equipment.
- Minimize distractions of noise, sunlight, intercoms, temperature, and so forth.
- Appoint someone to troubleshoot during your presentation.

19

Creating Favorable
Introductions

"It gives me great pleasure . . ."

—Anonymous

Overview

This chapter gives you tips for your introduction, which will help establish your credentials and whet the appetite of the audience. Your introduction should include details about your background that pertain to your topic and audience. It should substantiate your expertise and trustworthiness and set in motion the audience's acceptance of your ideas.

Television stars know the value of a warm-up comedian before their appearance; you can also benefit from a bright and perhaps witty lead-in to your speech.

Orson Welles was lecturing in a small midwestern town before a very sparse audience. He opened his remarks with a brief sketch of his career, saying, "I'm a director of plays and also a producer of plays. I am an actor of the stage and motion pictures. I write and produce motion pictures and I write, direct, and act on the radio. I'm a magician and a painter. I've published books; I play the violin and the piano." At this point, he paused and, surveying his audience, remarked, "Isn't it a pity there's so many of me and so few of you?"

One presenter told me, "I used to be somewhat cavalier about introductions, but now I write my own. I have had dreadful experiences with introducers who have ruined my credibility and I have had to spend the entire speech trying to get it back." I advise everyone to write his or her own introduction.

Send your introduction ahead if it is a formal occasion, but always carry one with you for extra insurance. You will have more control over the information presented. If you send a biography, expect to hear it read word for word. Arrive early at the speech site and immediately ask to meet the person who will introduce you. Review with her the proper pronunciation of your name and the title of your speech. If you have researched your audience and feel it is important to include your specific background in artificial intelligence or genetics, ask the introducer to precisely follow your written material. If appropriate, you could suggest the introducer briefly relate how she or someone in the organization was a former colleague or how she came to know about your work. If you have an accent, you might want your country of origin mentioned in the introduction so that the audience isn't distracted by trying to guess where you are from. Be visible when your introduction is being read so that the audience is able to relate to you and your credentials. Watch how the audience responds to the introduction, as it may yield important clues about how to proceed in your opening remarks.

Within a company, there will usually be no formal beginning of a business meeting. Someone will simply say, "John, let's hear from you," and you are in the spotlight. There is no need for you to give your background, but there is a need to have the audience focus on your subject. If the introduction says little about your credentials, it is perfectly appropriate for you to begin, "Let me tell you about the background I bring to this subject."

Why are *you* speaking at *this particular time* on *this particular topic* to *this particular audience*? When your background is described and you are introduced as an expert, you need only to establish your authority in relation to a certain aspect of your subject. It is not necessary to document your life after the high school debate team, but it may be important to mention a significant project or paper.

Many people include a personal note in their introductions, such as "She enjoys mountain climbing" or "recently wrote an article for the IEEE magazine." A witty line will have your audience smiling as you step to the lectern. Your introduction should place you in an advantageous position for starting your presentation.

KEY IDEAS

- Stimulate your audience's desire to listen.
- Establish credentials acceptable to the specific audience.
- Don't protest too loudly or too humbly to a flattering introduction.
- Review your introduction with your introducer.
- Write your own introduction. Keep it crisp and short.

20
Videoconferencing

"There is so much information being beamed around this world that it's almost as if there is another layer of the atmosphere. And it is going to become easier and easier to breathe that air no matter where you live."

—Irving Goldstein

Overview

A videoconference is a fast, efficient delivery system that allows companies to disseminate information in real time to employees, sales representatives, customers, and the general public. In this chapter you will learn techniques to help you become a compelling presenter at your videoconference. You can be calm, comfortable, in control, and enjoy communicating through this demanding but exciting medium.

The French philosopher Voltaire admonished, "If you are doing anything today in the same way you did it a year ago, you are probably doing it wrong." These words, written in the late eighteenth century, are especially applicable 200 years later. Organizations are becoming increasingly complex, global, and decentralized in the 1990s. Any company using yesterday's tools to compete in the current marketplace will soon be outpaced by its competition. A videoconference is a modern technological tool that can be used to build an accurate, relevant, and timely communication infrastructure within an organization. It can also deliver a message to targeted audiences without considering the boundaries of geography.

Videoconferences can be transmitted via microwave, via satellite, or over digital phone or fiber-optic lines. The term "videoconferencing" can apply to many different combinations of audio and video communication. In one-way videoconferencing, viewers at multiple sites can watch speakers at the originating site and interact by telephone. In two-way videoconferencing, participants at the originating site and receive sites (or downlinks) can both see and speak to one another.

The two major forms of videoconferencing are private business television networks and special event telecasts. A business television network is an industry-specific or company network that typically broadcasts programs from one site to multiple sites with one-way video and two-way audio. However, many companies conduct highly interactive electronic meetings with two-way video and two-way audio from multiple sites. Special event videoconferences usually combine one-way video with two-way audio. These onetime or ad hoc broadcasts use temporarily installed hardware. The event may be a simple day of training transmitted from headquarters to field offices or an elaborate sales promotion that is seen worldwide.

Advances in technology are making videoconferencing more convenient and cost-effective. The increasing use of fiber-optic phone lines, often combined with satellite transmission, provides high-quality, full-motion video that is readily accessible. For example, compact cabinets that contain complete dial-up videoconferencing systems are easily transported and set up at almost any location. Voice-activated multipoint switching enables a speaker at one site to be seen at all the conference sites, and when a person at another location speaks, the video image automatically switches to show that speaker. The not-too-distant future promises desktop videoconferencing using the existing telephone network. Another exciting breakthrough is the transmission of holographs (three-dimensional images) from one location to another.

As companies discover the cost-effectiveness and diversity of this versatile medium, videoconferencing has grown into a billion dollar industry. There are more than 200 private, industry, and special-interest networks. Pat Portway, president of ABC Communications, reports 80,000 receive sites are anticipated by the turn of the century. The number of international videoconferences is increasing as global competition intensifies.

High-tech organizations have embraced the use of videoconferences. Donna Collins, project manager for Apple videoconferencing network, comments:

> Apple today is a global company with more than 100 offices worldwide. We established the videoconferencing network as a way to increase the quantity, as well as quality, of our

communications, making it more accurate, including more people in the decision-making process, allowing for the timely exchange of information with groups in the field. In short, bringing all the parts of the world closer together.

Benefits of Videoconferencing

No one is excited about the prospect of attending additional meetings. But videoconferencing can be more efficient and productive than face-to-face meetings. Although this practical medium has reduced the expense and time loss of travel, it is no longer primarily being installed to keep corporate executives out of airplanes. Broadcasting the same message simultaneously to a widely distributed audience saves organizational time and energy. The attendees of an electronic meeting are there because the information is of particular value to them and they are prepared to participate. They must adhere to an agenda and accomplish their business in a minimum amount of time. Delays and crises can be avoided. And many companies speak of the exciting synergy generated by a videoconference. In a two-way videoconference, you can do everything you would in a conventional meeting: see people face-to-face, exchange documents and data, manipulate information in each other's computers—everything but shake hands.

A videoconference creates an opportunity for employees to identify with leadership and is extremely useful in cementing strong relationships with customers. Jeannie E. Tasker, executive producer for an international satellite videoconference for Hitachi Data Systems, commented, "Though we wanted to demonstrate the fact that we were global, we also wanted to capture a small family feeling that would let our customers know each and every one of them is important to us." She is optimistic that the enthusiasm generated by the videoconference will translate into new sales for Hitachi.

When Microsoft wanted to introduce its new Windows software to an international audience, the company announced the special event with a videoconference. The Law Enforcement Television Network and the Automotive Satellite Television Network use one-way videoconferences for training and informing its employees or dealers. Companies such as Federal Express, General Motors, Hewlett-Packard, and Unisys have employed two-way videoconferences to train and retrain employees, introduce new products, communicate with suppliers, promote special events, and inform employees about changes in top management, supervisory procedures, and policies.

Boeing engineers use the medium intercontinentally for problem solving when designing or testing airplane parts. Engineers can show and annotate blueprints and detailed engineering diagrams as well as display three-dimensional parts from site to site. The medium has helped the engineers and managers use time more effectively, shorten developmental cycles, accelerate decision making, and move products to market more quickly.

High-definition television is gaining more popularity with its sharper, fine-detail pictures and accurate color reproduction. Ford Motor Company has found these capabilities as well as the wide-aspect ratio and large-screen display helpful to auto design. And the medical community is showing particular interest in this new technology to train doctors in complicated and innovative surgical procedures.

VIVID Presentations

If you haven't already participated in a videoconference, it is inevitable that you will be involved in one, perhaps as a presenter, in the near future. At first, the unfamiliar terminology and process of a videoconference can be intimidating. Any number of important people may be watching. There will be no retakes. But like any new tool, you can learn what it does and how it will work most productively for you. Why not take advantage of this powerful medium and increase your visibility in your profession?

The acronym VIVID describes the concepts you need to keep in mind for any compelling videoconference presentation:

Viewers. Your viewers are your most important consideration. Everything in your presentation should be designed from the audience's viewpoint.

Interactive. Your viewers are not expected to simply watch passively as they do for commercial television. Design and deliver your message so that your audience becomes involved mentally, physically, and emotionally.

Visuals. Think in terms of images. Visuals reinforce and clarify your points, aid viewer retention, and add variety to your presentation. As you research your presentation, think about how the information can be translated into slides, viewgraphs, or preproduced video. Pay special attention to the legibility of your visuals at the receive sites. Handouts play an important part in any videoconference and should reinforce your message.

Immediacy. The biggest advantage of videoconferencing is the speaker's ability to relay up-to-date information to the viewers. You may need to incorporate late-breaking data and additional visuals at the last minute.

Delivery. Dynamic delivery skills are a must because video can make you appear listless. A compelling presenter will attract the audience's attention and encourage interaction.

William Mason, senior educational consultant for AETNA Institute for Corporate Education, says:

> I have the belief that television is part theater. One of our business writing instructors was dynamic and exciting. He saw teaching as an organic experience and a kind of dance, if you will, between the instructor and student. I didn't want someone who was merely knowledgeable. For a television audience, I wanted someone who had a kind of zeal and was energized by the dynamics of teaching.

Video can be a demanding medium. Audiences expect polished delivery skills, and they will check to see how you handle controversial questions and how you respond to comments. Your listeners typically will decide in the first few minutes whether they will give you their attention, and that decision will be based on the value of your material, your delivery skills, and whether they feel comfortable with you. Your listeners are accustomed to switching channels, and there must be something in what you are offering to interest or challenge them.

However, don't get caught up in trying to be the perfect presenter. A creative, informative program needn't be cosmetically perfect. A videoconference intended for your peers will not have the same production values as a TV program for a general audience. Remember that the single most important factor influencing how you communicate with others is your own self-concept. If you decide to enjoy participating in a videoconference, you will, and so will the viewing audience.

The Camera and You

It is to your advantage to know how to enhance your image in front of the video camera. Dynamic delivery skills can be the deciding factor in the success of your videoconference.

1. In a two-way videoconference, you will be able to see participants at the receive sites on monitors and should find it easy to converse naturally. However, during a one-way videoconference, you may not always be able to see participants at multi-receive sites or have a studio audience. It is frustrating not to have eye contact with listeners. You cannot read the audience's body language or sense how well they are receiving and understanding the concepts. It is difficult to talk to an unresponsive, mechanical object. Instead of letting the camera unnerve you, visualize one person you are comfortable talking with. Imagine that friend in the camera lens and speak directly to him or her in a conversational tone when presenting information.

2. Eliminate meaningless gestures or distracting mannerisms. These often distort, dilute, or confuse your verbal message.

3. Use your upstage hand (farthest away from camera) for holding objects or pointing. Be aware that if you cross your legs and your foot is close to the camera, it will appear larger than normal.

4. Avoid small talk or shuffling papers when someone else is talking. Every sound will be picked up by the microphones.

5. Review hand, verbal, and sound cues with your production staff. Work out a specific way to keep track of time. Plan when you will introduce a slide or preproduced video or use a projector. Learn how to tell which camera is focused on you.

6. Use good posture. Be comfortable but careful not to slouch when sitting at a table. During a special event videoconference, you may be moving around the set. Use colored tape on the floor to indicate blocking (where your feet should be positioned, moves you will make, and where you will end up). A dry run is imperative!

7. Discuss closeups or long shots with the director and the camera operator. Know when the camera will zoom in on you or an object you are holding and when it is taking in the entire set. Most two-way videoconferencing rooms have stationary cameras with zoom capabilities. Receive sites can usually control the camera zoom and

choice of shot. In a special event videoconference, camera shots are generally chosen by the director. Always rise from a chair slowly and give cues before moving to a different area so the camera operator can easily follow you.

8. Practice with all your props. If you don't have a steady hand, leave objects on the table or lectern or hold your elbow with the other hand.

9. Act as if the camera is on you when the videoconference begins or the director calls "action." Don't daydream, stare at the monitor, or allow your attention to wander.

10. Maintain a high level of energy and enthusiasm to keep your viewers alert and attentive. The camera will accentuate these positive characteristics.

The camera can be your ally. It can intensify your personality. It can reinforce the positive elements of your presence and delivery, and showcase naturalness and enthusiasm. After a few videoconferences, participants agree that the technology becomes transparent. They feel comfortable participating in electronic meetings and begin to focus on finding creative ways to increase productivity.

Rehearse Your Performance

Rehearsal and familiarity with the equipment dramatically increase the chances of a successful videoconference. Video broadcasts are usually tightly scheduled. Each speaker must get to the point and finish within the allotted time. Although it should look spontaneous, the event or the meeting must have a definite structure and organization to adhere to the time format. Rehearsal will help coordinate the roles of the participants. Write out your objectives and what you believe to be the expectations of the audience. Memorize your opening lines and the beginning and ending of each segment.

Ask for some objective feedback during run-throughs. Correct the mannerisms that may annoy your audience and intrude on the quality and effectiveness of your delivery. If TelePrompTers are available for special event one-way videoconferences, rehearse with them. Practice incorporating your props and visual aids into your presentation. Note where you will be referring to handouts that your listeners will be using at the receive sites.

The meeting or special event should move along at a comfortable but brisk pace and come to a conclusive finish. Run-throughs will minimize wasted time and inefficiency. Thorough preparation will prevent the frustration of not achieving productive results with this innovative medium.

Watch other commentators and presenters. Study their styles and note specifically what it is you like and dislike about them. Learn from them, and incorporate what you can into your own style. Be wary of imitating Ted Koppel or Diane Sawyer. Develop your own unique style.

It is now possible to reach anyone on earth with a live video image using a combination of three communication satellite transmissions. Voltaire's observation was accurate; traditional practices rarely offer opportunities. Investigate how you can become involved in videoconferencing. This exciting medium can extend your influence as an engineer, scientist, educator, or business professional. "Beam me up, Scotty!"

KEY IDEAS

- Make a decision to excel as a presenter during an electronic meeting.
- Concentrate on your delivery skills.
- Rehearse so that you can focus on your material and the audience.
- Talk to the camera as if it were a friend.
- Eliminate distracting mannerisms that can be magnified by the camera.

21

Analyzing
Model Communicators

"Circumstances? I create my own circumstances!"

—Napoléon

Overview

Analyzing why some individuals are clearly outstanding, successful, and effective communicators will help you improve your own speaking skills. A model communicator makes choices that work, especially in difficult, stressful situations. This chapter examines some of the behavioral traits of model communicators and suggests how you can become one yourself.

Marshall Ferdinand Foch, the brilliant commander in chief of the Allied armies in World War I, was trying to stop a powerful German drive to capture Paris. In the heat of the second battle of the Marne in 1918, he sent a message to the Paris High Command, saying, "My center is giving way, my right is pushed back, situation . . . excellent. I am attacking!"

In spite of the desperate situation, regardless of what was happening all around him, Foch took control, communicated strength, and eventually led his men to victory. Although you may not face the extreme danger of a battlefield in your profession, we have all experienced stressful situations, such as a meeting with an important customer, communicating with people who begrudge us their time, or making a presentation in an unfavorable environment.

Recently I watched a model communicator deal with less than

ideal circumstances. Robert Ballard from Woods Hole Oceanographic Institute was scheduled to speak at the Kingdome during the Seattle Boat Show.

After fighting a jostling crowd to gain entrance, I stopped to watch hundreds of potential buyers crawling in and out of the boats lining the floor of the stadium. Loud music was pulsating and the din of voices on the trade show floor reverberated in the huge space.

I asked a yacht salesman if he could direct me to the room for Ballard's lecture on his discovery of the *Titanic* and the *Bismarck* shipwrecks. The young man motioned toward the upper levels of the stadium. "It's up there somewhere," he said. I spotted a blue drape covering a movie screen high up in the bleachers. People were grouped behind the screen facing the yachts. I worked my way toward them.

Once Ballard was introduced, he began to speak passionately about science and his challenging discoveries. He showed incredible film footage. The noise and bustle of the Kingdome faded into the background as we were drawn into his quest for those two ships.

Ballard didn't draw attention to the boat show or the other distractions of the speech site. He simply focused on why he was there and his search for the sunken vessels. In spite of an extremely difficult situation, he made his presentation a memorable experience. He made choices that worked.

How Can You Become a Model Communicator?

In any skill, whether it is tennis or golf, you can cut down the time needed to perfect your technique by studying the performance of masters. Model communicators are experts in their fields, and their audiences perceive them to be trustworthy. This trustworthiness and expertise combine to create credibility. In general, model communicators display the following behaviors:

■ *They make an extra effort to thoroughly plan and prepare their presentations.* They use some form of the ten steps recommended in this book.

■ *They start from where the audience is, not from where they are.* They begin at the same level of knowledge as their audience and find common ground.

■ *They take responsibility for the audience's ability to understand the topic.* They have a gift for taking a large amount of material and breaking it down into smaller, cohesive units that can be easily understood and remembered by the audience.

■ *They personalize science and technology.* Model communicators use their own experiences to annotate their material as richly and elaborately as possible. They know that if they can interest the audience in their topic, their listeners will retain more of what they hear. A physicist told me, "Science is a personal endeavor and must be conveyed in a personal manner. You miss the resonance if you deal only with the facts."

■ *They illuminate and give insight rather than dilute scientific and technical information.* One model communicator told me, "A nontechnical audience will never be at my level in my field. But that's what makes me an expert. Rather than being arrogant about my knowledge and experience, I try to give general audiences a glimpse of some of the fascinating research that's going on."

■ *They are aware of the importance of delivery skills and of gaining rapport with the audience.* They have a natural style that is often like a focused conversation. They use variety and drama in their voice and body language to capture and keep attention focused on their complex technical and scientific subjects.

■ *They feel comfortable with themselves, their material, and the situation and feel free enough to get involved with their audience.* Their self-confidence is high, and they are responsive to feedback.

Physicist Phillip Morrison of MIT (Massachusetts Institute of Technology) describes himself as "very sensitive to what is going on in the audience or their lack of attention. I often put in a local reference or a small joke to see if they are with me. I go largely by sound feedback: breathing, muffled comments, the noise of people shifting positions. Based on what I hear, I may repeat a point or drop a point." The next time you give a presentation, listen to your audience. What you hear will provide you with valuable clues to help you adjust your material and delivery.

Making Choices

Model communicators make choices that work. San Francisco Forty-Niners football star Joe Montana knows all the rules, but that's not what makes him a great quarterback. He evaluates the entire situation and makes specific, creative choices that another quarterback might fail to consider.

People who "read" other people may be the most persuasive people in the world. Model communicators are sensitive to body language, vocal tone, and words of others and are flexible enough to change their behavior to get a desired response.

We can respond in various ways to difficult situations. What happens to your body language when you arrive at the speech site and discover no microphone, an inconveniently located overhead projector, and fewer people than expected? Do you become defensive, angry, or resign yourself to failure? Does your voice reveal irritation, disappointment, or anxiety? Model communicators make productive choices when confronted with problems. Be aware of any automatic negative responses and convert these responses into positive ones. Remember that you have choices; why not try humor or candor?

How you act and communicate under pressure is very visible and the rewards or negative consequences can be immediate. The ability to cope and communicate effectively under stress can make the difference between being an average presenter and a compelling one.

Having Options Available

During the San Francisco earthquake in 1989, the upper level of the double-decker Nimitz Freeway collapsed, killing over fifty people. It was a catastrophic structural failure. Even today in the age of computer-aided design, every part of a structure is only as safe as the weight and strength variables used in the structural analysis. Engineers know they have to provide for contingencies, and they factor these in. Nonetheless, there is an uncertainty factor within the margin of error; you can't predict every contingency.

We would like to have one set of rules that apply to all speaking engagements, but every situation is different. We can anticipate a variety of problems but can't predict everything that might occur. Start out with a plan, but be prepared to modify it according to the situation. Be willing to tackle the unexpected. You have choices—your choice may limit you or increase your effectiveness.

One of my clients was told that his audience would consist of staff interested in basic information about computer software. Before he began his speech, he was savvy enough to ask the audience specific questions about their background. To his surprise, he discovered that several computer maintenance people were present. He started out his presentation with general information to include everyone and was prepared to use the expand and contract approach. However, he realized he was losing some people in the audience when he mentioned anything technical, and the computer maintenance staff was clearly bored with the basics. He announced that he would present introductory information for the first part of his presentation and then, after a break, open up the forum for technical questions. Those not interested in the more specialized aspects could leave during the intermission. It was a difficult call to make, he explained, but he felt it worked out favorably.

Sometimes you will find that your audience at an association meeting will have widely divergent levels of knowledge, in spite of the fact that the published program clearly states the complexity of your subject. Engineers and scientists generally agree that you should present your paper as you prepared it, since the audience expects the level of sophistication stated in the program.

Passion and Charisma

The model communicators that I spoke with had a passion for their particular field of endeavor and were motivated to tell others about it. This fascination and involvement with their work is evident in their delivery. They renew this excitement and inquisitiveness in every presentation and follow author J. Samuel Bois' advice: "The important thing is to live over again the experience you had when the truth that you are now expounding to the audience became a discovery, an insight, a fresh learning experience for you as an individual." Many of them stress that they are constantly learning from each speaking experience and enjoy seeking new ways to convey complex information.

Model communicators develop a relationship with their audience. They encourage participation by getting out from behind the lectern, by walking into the audience, by calling people by name. They use the personal pronouns "I," "we," and "you" to create intimacy. They describe their feelings and invite the audience to share their viewpoint on the emotional as well as intellectual level. And they care about their audiences. If you are not concerned with serving your audience, there are no words in the English language that can help you communicate. That sincere concern for others takes a deep energy commitment.

Charisma is exhibited through personal confidence, as opposed to job confidence and a sense that you know what you are doing. Charismatic speakers always appear comfortable, no matter what the circumstances. Roger Ailes, communications consultant for President George Bush, says that "a charismatic person never auditions." Model communicators project confidence about themselves and their material, but they don't convey arrogance or try to compete with their audiences.

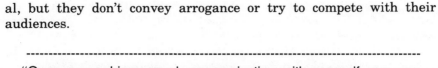

"Once you achieve good communication with yourself, you can communicate more freely and effectively with others."
—Carl Rogers

Communication is a two-way channel between the speaker and listener. But there is also another active channel: the dialogue that you have with yourself. "Do I look all right?" "Will I get through this?" "Hey, this is fun!" See the audience as a partner, and, at the same time, reassure yourself. Model communicators talk to themselves in positive but realistic terms. If things aren't going well with their speech, they don't hesitate to switch styles, ask questions, or depart from their notes. Don't allow the critic or doubter in your head to sabotage your performance. Be careful about comparing yourself to the previous speaker. And even if you see someone in the audience yawning or leafing through the handouts, there is no need to become anxious or tense.

Balancing Work With Other Interests

People who have strong interests other than their technical and scientific professions are the ones who can call on a variety of references and comparisons to aid their imagery. Ilya Prigogine, Nobel Prize–winner in chemistry, was educated in the classics, history, philosophy, and music. Colonel Milton Hunter, of the U.S. Army Corps of Engineers, has a background in architecture and says that, as a speaker, he is conscious of the structure and design of every presentation.

I spoke with an aerospace project manager who is an avid photographer, a physicist who is an opera lover, an engineer who rock-climbs all over the world, an expert in artificial intelligence who is an organist, and a programmer who grows exquisite roses. They all seemed to be able to add more variety and creativity to their communications because of their varied avocations.

British philosopher C. P. Snow remarked that it is as necessary for a truly cultured person to become acquainted with the second law of thermodynamics as with the plays of Shakespeare. "The Shakespeare canon and the laws of thermodynamics are, each in their own way, among the glorious artifacts that the mind has produced," Snow stated, "and neither is more humanistic than the other, for it was humans who created them both."

James E. Olson, chairman of the board of AT&T, agrees: "In today's world, we need the synergy that comes from an intermingling of ideas and perspectives. The engineer who's a closet poet, the administrator who ducks out to heavy metal rock concerts, the illustrator who's an inventor on the side. These are role models for the times, people soaking up the variety of life today."[1] Explore the arts and develop hobbies that are markedly different from your profession. Remember that good ideas are never born in the wrong places!

Observe Model Communicators

One of the best ways to learn how to be a model communicator is to study the behavior of successful communicators. Watch and analyze what they do, how they establish rapport with an audience, and how they are able to communicate their ideas clearly, accurately, and concisely. Note how they make choices based on the audience and the situation. Observe the use of stories, case histories, examples, comparisons, and personal experiences.

Read good speeches. The biweekly *Vital Speeches of the Day* records entire speeches of some of the best and brightest. Analyze why the speaker chose a certain organizational pattern, why he previewed his main points, how he brought humor into an unlikely situation. Learn by evaluating the delivery skills of keynote speakers at association meetings or well-known communicators who visit your city to speak. Attend city council meetings or watch press conferences to see how people respond to controversial questions or quantities of complex material. Borrow techniques from model communicators and adapt them to your presentation style.

Secrets of the Model Communicators

In my interviews with hundreds of model communicators, I questioned them about their secrets for success. Here's what they said:

- Start keeping a speech file with cartoons, jokes, quotations, anecdotes, and personal experiences.
- Avoid qualifying your viewpoint with weak language.

- Be a storyteller and tell your story as if you were sitting at the kitchen table talking to a friend.
- Write out your speech but write for the ear. Carefully select your words and then edit them.
- Increase your vocabulary by reading well-written prose. It will soak in and become part of your communication style.
- Keep the adrenaline flowing. Don't try to get rid of all your tension.
- Select images that call up vivid associations for your audience.
- Use active verbs. They will demand more exciting subjects.
- Use short, pithy quotations that are memorable, powerful, and insightful.
- Begin emotionally on a low key so you can build toward a dramatic conclusion.
- Avoid any kind of story that is even mildly offensive.
- Edit, edit, edit. Be brief. We don't need to pass on all the information we know.
- Use viewgraphs and slides to explain or highlight ideas, but don't let them dominate the presentation.
- Imagine that your presentation is a dramatic play and you are the scriptwriter. Consider the time, the place, the scene, what's happening before the play begins, and what happens after the curtain falls.
- Use strong eye contact to create the impression that you are talking privately to each individual in the audience instead of to a group.
- Be efficient. Speech preparation is hard work, so work smart. Make effective use of limited time or resources. Follow a system. Eliminate needless revisions.
- Listen to a tape of your rehearsal. You can make intentional changes and edit more effectively than by merely thinking through your presentation.
- Videotape and critique your presentation. It is the fastest way to improve.
- Evaluate and learn from past experiences. What can you do differently the next time?

Model communicators are interested in making something happen as a result of their communication. They are precise, well-ordered, and at ease with themselves. They have something worth saying and they say it in a way that is worth listening to. These are qualities that are certainly worth emulating!

KEY IDEAS

- Realize that effective communication is never an accident.
- Have options available for the times when things go awry.
- Use your time and resources efficiently.
- Balance your professional life with outside interests and use imagery from these activities to illuminate your subject.
- Study and learn from model communicators.

Note

1. James E. Olson, "The Spur of Ignorance," *Vital Speeches of the Day* (March 15, 1988).

Afterword:
Shaping the Future

"The only way to predict the future is to have the power to shape the future."

—Eric Hoffer

Overview

The electronic age has brought about revolutionary changes in science and technology that have produced equally revolutionary changes in how we think and work together. This chapter discusses the need for teams of experts from many disciplines to be able to communicate and cooperate in order to contribute to our quality of life. Scientists and technicians must also carry on a dialogue with the general public if they are to gain acceptance for their ideas; their new roles demand not only that the content of their presentations be of immediate value but that their messages be presented in a compelling fashion. The universal stage demands effective communication skills for professional success.

In the desert north of Tucson, Arizona, eight men and women are secluded in Biosphere II, a 137,000-square-foot glass and metal structure that may advance our ability to live in harmony with earth and may also be a prototype for the first colony on the moon or Mars. This self-sustaining living laboratory with specially selected animals, insects, and plants will be the home of the biospherians for two years.

The inhabitants represent a wide variety of disciplines, including engineering, medicine, botany, ecology, and management. Their survival depends on the development of a common vocabulary and an understanding of each other's point of view.

Biosphere II is a microcosm of the real-world situation. The global communications network ISDN (Integrated Services Digital Network) is an exciting and promising new global communications network. By moving voice, data, and video simultaneously over an ordinary telephone line, this all-digital transport system will collapse time and space. Universal translation will be instantaneously available. It is critical that professionals in different disciplines learn to drive on this "electronic highway" of information and be able to understand and work together harmoniously.

Funded or Forgotten

There is a wide communication gap between the scientists who live in theoretical worlds, the engineers who design a product, and the manufacturers who produce a profitable product. An equally broad distance separates the engineers and the investors who fund the project, and a similar gap exists between these groups, the politicians, and the general public. Perceptive communicators seek ways to diminish the gap between their knowledge base and that of their audiences.

People trained in scientific and technical disciplines have been accused of communicating as if they are plugged into a headset, hearing their own personal tunes. Rather than subdividing and classifying and separating, we should be trying to unify, to find common ground and common principles that will bring together technical and nontechnical people.

Scientists and engineers must recognize that, although excellence in initial research and design is extremely important, the packaging and sale of that research and design to management and consumers are equally important. The research can be original and the results positive, but an engineer must be able to explain the technology clearly and persuade the finance department that it's worth going over budget now to boost the company's future earnings. If an engineer can't defend a project, receive commitments of time, equipment, or personnel, or win the approval of a regulatory agency, he may be out of a job. He needs to have the ability to make a funding body—whether of investors, clients, or Congress—clearly understand what it is spending money on and why.

Douglas E. Olesen, the CEO of Battelle, urged his audience of biotechnical professionals to ensure a scientifically literate society for the future and to promote an understanding of the benefits of science and technology in the community:

This is not simply an issue of philanthropy. It's an important business issue, critical to public acceptance of scientific advances, and it is critical to our ability to succeed in tomorrow's marketplace. We must enhance our image by balancing our time in the lab with time in the community. Our task is communication. We know we have the ability to make the world a better place; we have to make sure the rest of the world knows that, too.[1]

The Public's Fear of Science

Innovative scientific discoveries and technological advances are not always welcomed by the public. The general population's resistance to programs promoting science and technology often occurs because questions about final proof, relative cost, and ultimate effects go unanswered. The public is frequently exposed to a flawed database of half-truths, rumors, and a clutter of statistics, and people end up bewildered, wary, or angry.

Scientists and technologists usually stay hidden behind the scenes until a crisis. Then they are called upon to explain why a bridge or building collapsed, why a species of whales is dying, or the effects of pollution on a community beach. Much of the defensive, hasty communication in the middle of a disaster poses more questions than answers and has had a negative long-term effect on the public's confidence in science and technology. It is critical for these professions to increase visibility and awareness of their work on a daily basis.

"Prizes don't go to the people who predict rain.
Prizes go to the people who build arks."

—Unknown

Model communicators are a minority in science and technology. Even though everyone agrees that communication skills are a number one priority, very few are willing to commit themselves to refining their talents. The ability to understand abstract data and to communicate it clearly is becoming an increasingly prized skill in the marketplace. Some of the most important decisions affecting a technical or scientific professional's career will be based on that person's ability to present ideas orally.

How many times have you been tempted to send in an abstract for consideration at an association meeting or a technical conference? You listen to the papers being presented and think to yourself, "I could do that. Is this speaker more intelligent or creative than I am?"

Take advantage of every opportunity to present your ideas. Your confidence and ability will grow with every experience. Commit yourself to becoming a good communicator—your participation in the exchange of information will bring you satisfaction and pride. Not only will you find that improving your communication skills affects the quality of your personal and professional life, but you will discover that people who are able to get up and speak about a subject are in demand. And if you can communicate well, you will be hailed as an expert, a leader.

Bigger Games and Higher Stakes

Several summers ago, I visited my parents in upstate New York. One night, around midnight, I was working on a speech at the kitchen table when my eighty-two-year-old dad returned from a fishing trip. He invited me to join him in a game of cards. When I told him that I had to complete a speech, he mused, "You know, there are a lot of similarities between making a speech and playing cards." I asked him to explain. He said:

> I like the challenge, the excitement, and the uncertainty of not knowing exactly how the game will come out. It always helps to be at the right place at the right time playing the right cards. You need to study and learn the rules of the game. Timing is crucial. Know when to move; know the value of your cards. Be willing to take risks and gamble. Otherwise, the game is boring. You have to calculate the rewards versus the risks and know how to minimize your risks. You won't end up being a winner if you are afraid to lose. Assess how much power you have, learn as much as you can about the other players, and be prepared. Play the hand to your fullest ability. If you have a setback, don't give up. Bluff when necessary. Watch the other players and be sensitive to their responses. Watch their eyes! Remember, there is always a certain element of luck. Commit yourself. Concentrate, and be highly motivated to win.

[Then Dad smiled]. Winners get asked to go on to bigger games with higher stakes.

To prepare ourselves for bigger games, we can seek out model communicators; their examples, experiences, and insights can be useful lessons. At a birthday party honoring Charlie Chaplin, the comedian entertained his guests by imitating his friends. Finally he sang a beautiful aria from an Italian opera. "Why, Charlie, I never knew you could sing so beautifully," a guest exclaimed. "I can't sing at all," Chaplin replied. "I was only emulating Caruso." When we use the best communicators as our models, we can bring out the best in ourselves, lift our vision to higher sights, and raise our performance to a higher standard.

Becoming an effective communicator can make your work easier and more productive. It can reduce the problems of dealing with customers, staff, and peers. It is an essential part of your job. All you have to supply is the motivation and the commitment to make your next technical presentation your best ever. Here's to your success in bigger games and higher stakes!

KEY IDEAS

- Commit yourself to breaking down barriers to communication.
- Build visibility and awareness of science and technology in the public eye.
- Emphasize communication skills within your organization as part of a smart business strategy.
- Take advantage of every opportunity to present your ideas and refine your speaking ability.
- Open professional doors with effective communication skills.

Note

1. Douglas E. Olesen, "Commercializing Agricultural Biotechnology," *Vital Speeches of the Day* (October 1, 1990).

Suggested Reading

Ailes, Roger. *You Are the Message*. Homewood, Ill.: Dow Jones-Irwin, 1988.

Alexander, Roy. *Power Speech*. New York: AMACOM, 1986.

Bartlett, John, ed. *Bartlett's Familiar Quotations*. Boston: Little, Brown & Co., 1980.

Boettinger, Henry M. *Moving Mountains (or the Art of Letting Others See Things Your Way)*. New York: Collier Books (Macmillan), 1969.

Buzan, Tony. *Use Both Sides of Your Brain*. New York: E. P. Dutton Inc., 1983.

Cole, K. C. *Sympathetic Vibrations: Reflections on Physics as a Way of Life*. New York: William Morrow and Co., 1985.

Cook, Jeff Scott. *The Elements of Speechwriting and Public Speaking*. New York: Macmillan Publishing Co., 1989.

D'Arcy, Jan. *Dr. Jack's Adventure in Videoconferencing Land: A Guide to Communicating Effectively on Camera*. Bellevue, Wash.: Jan D'Arcy & Associates, 1990.

_____. *Speak Without Fear—How to Give a Speech Like a Pro*. Chicago: Nightingale Conant, 1987. (Audiocassettes.)

Dellinger, Susan, and Barbara Deane. *Communicating Effectively*. Radnor, Penn.: Chilton Book Co., 1980.

Fadiman, Clifton, ed. *The Little, Brown Book of Anecdotes*. Boston: Little, Brown & Co., 1985.

Holcombe, Mary W., and Judith K. Stein. *Presentations for Decision Makers*. Belmont, Calif.: Lifetime Learning Publications, 1983.

Humes, James. *Podium Humor*. New York: McGraw-Hill, 1975.

_____. *Speaker's Treasury of Anecdotes About the Famous*. New York: Harper & Row, 1978.

Laborde, Genie. *Influencing With Integrity*. Palo Alto, Calif.: Syntony Publishing, 1984.

Leech, Thomas. *How to Prepare, Stage, and Deliver Winning Presentations*. New York: AMACOM, 1985.

Lessac, Arthur. *The Use and Training of the Human Voice*. New York: Drama Book Publishers, 1960.

Linner, Sandy. *Speak and Get Results*. New York: Summit Books, 1983.

Mambert, W. A. *Presenting Technical Ideas*. New York: John Wiley and Sons, 1968.

Martel, Myles. *The Persuasive Edge*. New York: Ballantine Books, 1984.

Morrisey, George, and Thomas Sechrest. *Effective Business and Technical Presentations*. Reading, Mass.: Addison-Wesley, 1975.

Pease, Allan. *Signals—How to Use Body Language for Power, Success, and Love*. New York: Bantam, 1984.

People, David. *Presentations Plus*. New York: John Wiley & Sons, 1988.

Rafe, Stephen C. *How to Be Prepared to Think on Your Feet and Make the Best Business Presentations of Your Life*. New York: Harper Business, 1990.

Seifler, Ann, and Doris Bianchi. *Voice and Diction Fitness*. New York: Harper and Row, 1988.

Smith, Terry C. *Making Successful Presentations*. New York: John Wiley & Sons, 1991.

Tufte, Edward R. *The Visual Display of Quantitative Information*. Cheshire, Conn.: Graphics Press, 1983.

Wurman, Richard Saul. *Information Anxiety*. New York: Doubleday, 1989.

Index